Notes from the Bedside,
A Physician's Memoir

James H Newman MD

Copyright © 2024 James H Newman MD

ISBN-13:

Dedication

I dedicate these remembrances to my children, Michael and his wife Jenna and my grandchildren, Porter and Riley; and Craig and his wife Courtney and my grandchildren Benjamin and Caleb.

It is my hope that on some future date one or more of them will take this book down from a shelf and learn about some of the adventures I had as I grew up and grew old. And in doing so they will become better informed about the parts of my life they didn't share or didn't see.

Just maybe, one or more of my grandchildren will catch a glimpse of the joy of being a physician.

And with this dedication, they all will know that I love them very much.

Grandpa Jim

Acknowledgements

Writing a book is like creating a sculpture or painting a work of art. It is a form of expression that appeals to the writer and in doing so, the creation brings great energy and joy personally and with the added hope that it will bring entertainment and insight to the reader. At least, that is what I have experienced and have hoped.

When you have dedicated your life to the profession of medicine, to raising a family, to loving a woman deeply.....well going off on an adventure in creative writing can be daunting. And whether you judge this memoir or my novels to be fun and interesting or poor excuses for the use of the English language, let me share with you that I could not have stayed behind the plow without great help from a few friends. Really too many to mention here. But I would like to thank Professor Emeritus Stephen Newman, Professor of Political Science at York University in Toronto, Canada for his observations and suggestions which, for their richness and depth, I have tried to include in my narratives. He's also my younger brother. I'd also like to thank Dr. Thomas 'Spud' Delaney for his support and his consistent enjoyment of everything I write. I have known Dr. Delaney for fifty years and had the joy of going to college and medical school with him. Finally, there was the encouragement of a small gang of doctors who I trained with at Penn. I fear mentioning their names lest I be deported, but here goes; David Henry, Tim Crowley, Arnie Cohen, Vicky Kusiak, Eric Neilson, Bud Relman, Larry Beck, Alan Myers, Sir William Osler and many more.

I would also like to mention some folks that I don't know but their thoughts and work have been often added to the beginning of each chapter. They are rock musicians who have been an inspiration, entertainment, relaxation and company during the many hours I have spent alone with my thoughts regarding this memoir and sometimes just relaxing in the sunshine. Eagles, Rolling Stones, Eric Clapton and his various bands and many others have enriched the writing. Thank you as well.

Whether I mentioned you or not, remember the important advice given to us by the august Founding Father, late of Philadelphia, Benjamin Franklin: "Gentlemen and Ladies, we must all hang together, for if we do not, we will most assuredly hang separately."

James H Newman MD

January   16,   2024

PROLOGUE

"Out in the shiny night

The rain was softly falling

Tracks that ran down the boulevard

Had all been washed away

Out of the silver light

The past came softly calling

And I remember the times we spent

Inside the sad café

Oh, it seemed like a holy place

Protected by amazing grace

We would sing right out loud

The things we could not say

We thought we could change this world

With words like love and freedom

We were part of the lonely crowd

Inside the sad café

Maybe the time has drawn.

Faces I recall.

But things in this life change very slowly

If they ever change at all

No use in asking why.

Just turned out that way

So, meet me at midnight, babe.

Inside the sad café

Why don't you meet me at midnight, babe?

Inside the sad café."

'The Sad Café'

Music and lyrics by Glen Frey, John Souther, Joe Walsh and Don Henley: Recorded by Eagles as the last track on their album, The Long Run. It is reputedly about the The Troubador Club in LA but there are many differing interpretations of individual lines in the song.

My story begins when I graduated high school and left home for college, never really looking back. I hope the timeline of my memoir is chronologically straightforward. Early drafts tended to be a bit scrambled, and I hope that I have corrected this. To set the record straight, events begin in June of 1967 and follow the history of my life right up until the present.... June, 2023, my 74th birthday.

My story is as close to the truth of it as I can get but my memory is sharp and clear regarding the stories and anecdotes recorded herein.

My purpose in writing this memoir is to entertain you, to give you pause to remember events in your own lives, and to understand how a young, naïve boy from Scranton, PA, matured into a physician who takes pride in his contributions to individuals' lives and the community he served.

The memoir is to be taken seriously but is not a serious read. What I mean by that is that I have tried to punctuate it with interesting historical and often humorous notes and avoided being officious, condescending or narcissistic. I'm not like that as a friend and I was never like that as a doctor.

I am going to tell you some rather personal aspects of my life. These are the things that happen in a person's life without planning. Unexpectedly. Sadly. Joyfully.

Let's   get   started......

Table of Contents

5

Chapter 1

"Out on the road today

I saw a deadhead sticker on a Cadillac

A little voice inside my head said

'Don't look back, you can never look back.'

I thought I knew what love was

What did I know?

Those days are gone forever

I should just let them go, but

I can see you

Your brown skin shining in the sun

You got your top pulled down

And that radio on, baby

I can tell you my love for you will still be strong

After the boys of summer have gone.......'

Don Henley and Mike Campbell....The Boys of Summer 1984 from the Building the Perfect Beast album

My story begins shortly after Labor Day, 1967. Cornell University College of Arts and Sciences which is in Ithaca, New York, roughly two hours north of where I grew up in Scranton, Pennsylvania six years after Joe Biden was born. President Biden often speaks of his early years growing up in Scranton and how he moved to join his father who had established work in Wilmington, Delaware, which is where, by chance, I came to practice medicine after all my education and training, and he began his highly successful life of service to our country.

My mom on learning we would be living in Wilmington, suggested I contact Senator Biden who might like to show us around. Right, mom. Like, first thing, I'll call our US Senator with two young sons and still mourning the loss of his young wife and daughter and ask him to take some time off to show my 35-week pregnant wife and I around. I'm sure if Joe knew this story, he would thank me for not calling.

My dad died when I was fifteen, early in my sophomore year in high school and my mother never re-married. As I think about it, my father dying suddenly when I was fifteen and my brother was 11; and my mother never dating or getting married again, says a lot about those times, about my family and my parents' priorities; and as clinical psychologists will tell you, your family of origin may be the major factor in shaping your growth and development into a functional and mature adult. You know, the disruption that occurred for my family probably explains a lot about my own growth and maturation. How many of us become mature adults throughout our life? I don't know, but I do know it's not one hundred percent of us. Right Arnie and Tim?

My mom went back to school and finished her degree which landed her a job taking some of the financial pressures off our family. Her commitment stressed the importance of a college education to me and my brother. And my father was a dentist who graduated first in his class with high honors. His practice was delayed by WW2, but it did get going. I seem to remember that he practiced general dentistry but was especially good with kids. One of his best friends had a pretzel factory in Scranton and kept my dad's office supplied with fresh and large tins of pretzels which my father would hand out as treats after the drilling with a warning not to eat the pretzels too soon after getting home.

Of course, my brother and I got fresh pretzels as snacks as well but my father, while being serious much of the time, was a softy when it came to Stephen, my brother, and me. I was into baseball big time and collected Topps baseball cards. In those days, a pack of cards came with a stick of gum and cost a nickel. The Topps company would release the cards at intervals so it would take an entire season to have a chance at a complete set. And the best cards were the hardest to find. Fortunately, another friend of my dad's was the distributor in the Scranton area for candy and he handled the Topps contract so when a new set of cards was released, he would drop off several boxes of card sets unopened, and my father would give them to me with the admonition not to chew the gum. Of course, Steve and I didn't listen which is why my father spent some time filling our cavities. So, between the cards provided by my dad's friend and the cards I won flipping them in the schoolyard, I had quite a collection which, unfortunately, my mom gave to my young cousins in Wilkes-Barre and Kingston, PA just before Hurricane Agnes destroyed their homes and my cards in June of 1972. I wondered at the time whether the value of all those baseball cards might have been enough to put new roofs on their new homes.

Truthfully, mom didn't have to stress education too much. It never occurred to me that college was not an option. I was a good student. I liked school. I love to read. I enjoyed learning. And I was always open to other students' (and adults') thoughts on any matter. All the kids in my classes felt the same way.

They were AP and Honors classes so I guess in hindsight they would feel the same way.

Nobody seemed to worry about how much college might cost. It certainly didn't occur to me. I assumed that things would just work out. And they did just work out with a lot of negotiating by my mother who knew a lot of "important" people in Lackawanna County. But from where I sit now, I know that a lot of my classmates who were plenty smart and hard workers went to Penn State or more local state colleges and universities because they were so much less expensive than private universities. Money was and will always be a factor which I guess is okay unless it is a barrier to a college education. For my Honors and AP classmates and friends, there was Harvard, Princeton, University of Pennsylvania, Columbia and I went to Cornell. I wasn't the Valedictorian at Scranton Central High School, but I was close. Still if it was a horse race, I was a good 8 furlongs behind Mary Jane. She was one smart woman. I believe she went to Berkeley which made sense to me since she wanted to get as far away from her family as she could. Then she got arrested for breaking into an army recruiting office in the middle of the night and pouring goat's blood all over the records. Smart and radical. It was the Vietnam War, you see. That kind of action was worth Honor Roll distinction at Berkeley. Not Cornell. Mary Jane grew up in a very strict Catholic home with many siblings and a father who was as strict as he was conservative. His job was commandant of the R.O.T.C. program at the Jesuit University of Scranton...a fine university. But I suspect all that conservativism and all those siblings molded Mary Jane into a progressive liberal who was seriously anti-war and so she looked to leave Scranton behind. I miss talking to her and I wonder where she is now. Probably hiding out in Yemen.

The college classes of 1971, where my high school mates who went to college were matriculating in 1967, had huge thunderclouds over the mountains in the distance. At least the men did. Almost nobody knew anything about Vietnam the week we graduated from high school. Not even where it was. And almost nobody cared. But a few did care and needed to know, so we read as much as we could about it. We discovered the New York Times, the Washington Post, the Atlantic, the New Yorker and Walter Cronkite. By the time freshman year was halfway through, every male in University Halls at Cornell (the freshman dorms) knew more than they wanted to about Vietnam. What I didn't understand was why we were there in the first place. What a waste of blood and treasure. For what? I felt patriotic...if it was the Revolutionary War, and certainly WW's 1and 2. I felt a duty to fight for my country and its values. But to die in the rice paddies of Que San, destroy a country of innocents over some half-baked notion of the domino theory of communism taking over Asia. I didn't think so. Like where is communism now? It's in the C countries: Cuba and China.

The last week of senior year at Scranton Central, the students of the AP and Honors classes met in front of the Scranton Public School Administration Building right under the Superintendent's office and sang "We shall overcome" until the cops came and broke it up and the Superintendent suspended all of us for the rest of the week. Maybe that's where Mary Jane began her radical journey.

My first few months at University Halls, Cornell, we still hung ties over the doorknob when a woman was visiting our room and the door had to be left partly ajar. That was the last gasp of a sea change that would re-shape my campus, change my attitude, and force all of us to consider growing up sooner than we wanted. I wondered whether I could leave my family to live in Canada. Of course, I ended up not having to consider that choice since med school was a deferment, but the eventual irony for my family was that my younger brother, Stephen, forged his career the past forty years teaching and doing scholarly work at York University in Toronto, Ontario Province.

Listen, we supported the enlisted men and officers that served our country so bravely in Vietnam and many who returned, suffered so needlessly. It was the politicians and generals that we questioned and sometimes held in contempt. My question was always why, why did we need to fight that war.

We no longer had late night conversations in University Halls about sex with co-eds. Conversation turned more political and serious. It would take another semester for all the dorms to be 'liberated' and go co-ed. We still stayed up talking over lit candles until 4 am, smoked weed and talked but the Cornell women were now our fellow students and our inbred misogyny was being scrubbed away by our real life experiences.

Martin Luther King Jr.'s assassination rocked the nation. Black Power as a political force and as a terrorist tool was growing under the leadership of new young men like Malcolm X and Eldridge Cleaver in the sixties as well as supportive white radicals sick and tired of the racism that the country had failed to expunge after the Civil War. Jim Crow was the new normal in large swaths of America.

Even feminism was growing popular, not just with our female classmates and faculty but also with radicalized male undergraduates. Formal and informal education was especially important in this new environment at Cornell: courses, guest lecturers, and books that everyone seemed to be reading... The Feminine Mystique, Sexual Politics, The Female Eunuch, Fear of Flying, Our Bodies Ourselves. Bella Abzug had been elected to Congress. By the end of Freshman year, the sounds of revolution were everywhere. A new day seemed to be dawning in America.

And over it all was the stench of the Vietnam War. Now there was talk of a draft lottery. Too many of the recruits lacked other options, and many of them were African-American. The country needed to balance the scales regarding race amongst the enlisted men.

My freshman year at Cornell was an abysmal failure in terms of academics. I had buzzed through Scranton Central for four years without doing much work that I can remember and getting straight A's every quarter. Cornell Arts and Sciences was different. They expected intellectual growth. Empty bullshit was out. Insightful and deeply thoughtful term papers were in. There was competition. By the end my GPA was a sad B minus taking courses that were reportedly easy and I enjoyed sufficiently to merit getting A's. I went home to Scranton and a job working at a Pennsylvania State mental hospital. At least they told me I was there because it was a job. On weekends I worked as a lifeguard at the pool of the downtown Holiday Inn. Now that was a great job.

Before I started working that first summer, I had an invitation to visit my freshman suite mate who lived in California. Of course, I had never been there. I had never been as far west as Pittsburgh.

Tim Harris had become a close friend. He lived in Beverly Hills. He took me on a tour of Beverly Hills High School. Taking him on a tour of Scranton Central seemed embarrassing. If I close my eyes, I can still see Central. The classrooms circa 1920, the large stairwells, the auditorium, the gym and lockers. Memories of those years in high school bubble up for me if I keep my eyes closed.

19

I remember hearing an inspirational talk by Jim Brown with all the school assembled in the auditorium. Brown was the largest human being I had ever seen. His neck size must have been greater than my waist. I guess he needed all that muscle to be one of the greatest running backs in pro football. The bizarre aspect, which never occurred to me in the moment, was that this very intelligent, very large Black man gave a great lecture to an auditorium full of white students. There was not one African-American in my high school.

When I was a high school freshman, it was in Mr. Caputo's Earth Science class that we learned President Kennedy had been shot in Dallas and that he had died shortly thereafter. That was my first taste of how life can throw some harsh curveballs at you. Kennedy's death was one year and one day before my dad died sophomore year.

But I was on my way to visit Tim Harris in his hometown of Beverly Hills. Tim's family lived in the flats while his grandfather lived in the Hills. Beverly Hills and Beverly Hills flats were divided by Sunset Boulevard as I remember it. Visiting Tim was like being in a movie. I spent an afternoon sitting and swimming by his grandfather's pool drinking Mojitos and smoking dope. You had a great view of Century City from the pool except for the fact that at midday the entire complex of skyscrapers was obliterated by smog. Eventually, Tim would take his law degree and set up an office in Century City.

That was a great two weeks. Tim and I drove all the way west with our new fraternity brother Loren who had a GTO which was a fucking burner: four forward gears, Hearst shifter, disc brakes. Whoa. Amazing that we made it in one piece since it was my first time driving a standard transmission. The entire 3500 mile drive in just over 48 hours. Somebody in

West Virginia took a shot at us but missed. I guess it wasn't Justified!

Tim's Dad took us to the Playboy Club in Los Angeles for lunch. My pro-feminism attitude took a nap for two hours. We hit Disneyland for twelve hours. We went to Tijuana for a day and almost got busted for soliciting prostitutes (which we weren't doing, you had to be loco to do that in Tijuana or anywhere else....we were living in the era of free love, only 500 miles south of Haight-Ashbury). There was even a small earthquake while I was there. It was a blast.

Except for one small thing that had a huge effect on me, on all of us, something that I still feel as I write this 56 years later.

Lyndon Johnson, you will remember, became President after Jack Kennedy was assassinated. About springtime 1967, he announced that "he would not seek, nor would he accept" his party's nomination to run for President the following year. To the extent that I was aware of this announcement by President Johnson who did a lot of great things as President, it seemed to me that this could be a nail in the Vietnam War coffin if he were to leave office. My view was that Johnson was older than his years, not well and tired of fighting with his generals about pouring more and more resources into southeast Asia.

So, Lyndon Baines Johnson of Texas would not be running for President in 1968. But there was a worthy field of potential candidates on the Democratic side: Bobby Kennedy, Eugene McCarthy, George McGovern and Hubert Humphrey. And it turns out that the candidate that would be the Democratic nominee for President would be the candidate that won the California primary which was held on June 4, 1968. Tim and I, being good Cornell progressives, did some work supporting Eugene McCarthy who was the most liberal of the bunch. I was still there visiting Tim when the primary election was held. There was a heavy turnout. After dinner, Tim and I went to McCarthy headquarters to wait and see who won and to party hearty if it was Gene. It wasn't. Kennedy won by a landslide and would be the Democratic nominee. Tim and I got into his car, an MGB, and drove five miles down Wilshire Boulevard towards the Ambassador Hotel where Kennedy's headquarters were located listening to the chatter from there on the radio. We were one mile away from the Ambassador. Kennedy was rising to the lectern to give his victory speech. He never made it. He was shot and killed by Sirhan Sirhan. He died just after 1 am on June 5, 1968. My 19th birthday.

It got worse. The following November, Richard Nixon was elected President of the United States.

As I write this book, I will tell some stories that I call small world stories. We all have experienced them but when they occur, they still make the hairs on the back of one's neck stand up. The Bobby Kennedy story is not really an example but shortly I will share a few of mine. Nevertheless, being so close to being in the Ambassador as Sirhan Sirhan went to take the shot, could we have stopped him? There could have been so many minor things that would have changed if we walked into the ballroom that may have led to a different outcome. It is a freaky thing to contemplate, enough so that my neck hairs are standing up again. That was not a great birthday present, Mr. Sirhan Sirhan.

I flew back to Philly from LA, then took a small commuter flight to Scranton. Those two flights were my first two times in airplanes.

I was bummed out. Two Kennedy's had been assassinated in a short time span, MLK Jr was gone by the same route, and, lest I forget, Malcom X was assassinated in the mid-sixties. The Black Power movement was trying to shove aside the more peaceful methods of MLK Jr. Black Power would be a startingly reality in my own idyllic college community in the not-too-distant future. The War was amping up as its successes kept creeping down. Now many of us knew men who were fighting and dying in Southeast Asia. And a few who were in exile in Canada and elsewhere. Anti-war protests were sweeping the nation during my freshman year, often focused on college campuses; in Washington, DC; and in recruitment and draft offices.

I wasn't the only new face at Cornell in 1967. My freshman year the Jesuit Order of the Catholic Church had appointed Daniel Berrigan as the Catholic Priest to Cornell. Daniel and Phillip Berrigan, bothers and Jesuit priests, had established

26

themselves as leaders of the anti-war movement. Daniel, in particular, was a prolific writer and poet with hundreds of publications and I was proud that he was a Cornell faculty member.

Despite everything that I describe that was brewing across my country, things in Scranton seemed to harken back to the days after the world war ended. All was quiet. No protests, no bombings, no speeches. Men lined up to enlist. Nobody drowned in the Holiday Inn pool in downtown Scranton, although I did pull one guy out who panicked in a pool slightly larger than his bathtub. The residents of the mental hospital were all tranquil being fully pharmaceutically zoned out. I guess you could say they were in the Goldilocks Zone of mental illness, not too sleepy and not too hyper. I formed a team and we painted the curbstones of the hospital campus white...all four miles of them. Then we played some basketball. Summer job numero uno.

I had a few dates but no girlfriends. The most interesting woman I dated became a nurse and moved to Manhattan where she got a job at Memorial Sloan Kettering Cancer Center. There was really nothing between us to follow up on other than the Archbald pothole. She lived in Archbald, a small town outside of Scranton, mostly known for the pothole which is a geologic structure that marks the southernmost advance of the glaciers that occurred during the Wisconsin Glacial Period, 15,000 years ago. Typical Scranton stuff. If you don't want to visit the pothole, there is also a park dedicated to the last operating anthracite coal mine in the area. You can ride in a coal car down its tracks to the actual mine where a guide gives you an excellent history and description. I took that tour. My recommendation is to skip it. It's not Disneyland.

One other comment about coal mines that I like to share with uninformed friends. Mine subsidence. A great deal of the Scranton area was built over coal mines. This was not strip mining. You dug tunnels down 500 feet to access the rich veins of coal. The entire process was very dangerous but also very interesting. Once a mine was cleaned out of coal, it was left, with a neighborhood above it. When I was a child, every now and then, a family would return home at the end of the day to find their house missing. It had fallen into a mine which no longer could support the overlying structure. And I guess, this subsidence also did damage to the infrastructure of the neighborhood: telephone poles, electric wires, gas lines if there were any. I'll bet every place in America has a comparable story as the cities came and went.

The only other thing I remember doing that summer was volunteering to help with the production of a Henrik Ibsen play, A Doll's House, which was

29

put on by a drama club at Marywood College, a small Catholic women's college in Scranton. I must have been very bored. Not sure, but I may remember the last line of that play, 'blow out your candles, Laura..' Nope that's not it. The play ends on a real feminist note.

Chapter 2

"Well, I don't know but I've been told

You never slow down, you never grow old

I'm tired of screwing up, tired of goin' down

Tired of myself, tired of this town

Oh, my, my, oh, hell yes

Honey, put on that party dress

Buy me a drink, sing me a song

Take me as I come, 'cause I can't stay long

Mary Jane's Last Dance.....Tom Petty and the Heartbreakers....1993....Greatest Hits album

My sophomore year at Cornell began with a fresh start. I said goodbye to University Halls and moved into a fraternity house where I shared a room with a sophomore fraternity brother. Tim and I were still close friends and in the same fraternity, but we also wanted to get to know new classmates. My roommate's name was Jay Goodwin and he didn't yet know it but he wanted to become a journalist. He was very smart, grew up in New Rochelle to the north of Manhattan in Westchester County, and was just a little bit more of a screw-up than me. Really a lot more. He was also in the College of Arts and Sciences, so I helped him with his organizational skills with the predictable outcome that I became more disorganized. He made up for that aspect by being extremely funny and enthusiastic about everything, which was a very good thing for me. He also came with a girlfriend who was at college elsewhere.

The last photograph I saw of Jay, much later, was a shot of his climbing from the roof of the American Embassy in Saigon into an American Evac helicopter. A Huey. I subsequently found out that he did that twice. He had left his journals collected carefully for five years in his hotel in the rush to get out and went back into Saigon, got his journals, made it to the same roof and left for the final time. I have tried to find Jay using the internet over the subsequent years with no luck. He did stop in Philly when I was living there and we visited for several hours in Rittenhouse Square, drinking coffee and talking about his adventures. I hope he is okay.

In retrospect, I question why I joined a fraternity, which at most colleges is called "Greek life". This seems odd to me since it has nothing to do with the Greeks then or now or the country Greece. Fraternities and Sororities do use Greek letters to identify themselves and many campuses across the US have chapters of the same fraternity which are governed by a national organization.

So here is the answer to this small mystery. The first fraternity was formed at the College of William and Mary in 1775 as a closed and secret club to distinguish it from other clubs on campus which were all about partying. They chose Greek letters to identify themselves with the thought that only intellectually savvy students would be able to understand the poorly known letters. This first fraternity in the nation was Phi Beta Kappa. Two years later, and for similar reasons, fraternities spread to Yale and Harvard and eventually, most colleges and universities. Aside from Phi Beta Kappa, the imprimatur of intellectual rigor was lost and Greek life became more synonymous with partying.

I am sure of this since much later in life I dated a Professor of Greek and Roman history and literature at Swarthmore College. She was from Milan and she swore to me in English and Italian that fraternities and sororities did not originate or become a college tradition in Greece or Italy.

Probably I joined a fraternity because I wanted an instant peer group who were friends that I could hang with....example, Tim and I drove cross country with Loren who was in the frat a year ahead of us and from LA, in that Pontiac GTO. I hated eating alone and the brothers ate together every night at the fraternity house. We had a full-time cook whose name was Ernie and he was very smooth.

Also, we partied a lot in the American-Greek fraternity tradition. That's where I first smoked hashish from a hookah. Also, the last time I did that. Smoking hashish and running through the gears of an exotic muscle car were college memories that were easy to hang onto. They were also a bit too rich for my experiences at that time. And today.

Drugs were plentiful on all college campuses in those days. It was part of the culture. 'Sex, drugs and rock and roll' was my generation's mantra. But they weren't for everybody. Most students that I knew from various peer groups would occasionally smoke marijuana and drink wine or beer. That was it. A much smaller group were specifically interested in hallucinogenic drugs, like LSD, psilocybin, magic mushrooms, and peyote buttons. There was very little interest in amphetamines except for some students who needed an upper to study for a test the next day. Similarly, I didn't see a lot of opiates used. If people wanted to get mellow, weed or Quaaludes seemed the drugs of choice and ludes are no longer on the market. On the other hand, marijuana is legal for recreational use just about everywhere and I don't see it as a gateway drug in 2023. More like a taxable commodity to help pay for infrastructure repairs. Call me naïve, but at Cornell weed and alcohol accounted for most of the drug portion of the mantra.

As I think about it, the one exception might have been rock concerts. And there were plenty of opportunities to go see great rock groups, at Cornell, in Syracuse at the War Memorial, and just about anywhere. At those celebrations there were likely to be more hallucinogenic drugs, especially LSD. I wasn't tempted.

My next-door neighbor growing up was as straight as the day was long. Smart, pretty and always good for doing the right thing. Then she went to Stanford.

She came back as a flower child. She had changed her first name. She spent half the summer in NYC playing bongos with a street band. She told me that she would go to parties at school where her friends would dump un-identified pills in a large bowl and the party goers would take handfuls and just swallow them. Her grades were mediocre, but I could tell she was still smart and still beautiful and even though she seemed stoned 75% of the time, she was always capable of interesting conversations. For me, looking at things from slightly outside, I did not see any evidence that her parents were concerned. She went back to Stanford. The last thing I heard about her was that she was living in Israel.

Stanford was known as the Cornell of the West. No. But that would be wrong. At least in 1968. Stanford was more the West of the West along with Berkeley.

This might be a good time to share with you why all my friends and acquaintances in Scranton seemed to me to be 'brilliant'. Two simple reasons. Brilliant is slang in England for doing something stupid as in 'I left the car keys in the trunk.' So, I could call someone brilliant, when I meant they were dumb, but they wouldn't be insulted. The second reason had to do with Scranton's population. Never the most progressive or interesting of cities, when I was a child, the population was around 140,000. Now, the population is 60,000. All my friends who I considered smart never came back and this trend was generation after generation. Brilliant, which in this situation meant smart.

When you join a fraternity, at the beginning they call you a Pledge, a demeaning title that is supposed to suggest that you must pass an initiation test to become a full brother. Which is bullshit since, as usual, it's all about money. Which, during college, was one of my problems. I did not have a significant

40

allowance for spending money, like almost none. That was one of the good things about being in a fraternity. Your friends had much more generous allowances and they understood my problem: single parent, no father, brother who needed to be educated. I made out okay although I was careful not to free load. And I started to find jobs which helped enormously. For example, I became the dishwasher at the fraternity house. I have always enjoyed washing dishes. Sounds weird, I know. But it is a task which has a beginning, a middle and an end. Comparing that to being a physician where there is never an end in sight.

I don't want to spend any more time on 'Greek life'. I quit after the year was over anyway, as did Jay and Tim. In fact, that fraternity fell apart on Cornell's campus. Everybody quit. Not because it was a bad experience. It was a really good experience. It was just that my brothers at Phi Epsilon Pi were not "Greeks". They were just cool.

I told you that I considered myself an academic failure freshman year with a B minus grade point average. This was 1967-1968. The courses I took Freshman year came from what can only be described as a Chinese restaurant menu. You needed to take 15 credit hours each semester. Most courses were worth 3 credit hours. In the Arts College, you had two columns to choose from each semester, picking two courses from one column and three courses from the other column. Five courses a semester equals 15 credit hours a semester. The University's intent was that you would start with a rather broad, liberal arts curriculum. Maybe they thought it would help you decide what area to focus on during your remaining three years. I considered it non-relevant with only a few interesting choices. That only happened during my freshman year.

Most of my friends' criteria for choosing classes were that they did not have lectures earlier than noon, or later than five, which seemed to me to thwart the University's intent. It was obvious to me that my friends wanted to maintain the option of staying out late every night. Okay, but college costs a lot of money so what was the point if you missed out on great courses. The point didn't matter. We were young and had our priorities. Freshman year ended with two freshmen in my corridor in University Halls Four flunking out. They never studied, ignored course work, blew off meetings with TA's and Professors, and played chess, smoked weed, got drunk and slept. I never wondered what happened to them. I only wondered why they went to college in the first place.

The first week of sophomore year, you had to choose your predominant area of study or what was called your Major. Some manic students, likely the only child in their family, chose a double-Major. A

43

few depressed students chose a Major and a Minor. The majority just declared a Major. Like me. Still, in considering these decisions, it said a lot about the inherent mental illness in our society. But whatever you did, it meant you committed to taking a specific number of credit hours over the next three years in your Major and your Minor if you had one. Plus, depending on your field of study, you may be required to participate in a professor's research project or write a term paper that was like a mini-graduate thesis.

I wanted to keep my options open. But, if I was honest, I really thought what turned me on the most would be going to medical school and becoming some kind of doctor. I got a lot of help with that decision because every friend I ever had at one time or another, and particularly the women, took me aside and told me that fate decreed that I go to medical school because they couldn't imagine anyone that would make a better doctor than me.

Very gratifying. It seemed I was heading in the right direction. Now I realize it could have meant that they couldn't imagine anything else that I could do.

I needed a Major to graduate from Cornell and I needed courses where I would do well enough to compete with the growing number of medical school applicants and the shrinking percentage of medical school acceptances. How about biology? That seemed logical.

At the beginning of sophomore year, I chose an interesting set of courses, the most difficult one being 'Comparative Anatomy of Vertebrates'. Two lectures and two labs a week and worth five credit hours. I walked into the first lecture a bit early. This lecture hall looked like the room where Indiana Jones gave his lectures before he left to find the The Lost Ark. A grad student with good drawing skills had drawn across the entirety of a huge blackboard at the front of the lecture hall a gigantic eel, one of the lowest, if not the least evolved, of the vertebrates. And then inside the eel he had drawn at least two hundred small organ like structures that made up the inner workings of the eel.

If the eel was the subject of the first lecture, what would a pigeon look like? I stared at the eel for about five minutes, my mind blank. Then I turned on my heel and walked out, went over to the Dean of Students office, crossed out my enrollment in that course and changed my Major to psychology, changed my courses for the semester and wandered out wondering what I had just done.

As an aside, have you ever eaten eel? Freshwater eel is considered a great delicacy in many parts of the world and usually offered as a first course. I ordered eel once in Prague visiting my older son who was volunteering defending Roma (the gypsies) at the International Court in the Hague. I couldn't get past the rows of razor-sharp teeth at the front of the animal.

Now the historical part of this is that the lecture hall with the big eel used to be the Cornell Medical College until about 1900 when they ran out of live patients for the students. So, they moved the Medical College to Manhattan as part of the New York Hospital campus which included Memorial Sloan Kettering, Rockefeller University (home of many Nobel prizes), the Hospital for Special Surgery (orthopedics), Manhattan Eye and Ear Hospital, several dorms and residences and a bunch of hospitals in the general vicinity. Plenty of patients. New York City. Lots of trauma and cardiac disease. Tons of sick patients for the rest of us. The city even seemed to have a monopoly on tropical medicine. You know, worm infestations, like the fiery worm of Ethiopia.

So now I was a psychology Major who wanted to go to medical school. I decided to map out my courses for the next two years so I would be sure to get those courses which I needed to apply to med school by my senior year. It was then that I made a few lucky, but brilliant (smart) decisions. Specifically, I decided to take a two-semester organic chemistry course Junior year. There was also a one semester organic chem course, but I decided against that. This was an uninformed but outstanding choice for reasons that you will learn about. I also decided to take the two-semester physics course junior year and the one semester calculus course during the second semester of my sophomore year. I did this with the hope that the two-semester physics course would be easier for me to pad my grade as an experienced Junior and the one semester calc course I just wanted to get past it, math not being my favorite subject. If anything would drag my GPA down, it would be calculus and physics. And they were required for applications to med schools. Why? A brilliant (smart) question, no doubt. I have practiced medicine in one form or another for 43 years and nobody ever asked me if I knew the answer to dividing Pi by the square root of 6,702. Or, if two trains were traveling in the same direction in different states at 90 miles an hour, which would get to Dubuque first? Yet choosing to take these courses when I did really helped me find my way into med school.

As far as psychology went, meh! I didn't even know that Cornell's department was focused on experimental psychology and not clinical psychology, which would have been a lot more useful, both to me personally and to me as a physician. The two things I remember from my studies of psychology are 1.) the visual cliff experiment which made the department temporarily famous. In this experiment, babies who can crawl are put on a tabletop in the middle of which is a safe, supportive, glass insert. At a certain stage of development, the babies will recognize the potential for falling and not venture onto the glass. That's it. The Visual Cliff. Now 2.) was Professor Eric Lenneberg who was my Major advisor, and a nicer man was never a professor at Cornell. Professor Lenneberg's area of study was the neurophysiologic correlates of language, and it would have been a joy to work with and learn from him. Unfortunately, he died after our first meeting. Not because of it. My next advisor was an asshole whose most prominent characteristic was narcissism.... which, as you must know, is a clinical psychological diagnosis. Likely that the hiring committee missed the diagnosis.

Some of you might remember Alan Funt and Candid Camera, an early TV show in which Funt's crew secretly captured unsuspecting people's reactions to embarrassing situations on videotape and showed them on TV. Alan Funt was a Cornell graduate and after the show was cancelled, he donated all his tapes to the Cornell Psychology department to see if they could learn anything from them. My advisor was the recipient of those tapes. He was less than helpful to me. You know, if I ever run into him and recognize the bastard (I heard he was at Penn now), I think I will kneecap him. Kneecapping is a Philadelphia tradition.

Meanwhile, the problems of the world were getting worse. Richard Nixon was now President and he liked feeding the war machine. Racism, misogyny, bigotry of all types (anti-gay riots, antisemitic acts, anti-feminist demonstrations) were dividing the country like I had never seen although it had always been there under the sheets, so to speak. The right wing, fascist, Ku Klux Klan sheets. Draft cards were being distributed in preparation for a draft lottery. The United States was in a world of hurt and there was a lot of shit to work through.

I noticed something on campus, reverse segregation. The African American students were pulling away from contact with the Caucasian students. They had their own area of the student union's dining hall, they rarely dated white co-eds, they didn't party with white groups like fraternities (and I can't remember one Black student joining a white fraternity while I was there), they had their own separate protests and rallies, and they lived in their own residences. This made no sense to me. In my mind, Cornell was a liberal, progressive university which should exhilarate in its diversity. I was constantly trying to understand the tensions in American life between Blacks and Whites since slavery was abolished and this wasn't helping. I didn't have any Black friends to discuss these issues. I substituted reading those books which provided insight: Soul on Ice by Eldridge Cleaver; The Autobiography of Malcolm X; Man child in the Promised Land by Claude Brown; Black Boy by

Richard Wright; and The Fire Next Time by James Baldwin. In fact, anything by James Baldwin.

This is a brief story about a girlfriend I had during Freshman year named Carol and it has a bearing on this race conundrum I was experiencing. We have remained friends through the years and occasionally communicate by emails or birthday cards. For some reason, she always asked me to help with new boyfriend problems. After we broke up, and during Sophomore year, she started dating a Black student. But they had a problem. He was concerned that if his peer group found out he was dating a white woman, even though she was from St. Paul, MN, the progressive center of middle America, he would in some way be ostracized. Could I help? Of course. I would meet Carol for a 'date' and very quickly we would meet up with her boyfriend who I think may have had a car which made things easier. I would say good night and slip into the shadows. My personal contribution to integration on campus.

As a sophomore, my GPA slowly began to rise, perhaps because psych professors were easier graders. Who knows? I was taking other courses as well. But now the second semester was going to start. Calculus. To make things worse, the mathematics department focused on theoretical math rather than practical math which I found particularly daunting.

But as the war in Viet Nam was worsening, the protests here at home were also getting larger and more violent. I went to DC and found myself being tear gassed as the police tried to dispel the thousands of people who had rallied to protest the war. At some campuses, fake bomb threats were made to escalate students' discontent. Then, suddenly, they were no longer threats as a few campuses suffered real fire bombings of both campus offices and army recruitment centers. A student self-immolated in front of Congress to protest the war. A year later, the inevitable escalation of protest led to a peaceful protest at Kent State University being shattered when National Guardsmen called up for crowd control fired into the assembled students killing 4, memorialized in the folk song by Crosby, Stills, Nash and Young ('Ohio').

And, only a few months after Kent State, the peace and quiet of a college town in Wisconsin was shattered by a huge bomb blast that destroyed a large math building and parts of a hospital across the street. It could be heard ten miles away and killed one graduate student in physics, a PhD candidate and father of three. The University of Wisconsin – Madison bombing electrified the student protest movement nationwide. Nowhere seemed safe. The FBI called it the biggest act of domestic terrorism ever seen. The perpetrators fled the country, one has never been caught and remains on the FBI's most wanted list.

It was clear to me that our innocuous protest beneath the office of the Superintendent of the Scranton Public School System in June of 1967 had, in front of my eyes, grown at times slowly and at times by quantum leaps. But one thing was clear. My generation was not going to tolerate what had become Richard Nixon's War. One way or another, America was going to leave Vietnam.

Second semester, sophomore year was thankfully quiet in that there were no bomb blasts. But there was a rash of bomb threats called in at Cornell that disrupted many classes including my calculus course.

The University, in their wisdom, decided to give students a choice that semester.... they could take their grade in each course; or they could take a pass/fail option. That meant that at the end of the semester, if you had a passing grade and you chose pass, your transcript would show pass. This may surprise you, but I chose to pass in calculus since I was passing. And I was getting A's in my other courses, so I chose my grades in those courses. This helped my GPA. And remember, this was a year before Kent State and the University of Wisconsin – Madison bombing. Bomb threats and bullets were just threats but not the real real.

Meanwhile we still had lots of energy for all the other problems in our society which irked us. Every day there were protests at lunch time in front of Willard Straight Hall, which was our primary Student Union, against Cornell's investments in South Africa because of their racist policy of apartheid. The Black students still separated themselves from the white students. There were many events heralding the feminist movement. And there was still 'sex, drugs and rock and roll' with parties, concerts, love affairs, group sex and so on.

Then something happened that powered its way past all the demonstrations, all the agitation, all the political engagement that had consumed campuses including Cornell's through the mid-point of second semester Sophomore year.

I hope that your reading of this has instilled in you the rising degree of racial tension that existed in the country at large and was paralleled by the racial tension that was occurring on Cornell's campus. This tension exploded in early April 1969, when there was a cross burning on the lawn in front of a dormitory designated for African-American women and shortly thereafter what was considered unfair disciplinary action taken against a Black student who was protesting institutional racism at Cornell. Parents weekend commenced April 18th, 1969. Because of the above events, the perceived institutional racism of the University, a perceived biased judicial system and slow progress in developing a promised Black Studies program, members of the Cornell Afro-American society escorted visiting parents, some of whom were staying in the student union guest quarters, out of the building and took control of Willard Straight Hall. Taking over a classroom or rooms was one thing, but taking over the Student Union and throwing out the parents on Parents Weekend was a quantum leap beyond. Worse was to come. When this news spread across the campus, members of a white fraternity where many athletes lived tried to retake the building by force. This was not a university administration choice, it was the brothers' choice in that fraternity. In response several Black students slipped away from the Union, returning armed with rifles and shotguns. It is not clear from the reporting, but the Afro-American students holding Willard Straight Hall under arms remained for a few days, protected in part by a cordon of white student members of a radical group

59

(present on many campuses) named Cornell Students for a Democratic Society (SDS).

The stand-off ended peacefully with the Black students leaving with their weapons and no shots being fired after the University agreed to form a University Senate, restructure the Board of Trustees, reform the campus judicial system and found an Africana Studies and Research Center; essentially all the Black students' demands. James Perkins, Cornell's President during this period, was forced to resign at the end of the academic year presumably because of his willingness to negotiate with the students.

This was 1968. There was extreme racial tension. There was a lot of animosity. There certainly was bigotry. There were guns. There was rioting at the Democratic National Political Convention in Chicago. I could go on, but my point here is that no shots were fired, nobody was badly hurt, there was some compromise and a peaceful resolution of problems that had been festering for a long time. There were no AR-15 style weapons. Nobody went off the rails and fired at crowds of students (except at Kent State), police or anybody else. The authorities, and here I mean the cops, kept their cool and followed their protocols.

So why do I have to listen nightly to mass shootings with long guns meant to be weapons of war, killing innocent children and teenagers and adults. As I write this, the year is 2023. 55 years after the taking of Willard Straight Hall. What the fuck are we doing?

I sat transfixed every night for more than a week watching my university lead the CBS Evening News with Walter Cronkite reporting. Photographs of the entire affair filled the New York Times,

Washington Post, Time and Newsweek and dozens of other newspapers and magazines. I want to acknowledge the small amount of information I gleaned from my extensive review of the internet regarding this affair. Had things not come to a head as they did, people might have died. But they didn't.

I did notice one change when I returned to campus for Junior year. The campus police were now armed.

As the end of the year approached, Jay and I decided to rent an apartment around the corner from our abandoned fraternity house. I think it was on Ridgewood Road. I know it was about 50 yards away from a sorority house, Sigma Delta Tau, where I had a lot of friends several of whom I would have liked to know better. Tim had a car now and he rented a house with three others in downtown Ithaca but I still saw him all the time.

I was going home to Scranton where the dull aspects of my life there might have been a relief from the events that had shaped and sharpened my sophomore year. But I didn't feel that way. I was excited to get back to campus for Junior year, two semesters which promised to decide whether I would be going to med school after graduation. After two years, my grade point average was hovering around 3.4, still too low, but I had those two semesters of organic chemistry to look forward to and the MCATS (these are the standardized tests used to some extent in determining admission to medical school, sort of like the SAT's.) Plus, what would be the fallout from all the stuff that happened on campus. I knew that President Perkins was gone, but who would replace him?

And the Cornell men's ice hockey and lacrosse teams had a real chance at winning the NCAA

Division One championships. My junior year would be interesting.

But for now, it was back to painting curbs with tranquilized residents of the PA mental hospital and saving panicked visitors at the Scranton Holiday Inn pool.

This might be a good time for a little pause to discuss a few items I wanted to share. One of life's needs is that few people who can do it, take the time teaching you how to mourn. How to grieve loss. Unfortunately, I had an enormous loss as a very young man. Being 15 in 1964, you are a lot younger than if you're 15 in 2020 and your father drops dead. Kids grow up faster now and I am not so sure that is a good thing. When I was in high school, a classmate of mine got pregnant at age 17 and it was considered sinful and embarrassing and had to be hidden. That just wasn't right. What if my classmate wanted to keep the pregnancy and baby?

Anyway, I never got to participate in a lot of things that sons do with their fathers. But in the year before he died, he did three things that I thought were a bit unusual for him but now I consider them in a different light.

For one, he took me to the old Yankee Stadium (he was a big fan, as am I). This must have been a strain for him because of unstable coronary disease and how hard he worked.

Second, he had a serious conversation with me about a boy who belonged to our synagogue and was two years older than me. I didn't know him. But this boy's father had died suddenly, and the boy had followed the traditions associated with mourning for a parent. That really impressed my father.

Finally, and most uncharacteristically, he took me on an unusual drive to the home of one of his patients after he finished in his office. This was some distance from our own home. He told me I was the only one who knew what he was doing. There I found that his patient's bitch (female pregnant dog) had a new litter of puppies, the Heinz 57 variety. My Dad said pick one and his patient smiled. I did and put her in my gym bag, she was so small but so, so adorable. I knew my mother had said long ago that she would never tolerate a dog in the house and boy was she pissed when we got home. I have never seen her so angry with my dad, but he calmly let her settle down and my brother (who was over the moon) and I named her Pepper because she had black and white spots, fed her and got her set up in the basement where my mom insisted she sleep until she was housebroken. And we had to clean up her messes in the morning. Soon enough she was sleeping alongside our beds.

I believe all three of these events were connected and were carefully planned by my dad, to teach me lessons and give me tools to accept and overcome my grief when he died, because he knew it would not be long. And it wasn't. Just five months later. Tears come to my eyes as I write this, and I am glad for those tears. Andrea, just know that those twelve years of therapy were worth it. Thank you.

You see the treat of going with him to Yankee Stadium and seeing the likes of Mickey Mantle and Roger Maris, Whitey Ford and Yogi Berra for three whole games and staying in a hotel was a memory that I will hold onto forever. It was not a common occurrence to do something special like that with my father.

Impressing in me a tradition related to grieving a parent was important to him, and, I have come to believe that he knew it would be crucial for me in finding closure for my loss. It was onerous, going to the Temple twice daily for ten months to pray with the adult men conducting the early and late afternoon service to say the Kaddish and remember my father. The men were great, very supportive, and helped me mourn.

But the puppy, against the oft stated insistence of my strong-willed mother, coming to the house hidden in my gym bag with nowhere else to go, must have been a very difficult thing for my father to pull off but he did it with grace, patience and aplomb. And for all my mother's anger, Pepper lived to be 19 years old, was never sick a day in her life, was brilliant (smart) practically taking care of herself and served as company for my mom for years after Stephen and I had left home. Pepper died of a stroke at age 19. I was a freshman in high school when we brought her home. I was married and in the final stages of my fellowship training in rheumatology at Yale when she died. Good going, dad. And Pepper, may your memory be a blessing....

So, my dad helped me deal with his death in advance. At least I believe that. But several months after his death, my mother encouraged me to start going out with my friends. It was a lovely thing to do because I was sort of frozen socially, in an unstable goldilocks zone between being at home with my family and going out with my friends. But once I got started, I hardly ever came home and soon enough there was college and my distance from my family of origin, my mother and my brother, and Pepper and Scranton grew wider and wider. The same thing happened with my faith.

I was raised in a Conservative Jewish home. That is to say that we belonged to a Conservative

Synagogue, we observed all the holidays and celebrations and many of the youth activities. I went to Hebrew School and was confirmed, I was Bar Mitzvah, I was in the youth choir, and I would periodically go to services just to go. But I was drifting away from all those things and by the time I got to Cornell, I considered myself an ethnic Jew but not a religious one. I knew a lot about my religion and its practices, and I could speak practical Hebrew. But I questioned why we needed to believe in a God. A deity that could allow the Holocaust and not just the Nazi Holocaust but smaller holocausts all over the world for a long time. And what about racism and antisemitism and misogyny and on and on. I had no time for Rabbinic discussions. I guess I settled on the idea that religion in general was a common theme that allowed families to come together and learn how people should behave in a society and set up a system of rewards and punishments to reinforce these ideal behaviors. And I felt that way for a long time. All through my education, my clinical training, my marriage, having children, and my divorce.

It was a dog that changed my mind. My dog. A dog as close to my heart as any human being. My beloved Gabriel. Those tears are there in my eyes again when I think of him. Let me tell you how he restored my faith.

Remember you left me pondering summer in Scranton waiting for my all-important Junior year to begin. Well long after that summer I was married and blessed with two wonderful sons, Michael and Craig. Craig was younger and desperately wanted a dog, taking every opportunity to remind his parents. Leslie and I weren't opposed since we both grew up with dogs, but Michael had bad allergies and mild asthma when he was young, and we were concerned that a dog in the house could make it worse.

Michael's asthma and allergies got better. Finally, Craig won the day. His instructions were to search the American Kennel Club website and find a breed of dog that appealed to him, but we gave him some restrictions. We wanted a dog that was in the Goldilocks Zone: not too big and needing lots of exercise and not too small with a lot of yips and manic behavior, but just right. Maybe 40 pounds, calm personality, good with children, and, oh yeah, the dog couldn't shed. It took Craig about an hour to find his choice. A soft-coated Wheaten terrier. A male. It was a great choice and we set out trying to find one. This wasn't as easy as it sounds. Wheaten breeders are extremely picky as to whom they will sell a pup. We did find one eventually. That turned out to be Spencer. Craig named him after the little boy in the movie 'As Good as it Gets'. Good choice, Craig. Spencer was a very good pet. Craig was a freshman in high school when Spencer came to us, and Craig took incredibly good care of him. But four years later, Craig was off to college in Washington,

DC. Michael was already gone 4 years. Spencer was my dog now and I was happy. Leslie was good about helping. But Spencer developed a spinal cord malignancy and became incontinent, so we had to put him down. Leslie was happy to be a true empty nester. I was sad because I missed Spencer....and my boys. Eventually, everything came together when Leslie and I were taking a break for a long weekend in Florida and saw a young couple walking a Wheaten Terrier. Les looked at me and said, 'I think it would be okay to get another Wheaten if we rescued one.'

Within two months we found ourselves at the Kansas City airport which I think is in Missouri, waiting for the Wheaten rescue lady to bring Gabriel to us for a look-see (as they say in Missouri). The Vet that she had taken him to felt by his dental exam and bone x-rays that he was probably 4-5 years old and in good health with none of the bowel or kidney problems this breed can sometimes have. I swear this

73

is what happened. He jumped right out of her truck and right over to me giving me that initial Wheaten jump hello. I snapped on his leash and told him we would go for a walk, and he flowed into my gait as we circled another Holiday Inn not nearly as nice as the one in downtown Scranton and with no pool. There was no question that he was coming back with us to Delaware. I had already booked his flight for the next morning. Tired, we settled in to sleep at the Holiday Inn, and in a split second, Gabriel had nestled in between us and was asleep himself. Gabriel adapted to us and to Delaware like he had lived there all his life.

Flash forward to the summer when Gabriel was eleven years old. That summer he was diagnosed with an incurable mast cell tumor around his anus which had spread to his pelvic lymph nodes. This is a very rare cancer in this breed, but shit happens. We visited our vet who I adored. He told me what I already knew.

"Gabriel is suffering and it's only going to get worse. You could take him to the Veterinary Medicine School at Penn, but they will offer radiation therapy that will bankrupt you and won't help Gabriel. Doesn't matter if your decision is tonight, tomorrow or the next day; I'll be here for you, it will be quick and it will be painless. For Gabriel. Maybe not so much for you."

I looked at him and shook my head affirmatively to go ahead. He left us to gather what he needed. Truth be told, my six years with Gabe had been difficult for me. I may not have gotten through them had it not been for my dog. Gabriel's loyalty, gentleness, friendliness, overall happiness and genuine empathy had supported me through the tough years.

I knew what would happen. The Vet started an IV after shaving part of his right front leg. He looked at me and confidently said we must do this. It is the right thing to do and there are no other options. Now go stand by Gabe's head. I stroked the soft silky coat of his head and neck. The Vet pushed propofol through the IV and Gabe's legs buckled. Then he pushed a second slightly pinkish fluid rapidly through the IV. Within seconds, Gabe stopped breathing. It was sudden and peaceful. The Vet listened for a heartbeat. There was none. He nodded and told me to take as much time as I needed and then he left Gabe and I alone. A tech came in and told me the body would be picked up by an animal crematorium and in a few weeks, they would call and have me pick up his remains. Then I was truly alone.

I started to sob uncontrollably. Tears poured from my eyes. I hugged his head. I cried for Gabriel, for myself, for Spencer, for my parents, for my dead child, for all the loss and grief that I had never let myself feel. It was as if all my dad's preparation and Gabriel's love and devotion had collided in one gigantic melding of feeling, emotion, love and grief. After 5, maybe 10 minutes I tore myself away from Gabe and ran to my car. Inside the car, I started to sob again. Suddenly I felt sick, nauseated, lightheaded, breathless. Maybe I would die right then and there. But after 20 seconds it passed, and a calm passed over me and I knew that Gabriel was with me in that car. It had just been a panic attack, most likely. But Gabriel's spirit or something like it, had calmed me and somehow let me know that while he would move on, he would always be near enough to me if I called for him.

I buried Gabe's ashes which were in a small burlap sack three feet under a bush that grew under my bedroom window in front of our home in Delaware. Four years later I sold my home and chose apartment living. I took the small plaque that says Gabriel and has his paw print embedded in it with me. The sack with Gabe's ashes remains buried in front of the new owner's home, but Gabe is not there. He is with me all the time. If I quiet my thoughts and search for him, he is there. If I catch a movement out of the corner of my eye where no movement should be, and I look but there is nothing there, I smile. In 2017 I went on a road trip with a friend. We had heard that there was a grey wolf pack hunting elk in the northeast corner of Yellowstone National Park while we were staying at the Lodge at Old Faithful. We got up very early and drove the three hours to the spot where the wolves had been spotted by Rangers at dawn. We arrived at the right time but did not see any wolves. I would have loved to spy on a Grey in the wild at dawn. But I did feel Gabe's presence and keen interest in the back seat of our car.

Gabriel, this message is for you. I am dying. I have something humans call leukemia. It won't kill me right away but eventually it will overwhelm my defenses and my treatments. I am not afraid to die. You taught me that. And I have so many other wonderful gifts from being your human. Always stay close and I promise the same.

Chapter Three

"Tell us what you're gonna do tonight mama

There must be someplace you can go

In the middle of the tall drinks and the drama

There must be someone you know

God knows you're lookin' good enough

But you're so smooth and the world's so rough

You might have something' to lose

Oh, no, pretty mama

What you gonna do in those shoes?"

Those Shoes....Eagles....1979 from the album The Long Run

There really wasn't anything major to report about that summer in Scranton. The curbstones looked even better with a second coat of white paint. Nobody panicked in the Holiday Inn pool. But we did have two sets of interesting guests that I can remember.

The first was a couple of middle-aged guys in suits and ties that they wore sitting by the pool. Since they obviously weren't going swimming, I ignored them except to ask if they wanted to order food or drinks. Which they didn't. Finally, they called me over and asked what you did for fun around Scranton. Funny question. People worked, ate and slept in Scranton; maybe went out for a beer or movie. Then they wanted to know what I did for fun. I told them they were looking at it. Since they weren't getting anywhere with their line of questioning, because I had no idea what they wanted to know, they tried a different tack.

"Look son," the bigger guy said, "we're here on business. A special kind of business. So, you can be honest with us about stuff in Scranton, and the surrounding area."

Why did these two think I wouldn't be honest or if I chose to be dishonest, that I would change my mind because of some business they weren't telling me about. I didn't want to be impolite or appear like a dumb lifeguard, which I was, so I thought about it for a few minutes.

"Well, Scranton has a lot of pretty good Italian restaurants. We have three movie theaters within walking distance of here and the front desk can tell you what's playing. If you want to take a drive, you can visit the state park they built around the Archbald pothole, but you would have to do that during the day. Also, there are some beautiful churches and the University of Scranton is a great Jesuit University so you could tour those things."

I was quickly running out of ideas for them. The attractions that are available today, like Steamtown, dedicated to steam railroads, or the tour of the last operating anthracite coal mine, weren't in existence yet. Each new inventive attraction just shrunk the population more. Really reaching and about to give up, I told them about Nay Aug Park, the city park which was notable for the smallest and smelliest zoo in America which at that point housed only a geriatric elephant. Oh, and a museum dedicated to John James Audubon, a naturalist who studied American birds and in which there was a small but functioning planetarium although I don't know what that had to do with birds.

These two guys. They couldn't be called gentlemen or even men. They were guys who reached into their suitcoat inside pockets and pulled out two wallets, opened them and showed them to me. Holy Shit. These guys were FBI Special Agents. I figured I was a dead duck. They probably had all kinds of photographs of me attending Cornell SDS meetings, getting tear gassed in DC, letting my hair get long. I was just going to confess, come clean and take my punishment. I had heard that Federal Prisons were nicer than state penitentiaries.

Nope. I wasn't who they were after. Their questions were all aimed at finding out where the good brothels were. They wanted to get laid. I never knew this but apparently Scranton was well known during the 1930's and 1940's as a hub of the prostitution industry. No wonder the population had swollen to almost 150,000. But the genteel 1950's and the political 1960's along with a steadily declining industrial and professional base had gutted whoring, if you can say that without being accused of a horrible allegory.

I gave them the bad news. Could someone else, perhaps older and more jaded help them? I told them to ask at the desk and never saw them again.

Now, ironically, several weeks after the FBI fiasco, we had a large group stay at the Holiday Inn for an entire ten days. There were probably twenty people in the group and 16 at least must have been women in their twenties and thirties. They spent the day by the pool in bikinis and drank and gossiped and ignored me, then disappeared after 7 pm. Now I worked the pool on Friday, Saturday and Sunday. The group checked-in on Friday and when I returned the following Friday, they were still there sunning themselves, drinking and gossiping. Nobody went into the pool. After cleaning the pool four times Friday morning, I finally got up the nerve to start a conversation with one of the women who appeared to be about my age. At least, she was younger than the rest. And this is what I found out.

Wayne County is roughly in north central Pennsylvania, and it is rural with some agricultural activity but no real commercial or residential development. Every summer the main event was the

County Fair which I suppose is not much different from other similar fairs, just smaller. You know, who has the largest pig; a pie-eating contest; etc. But the Wayne County Fair had a tent with a strip-tease show. If I was aware of that, it was only by vague rumor. Right here, sitting around my pool with their legs dangling in the water, were the actual strippers. Wow! Did those FBI dudes miss their opportunity! Of course, being a stripper did not mean you were a prostitute, but somehow, I had the feeling that there was some commingling of the professions. They stayed the weekend, and we had some interesting conversations in which I learned a lot about the art and skill of stripping and they learned a lot about being a student at Cornell. They did most of the talking.

But now summer was over, and I was moving into my own apartment with my apartment mate, Jay Goodwin. This was going to be fun. (I imagine saying that last sentence out loud and sounding just like Tom Petty performing Spike from the Southern Accents album as he and his buddy guitarist Mike sat in the darkness of the Cypress Lounge. You have to have heard the track Spike which is the story of an adolescent boy who wears a dog collar and leather jacket in the summer in Gainesville, Florida.)

One thing I should mention, both last year's fraternity and our new apartment were in Cayuga Heights which was on the other side of a large gorge from the lower campus where most, but not all, of our classes were held. And that was where Willard Straight Hall, the student union, was; and the student infirmary; and the Arts and Sciences quadrangle; and Uris (undergraduate) library with it's famous bell tower and bells; and the block like Olin (graduate) library; and the chapel where an occasional couple could get married; and Schoellkopf field where our football team played and lost; and Lynah Rink where are ice hockey team won and won and won and won.

You can see that the lower campus was a beehive of activity. I didn't even mention all the buildings holding classrooms and professors' offices and labs. But the upper campus had a lot of stuff as well, particularly if you had matriculated in the Agricultural College or the Human Ecology College.

When I was a freshman, Human Ecology had a different name, Home Economics. The name home economics was passe', insulting, misogynistic and was suddenly, with the same courses and faculty, the College of Human Ecology. Sometimes everything is in a name. I am really sorry, and I apologize in advance to my schoolmates from Cornell, but I just now had this image of politically aggressive braless co-eds taking over Bailey Hall armed with egg-beaters and rolling pins. That never happened. It was just a passing image somehow mixed together with two middle-aged FBI agents. Just too many sit-ins and occupied buildings with which to keep up. After the conference with the strippers, I needed to turn the dial back to feminism to be in the correct frame of mind, now being a Junior at Cornell.

I got carried away there. Please know that I have been back to Cornell numerous times since I graduated, and the campus has changed but not drastically. It is still one of the most beautiful universities on the planet. One thing that has drastically changed is the impact of computers, which I will not talk about further.

It was a hike from our apartment to the Arts quad (or anywhere else on campus). There were several ways to go but my preferred way was via the Suspension Bridge which the Engineering College had designed and was a marvel. It was a long bridge over a great height, but it was beautiful and as the seasons changed, the beauty changed but never diminished. Just like the Eagles sing in Hotel California, "anytime of year, you can find it here."

You may find that I will make occasional references to the rock band Eagles since they are identified as California Rock even though only one of the band members was from California. The reason I do that is to memorialize Tim Harris who you will remember as my freshman roommate and lifelong friend who died too young. I miss you, Tim.

Organic chemistry had three early morning lectures a week beginning at 8 am in an Arts Quad building. That meant I would have to leave the apt. by 7:15, particularly if I wanted to stop and pick up a coffee at Zeus which was a favorite coffee place in the lobby of a main Arts Quad building, Goldwin-Smith, the tables intermingling with fake Greek statues. Now for the life of me, I am blocking on my professor's name. C'mon, Jim, it's only been 53 years since you last spoke with him. I can visualize him. He taught Introduction to Organic Chemistry, Part One in the fall and Introduction to Organic Chemistry, Part Two in the spring. I had made the decision to take both courses instead of taking the single organic chem course. I went searching for this chemistry professor's name but I could not find it on the internet. There were a lot of Cornell chemistry professors who won important awards, like the Nobel Prize, but not my professor. I discovered that Linus Pauling PhD, etc., taught at Cornell. He was an avid anti-war activist and considered by those who should know to be one of the 250 greatest chemistry scholars of all time. If they made a movie about him, they would have called it 'The Imitation Molecule'. Tom Hanks could have played Linus Pauling. But my guy was not listed anywhere on Google or Wikepedia. However, in searching, I discovered an old photo album with a collection of my transcripts. Maybe his name would be on my 'report cards'. Nope. There were two organic chem courses, each carrying an A after the title of the course. I had also taken the two-semester Introduction to Physics courses my junior year as well. And unbelievably to me, there were A's after both physics courses. I have gone through most of my life thinking that I had taken a Pass/Fail in physics but instead I had ace'd the two courses. The only course I had wimped on was calculus. I earned a pass. Or maybe I squeaked by with a pass. 'Earned' sounds too grandiose.

Thinking about The Imitation Game (the excellent movie about Alan Turing, a British scientist who against many melodramatic odds invented a computer during WW2 capable of breaking the Nazi's Enigma coding machine.), several things came to my overactive mind. In college, movies were called flicks, not movies, even though the term flicks would seem better applied to Casablanca or The Maltese Falcon. It was fantastic how Bogart could look like he was sneering when he was smiling and vice versa. If I had the part of Rick Blaine in Casablanca, after shooting Major Strasser in the penultimate scene, I would have shot Louis Renault, Victor Laszlo and the pilot of the plane and driven off as fast as I could with Ingrid Bergman. That would have been more realistic. No soap radio.

Finally, a historic note regarding Alan Turing, the hero in The Imitation Game who worked tirelessly to crack the codes created by Germany's Enigma machine. For his patriotism and dedication to his country, England, he was assassinated by the British Secret Service in the 1950's because he was gay and therefore considered a security risk by the boys at MI5. You will remember that MI5 was a hotbed of Russian moles as written about in Tinker, Tailor, Soldier, Spy by John LeCarre. One wonders what would happen to British Intelligence if it ever came out that James Bond was homosexual. Personally, playing the part of Rick Blaine, I felt safe from MI5, MI6 and all the European homophobes as I drove quickly around the curves of the Amalfi Coast with Ingrid Bergman by my side. Nobody would mistake me for a gay American barkeep most recently in business in Casablanca.

Now in Chapter two, my sophomore year, I chose my major and told you about poor Prof. Lenneberg and the asshole that replaced him as my advisor whose name I have wiped from my memory banks. I really wasn't very gracious. Which sometimes I'm not. That's one of the great things about Cornell and one of the great things about being at Cornell in the sixties and seventies: No Limits. Except you can't kill or maim people or animals. Sometimes people did commit suicide, though. The preferred method was called 'gorging out' and I will leave that to your imagination.

To the extent that I have mentioned the professors at Cornell, I have said very little. My first Major advisor I liked but didn't get to know and the other I got to know and was convinced that he was an arrogant, narcissistic, ass. But I wasn't contemptuous of my teachers at all. Well, maybe I am being inconsistent. Most I liked and some I absolutely loved. And that was true of my organic chemistry professor. He lived several blocks from my apartment. After learning where I lived, every Monday, Wednesday and Friday he would drive by my building and wait for me to exit and offer me a ride which I would accept when the weather was inclement. That way we got to be friends. He was married with two young children, this was his first academic job, and he was Jewish, though not religious. I asked him why he was teaching the two-semester organic chemistry course and this is what he told me.

Undergraduates working on an Engineering degree had their own requirements like pre-med students if they wanted to go on to get specialized graduate degrees. One of those requirements was taking the two-semester introduction to organic chemistry courses. The other organic chemistry professor preferred to teach the one semester intro to organic chemistry because it was full of pre-med students who were busting their hump trying to get a good grade, which the professor found amusing. He added that the other chem prof was pro-Vietnam war and he liked to have the opportunity to screw the pre-med students who he felt were just trying to duck their military responsibility, particularly the Jewish ones. He finished by telling me that he thought his colleague's salary came in large part from a grant from Dow Chemicals, which among other interesting compounds, made napalm. What I took in was that the other guy, who I would not ever see, hated Jews, was pro-Vietnam war, and was paid by at least one company that made particularly noisome weapons of war that were destroying this country where we had no business being. I was warming up to my organic chem prof.

Then he went on to tell me that the requirement to take a two semester intro to organic chemistry for engineering students was questionable and definitely not well received by the engineering students who hated his course because they felt they didn't need to be exposed to the material and it was a waste of their time...which led to them blowing most of the work and tests off and this would likely have the effect of skewing the curve in the favor of anybody who actually cared about the course material. He glanced at me. And he smiled. I loved this guy.

It got even better. I liked his teaching style, and I liked the course material. Fifty percent of the final grade was going to be based on the final exam. Two weeks before the Christmas break, I ran into him, and he said he wanted to give me a hint about the final. He told me there was only one question, but it would take about 8 pages to answer it and it happened to be his research topic for his PhD. Did I want to know the question? Hell, yes. Starting with a few basic molecules, demonstrate the construction of the complex organic chemical: Delta 9 tetrahydrocannabinol. Great question. Now I knew I would ace the final and ace the course. Delta 9 tetrahydrocannabinol, the chemically and pharmacologically active moiety in marijuana, is responsible for its psychoactive effects. This is what my professor demonstrated to earn his PhD.

Most other professors were fine. They had good days and they had bad days. Some days they would make the effort to be more interesting than usual. They were professionals doing their job with many varied responsibilities. From where I sit today, I recognize the pattern. Humans are complex and nobody really knows what could be motivating their behavior. It's true of doctors, lawyers, truck drivers, dry cleaners, waitresses, and cabbies. Also, strippers. You name it. Understanding this is one of the burdens but also the joys of being a doctor.

The only human being that this variability and unpredictability may not be true of are soldiers. This is my bias and my hope. The people who choose to wage war are trained very hard to act as a team and sometimes as individuals and they must do that perfectly every time if they are to survive and win. And if they are American soldiers they must win and they must survive. The Vietnam war was confusing to more American young men than most people of that era realize. It may have been the first time that Americans (mostly men) had very strongly held beliefs that America was on the wrong side of the conflict and was worsening the situation. These beliefs were so strongly held that they prevented many from serving their country when called upon to join the military. Some went to Canada. Some to Europe. Some just disappeared. Some went to jail. For most, this was not cowardice. This was principle. I know. I went through the entire process in my head again and again. But as fate would have it, I went to

101

medical school because I wanted to, and I was lucky enough to beat the odds and get accepted. This was an automatic deferment. Had I been rejected from med school; I still don't know for sure what I would have done. My draft number was 23. I knew exactly where I was when I found that out. I was working a job in the Map Room of Olin Library, and it was just after 8pm. It stands out with only a few other events in my life: my father's death, the assassinations of the Kennedy brothers and Martin Luther King Jr., putting Gabriel down, my father-in-law's death, my middle son's death and the birth of my two children. So much sadness. So little joy.

It seems to me that since Vietnam, we have been involved in endless war. That would be my entire adult life. We have had troops and personnel stationed in Syria, Libya, Kuwait, Iraq, Sudan, Pakistan, the Levant, South America, Europe. Maybe the only two places we don't have military presence is China and Russia with whom we seem to be always on the verge of war. And if you name a country without any American military presence, I will wager we have human intelligence on the ground. Wait, that may not be true for North Korea but then again, who knows. I pray for those men and women now that I have had my faith restored. I respect their patriotism, their selflessness. But why in 2023, on the very edge of colonizing the moon and sending manned (and womanned) missions to Mars, should we have so much conflict? Have we progressed so little? What will the Martians think of us Earthlings. Ahh, that's someone else's book.

There was another professor who I thought little of although as I consider him, I may have been unfair. He had a thankless job at a difficult time. I don't even know what his department was. He was the pre-med advisor, and it was the responsibility of every undergraduate intending to apply to medical school to make an appointment with him to be advised. My meeting with him was abrupt, unfriendly and unhelpful. He glanced at my transcripts and told me the competition was so fierce to get admitted to medical school because of the war that I had little chance of acceptance barring some miracle. We didn't have a pleasant 'shoot the shit' preliminary sit down. He didn't ask me if I had any questions. I am not sure he even made eye contact. That was it. Meeting over. On my way out, he stopped me and added that I looked out of shape, and I should start exercising with weights if I was going to war. People have been giving me that advice since I was 6 years old.

Nobody took over any buildings during my junior year although there were plenty of sit-ins, sometimes with students who handcuffed themselves together and to the furniture which made for some full bladders.

Probably the biggest sit-in of my college career took place in April, 1969, when I was still a sophomore and prior to the taking of the Straight. It was an all-night affair in Barton Hall, the military science building and gymnasium with many speakers, burning of draft cards, ubiquitous marijuana and protests in support of the Afro-American Society, against the Vietnam War and the generally held concept that the country was corrupt, and the University was complicit. I was there along with at least 2000 others. In the morning, I called my mother to let her know I was okay because only God knew what the media was reporting. Her take: 'try to be politically apathetic.' My roommate Jay found this hysterically funny. So did the rest of my friends. I knew that mom was only looking out for my welfare and didn't realize I had taken on all the ills of American culture personally.

Junior year, only the campus police had firearms as far as I know, and they never had to draw on anybody. The Afro-American Society of Cornell kept their distance from the white students to my dismay, but they seemed to be getting along better with the new and improved university administration. There was so much napalm being dropped on Vietnamese villages and fields that the people started to just self-immolate so they wouldn't be caught up in the inferno. This led to some of the most graphic, historically important and emotionally wrenching war photography of all time. Things weren't going too well in Cambodia and Laos either. That whole business is a bit fuzzy to me but my sense of it was that this was not the 'domino theory' of communism but rather neighboring countries that were so damaged by our war that they were developing their own radical anti-Americanism. It was Cambodia, I believe, that gave us the apt term, 'The Killing Fields'. That's what we created. The killing fields. Our gift to southeast Asia. And didn't the CIA have something to do with our incursions into Laos and Cambodia?

Now, more than fifty years later, these countries are close friends and allies of the United States, terrific tourist destinations, fantastic commercial and trading partners, helpful intelligence operators. Did you ever talk to a Vietnamese who has moved to America? You couldn't find a kinder, nicer human being. It boggles my mind.

As the second semester was inexorably moving to springtime, I got some good news. I had applied as a volunteer to a hospital just outside Tel Aviv and been accepted to their program. They would provide me with room and board but couldn't give me a spending allowance. Gee, miss out on the annual Wayne County strippers stay at the Scranton Holiday Inn? At least I felt good that the curbs at the state mental hospital would still be looking good as we had a mild winter in northeastern Pennsylvania. In those days, many of my friends were taking the summer after Junior year and back packing around Europe. The central hub for so many American college students was the local American Express office. This image in my mind stands in stark contradistinction to what was happening in Vietnam. Still, it was an important period of growth for many and an incredible educational opportunity. And my dorm room at Tel Hashomer in Ramat Gan became the central hub for my friends who decided to stop by Israel for some Hummus and Tahina on pita bread with a hot pepper. Tel Aviv did have an Amex office, but nobody spoke English there. And I spoke Hebrew. Ramat Gan is a suburb of Tel Aviv. Or was. Now it may be a major metropolis.

I could write an entire book about my four months in Israel, but I will just give you a few highlights because I know you are anxious to get to my Senior year at CU. So here are a few interesting and mercifully brief stories from Eretz Yisrael.

Perhaps the most curious thing that happened was on the way home. I had a flight from Tel Aviv to London non-stop and I was scheduled to stay a week in London since I had never been there. I was kind of an exotic; aside from the country of Israel, Los Angeles, Tiajuana, London, Ithaca and the Archbald pothole, I had never been anywhere. Still, I could have been less traveled. We had a comfortable flight on El Al and I noticed we were beginning our descent early. Great. Soon enough we were landing.... At the Zurich airport. An unscheduled stop. We taxi 'ed to an arrival gate and we were asked to dis-embark but remain in the lounge which had been cordoned off. Nobody said anything else to the passengers in any language. We watched from the windows as all our baggage was taken off the plane and several officials got on board. Three hours went by. Then they put all the luggage back and we were asked to resume taking our seats on the same plane. This was El Al, of course. We took off and

109

arrived at London's Heathrow airport uneventfully but late. I thanked the crew and said 'Shalom' and headed for my hotel. I never found out what that was all about. The Israelis just left it up to our imaginations. Israelis. You just can't fuck with them. Especially if it involves El Al. While I was in Israel there were several terrorist attacks at Ben Gurion airport. Nobody Jewish died.

The summer I was there, there was a war on with various radical Palestinian factions led mostly by Yasir Arafat who I suspected would have made a great Senator if he was born American. One of the greatest bullshit artists of all time. Golda Meier was Israel's Prime Minister. In front of my dormitory, which was modern, was a large flat lawn about fifty yards square and beyond this lawn was the operating rooms of the hospital. Every night there was a flash point somewhere: Gaza, Golan Heights, Lebanese border. About 2 am the helicopters would start to come in and land on our lawn and we would all exit the dorm to help offload the wounded and get them either to a triage area outside the ORs, or directly to an empty OR. That was the closest I have ever been to actual warfare. It was nothing like MASH. It was hard to get back to sleep so we would stay up talking and wait for dawn, just a few hours away. Then we would go onto the small, pleasant balconies that overlooked the terrain behind the dorm where we could watch tank maneuvers and various other activities. As strange and upsetting as all this must have been to me, it wasn't as bad as touring the country and everywhere I went to were young men and women, Israeli teenagers really, in uniform armed with rifles, going about their chores. Military service was mandatory for everybody, I'm guessing between 18 and 24, with reserve responsibilities until age 50. That's a good guess. Now that was the summer of 1970. I returned to Israel with my family to celebrate my older son Michael's Bar Mitzvah. 1993. There had been enormous change. In 1970, Israel still maintained so many vestiges of Jewish life in the shtetels of Europe and Russia. There were many, many people who had escaped Europe's Holocaust, come to build a Jewish homeland or traveled from Africa to make a new life. Six of them were my relatives, although somewhat distant, but I got to know them. They were very kind to me. But I lost contact with them eventually.

If I try to summarize the prime areas of Israeli brilliance (in this case intelligence and know-how) that occurred to me that summer of 1970, there would be three: medical science, engineering/computer technology, and greatly in the lead ahead of everything else, military tactics and intelligence gathering. In America, 'Never Again' was a slogan. In Israel, it was a reality. In 1970, and even today, the rest of the world outside Israel is both an existential and real threat.

I didn't have to spend all my time volunteering. I could go and do anything that appealed to me that was legal and most of what I wanted to do was see the entire country and speak to the people. To this end, the Israelis provided plentiful youth tours on buses everyday which were very inexpensive and left from central Tel Aviv. I have several sharp memories of moments on these tours. Israel has great beaches, both on the Mediterranean and the Red Sea. Back then swimming in the Red Sea was safe. The far eastern edge of the beach belonged to Sharm al Sheikh, a Jordanian resort town that some of you might remember from the movie Lawrence of Arabia. As it turns out, Sharm as it is referred to by the locals has become the most prominent destination for Great White Sharks in Middle Eastern waters. They stay away from the Eilat beach waters on the western edge of the long crescent shaped beach which is in Israel. Even Great Whites know you don't fuck with the Israelis.

Public transportation shut down on the Sabbath which began Friday night at sundown and ended on Saturday night around dusk. I was fortunate to have befriended a junior attaché at the American Embassy which at the time was in Tel Aviv. You may remember that a recent American President facilitated moving it to Jerusalem to the great dismay of the organized Palestinian movement. Guess what, this attaché was from Scranton, PA!!! And I think his first name was Tom, Tom Killeen actually, and he was a great guy. I stayed in his apartment every weekend and he didn't mind since he was working anyway, and I practically lived on the beach. I probed him a little, but I could find no evidence that he was a spook.

One time, four friends and I found our way to a beach we had heard about which was at Ashkelon, a small village south of Tel Aviv but a distance from any fighting in Gaza further south. There were many Roman ruins along the road that ran along the beach, and it was a pretty place just to swim, sunbath and not crowded, which was never true of Tel Aviv beaches. We lay on our towels with rocks as our pillows when we became aware of a disturbance in the air we could not quite identify.

The history of the IAF, the Israeli Air Force, is fascinating. I have read about it, and I would urge any of you that find military aircraft interesting (all you Tom Cruise fans) I recommend a quick internet read. Before the Six Day War in 1967, the United States became progressively involved in providing planes and techniques to the IAF which up until that time relied on re-commissioned old WW2 junkers.....not German fighters but planes that were piles of junk. The US involvement sounds roughly parallel to our current decision-making process regarding modern war planes provided to Ukraine. By the time my friends and I were lying on the beach at Ashkelon, the Israelis had at least 100 American made F4 Phantom jets, considered at the time the fastest, most maneuverable and most dangerous fighter jets in the sky. The general word around Israel was that the IAF tore the jets completely down and then rebuilt them, improving on every aspect of their performance. Brilliant.

We were lying on this beach, the ocean in front of us, the ruins and the southern desert or Negev behind us and the Gaza strip to our left or south. There was this weird air disturbance for a few seconds, then four Israeli F4 phantoms flying wingtip to wingtip, on the 'deck' no more than a thousand feet off the ground screamed across the sky coming from the desert and headed for Gaza. These pilots were on the deck avoiding radar. The planes were there and gone in no more than two seconds. Then another wave and another. Four waves of Phantoms headed for Gaza. No one ever feels safe when they are in Israel. But that day I felt safer.

There are too many events, people, experiences, observations to share about the four months I was there so I will just describe the hospital a little bit since I found it so interesting. As Americans we all have a sense of how hospitals are put together and how they have changed over time. When I arrived at my destination, Tel Hashomer Hospital, it blew up all my assumptions. Tel means hill in Hebrew and if you excavated straight down on a Tel in Israel you would often find evidence of prior communities that lived there. If you have never read it, I recommend The Source by James Michener as a great read. (An interesting tidbit about this book. Michener never went to Israel. He wrote the entire 900 page book from the notes of his assistants who did the research in Israel.) Hashomer means the guard; so Tel Hashomer means the hill of the guardsman. It is just outside the village of Ramat Gan which is suburban to Tel Aviv.

Before Tel Hashomer was the major hospital for Tel Aviv and the medical school there, before Israel was an independent country, Tel Hashomer was a British army base. The British occupied and controlled Palestine, as I am sure you remember. If not, read Exodus by Leon Uris or watch the movie with Paul Newman. When the British left, the Israelis converted it to a hospital...a horizontal rather than vertical hospital. Each barrack (think long narrow hut like structure with a canvas roof and beds on either side) served as a hospital ward. There were rows of these barracks on either side of a walkway shaded by trees the Brits had planted. These groups of barrack/wards were scattered around the campus of the hospital. In the middle of all this was a small Tel and on the Tel were the operating theaters I mentioned earlier. One of my 'jobs' was to retrieve a pre-op patient, transfer him to a gurney and bring him to the OR and return the post-op patients. I was an orderly. After they got to know me, they moved me into some of the research and clinical labs.

The Tel Hashomer I knew is gone. Now on the site is a modern hospital, Chaim Sheba Medical Center named after the physician who founded the modern medical center as well as the medical schools in Tel Aviv and Jerusalem. Israel changes so quickly that if I went back now, I probably wouldn't recognize it. The one thing that seems to remain is the emotion, the animosity, the disdain, the jealousy, the anger between Israelis and Palestinians. The feeling of being robbed of their land. That doesn't change. It makes me sad. So much progress. So little progress. That summer, I would meet up with a cousin of mine named Serl who was from Scranton and was spending a year at Hebrew University in Jerusalem. This one day, waiting for her to get out of class, I took a stroll outside the immediate campus and found myself resting on a pile of rocks when a boy about my age walked by and I said hello in Arabic since I guessed he must be Palestinian. He sat down and we talked for a while. He told me about

119

his life in a small village. I asked him if he ever thought there would be peace in the land between Palestinians and Israelis. He said, 'no.' His reasoning ultimately was that both lay claim to the land and that would never be resolved. God had given the land to the Jews three to four Millenia earlier, but the Palestinians had been living there for almost 2000 years. I guess it was the Middle East's version of squatter's rights. The Holocaust, the Shoah, had changed everything, for now European and Middle Eastern Jews felt they needed their own Homeland, their own nation, and preservation of that nation was there first and only real priority. Never again.

So, my Palestinian friend, after a few minutes said that this was a multi-generational feud that would never be resolved. I hope he was wrong. But my observation today is that Israelis are arrogant, strong and committed while the Palestinians lack the leadership and guidance and strategy to force peace

that would benefit both cultures, both peoples. It is
an   on-going   shame.

Chapter 4: Senior Year

"Well my time went so quickly

I went lickety-splickly out to my old '55

As I drove away slowly, feeling so holy

God knows, I was feeling alive

And now the sun's coming up

I'm riding with Lady Luck

Freeway, cars and trucks

Stars beginning to fade

And I lead the parade

Just a-wishin' I'd stayed a little longer

Lord, don't you know, the feeling's getting stronger"

Ol '55.....Eagles...1974 from the On the Border album

Returning from an eventful summer in Israel and an enjoyable week in London, I had just enough time to kiss my mother hello and goodbye, throw Pepper a treat and wave to my brother who was on the phone. Then I drove back to Ithaca.

Did you get that. I drove back to Cornell. My uncle Danny, my father's older brother, gave me his car. A 1964 Chevelle four door sedan with the shift on the steering column (it was an automatic), 172,000 miles on the odometer, a cracked engine block, no discernible suspension and very worn brakes. The car stalled every single time it stopped. But it had a very good battery and starter. It got me through my final year in Ithaca, which was no small feat, and back to Scranton where I promptly gave it to my brother who sold it for $100, and it was probably used for scrap and worth more than that. Thank you, Uncle Danny, it really made my senior year more enjoyable. I later found out that the Chevelle was the most popular, durable and recognizable Chevrolet for 15 years until it was discontinued by GM.

There was a second immediate change once I got to campus. I was moving into new digs. I had gotten myself a cool job which provided room and board and an hourly stipend for work done at night and weekends. I was one of two on call phlebotomists and emergency technicians at the Sage Infirmary. Sage was an enormous old Victorian home halfway down the hill to Ithaca proper from campus. A portion of it had been converted into a ward with about ten beds for students who were sick enough that they needed nursing attention at night and on the weekends when no one was around on campus to care for them. The most common reason for admission to Sage was mononucleosis causing inflamed tonsils and lymph nodes that prevented the ill student from swallowing, thereby needing

126

intravenous fluids. Viral hepatitis was also a common admission diagnosis. These students with viral hepatitis had no appetite, complained of severe fatigue and were potentially infectious to their friends. It also needed to be followed carefully, lest the liver begin to lose its function causing potentially lethal complications. Hepatitis sufferers often had blood drawn twice and even three times daily. Luckily, I was an excellent phlebotomist, having learned the tricks of that trade while working summers in a tiny community hospital while in high school through family connections. The medical director of the hospital had been a close friend of my dad's and he, himself, was a physician.

My partner at Sage was a second year Cornell Veterinary student named Kevin who studied all the time. It was sort of like watching a second-year medical student, I guess. But he was an asset to me. The two of us divvied things up and helped each other out and I learned a lot from him. Sage was such a big house that it had its own library. And the two of us studied there. Well, he studied. I read the New York Times. It also had a laboratory which was like the one at the tiny hospital where I learned to draw blood and start IV's, so I felt right at home. And we had to carry pagers which made me feel very important and very sexy.... for about two months when I figured out that the pagers were going to interfere with my life. Kevin and I each had our own apartment inside this big home. My apartment was bigger than the one I shared with Jay during junior year. Our apartments had their own bathroom and dressing area and phenomenal bed (a four poster with a new mattress.) Having a guest for the weekend was a pleasure.

Sage also came with a huge kitchen, sort of like Upstairs/Downstairs or Downton Abbey; and with two cooks who made us breakfast and sent us on our way with bagged lunches and a menu of what to expect for dinner.

Now here's the thing. Lunch and sometimes dinner was constructed around Spam. Not spam calling you on your cell phone, the original Spam. I had never smelled, tasted, felt or digested Spam before. I did know it was on the shelf of the supermarkets in those days. When I asked my mother about it, she told me it was a generic food consisting of whatever was left over after they butchered pigs, cows, chickens, and in southern Delaware, stewed muskrats (a delicacy in southern Delaware.) After all the identifiable and edible parts of these animals were removed and prepared for sale, what was left over was made into Spam. Jews were not allowed to eat Spam because it wasn't Kosher and I grew up in a Kosher home, although this must have been a special variety of Kosher because when we ate at restaurants I ate shrimp, oysters, moo shu pork and many cuts of beef that were not Kosher. I suspect that Spam just wasn't a healthy food and should be avoided. It was easy to

129

serve. Open a can and flop it onto a slice of bread or a plate with some butter.

Yes, I said butter. I got an education at Sage regarding what I suspected was the common daily diet for Americans. Breakfast was always eggs, bacon and toast with butter. Lunch was always two sandwiches and two apples. The sandwiches were lathered with butter on the inside of both pieces of bread and the Spam, or sometimes peanut butter and jelly, sardines or chicken salad, would be stuck in between the butter. This was a time that cardiovascular disease was rampant in the United States. Please note that my dad did not eat spam or butter on every piece of bread, but he did smoke a lot of cigarettes. Dessert for dinner would be various flavors and color shades of Jello or pudding. Best part of the meal.

Sage meals were not even close to Ernie's menus in the fraternity house and light years away from my mom's cooking and, at best, she was a bland cook although she made great apple pies. All this explains my affinity for ketchup which I put on everything except the Jello and the apple pies when I was at home. I started using Heinz ketchup liberally as a young boy in Scranton, adding it to my plate for chicken dishes, roast beef, steaks, hamburgers, hot dogs, canned vegetables (mom thought fresh produce was contaminated.) I didn't know mustard was a condiment until I got married. Steak sauce and the various hot sauces were not in my sphere yet.

I will admit it here and now, that I gave away all my lunches to those that liked spam and if nobody was interested, I secretly threw it away fully realizing that there were places in the world where people went hungry, and I felt guilty in the process. Just not guilty enough to eat a spam sandwich.

I have a friend who I have stayed in touch with since college days named Joan. I was sweet on her, but this was early in my undergraduate career, and I hadn't learned to be aggressively cool with attractive women. Joan had two truths that bind us forever. First, she is the only Cornell co-ed that visited me in Scranton; and two, we ate hamburgers the same way. We would pour a large dollop of ketchup in the middle of our plates and dunk the hamburger and all the stuff on the hamburger into the ketchup mountain in the middle. We had developed this technique independent of each other but were delighted to find out we shared this trait. My personal feelings were that hamburgers and French fries were invented to eat ketchup. She agreed. I thought we might have had a future if only I had the courage back then. Recently she told me she always had a boyfriend, but he was never at Cornell, so I am not sure whether he would have been a huge obstacle. I guess I will never know for sure, but ketchup can make up for a lot of shortcomings. Could have worked out.

Dinner in the kitchen at Sage was sad. Dried out baked chicken, dried out tilapia and dried out ham with canned string beans as a substitute for salad. I ate in my apartment where there was a small accessory kitchen and a case of ketchup. Heinz. Not generic.

My year living at Sage with Kevin offered two surprises, the most interesting one being the admission to Sage of a graduate student in sociology named Harry Edwards. Now Professor Edwards, since I believe he is still working at a West Coast University, either Berkely or Stanford. I wonder if he ever met Mary Jane. But the week he spent as a patient in Sage Infirmary, he was not yet nationally known as a famous African American sociologist who organized the protest movement at the Olympics in Mexico City and was considered radical by some and peaceful by others. This gave me the chance to sit and discuss race relations with Harry every night, with his permission. Finally, a Black student willing to have a conversation with me and all I had to do was hold a venipuncture needle to his arm and tell him it wouldn't hurt. He taught me a lot and I thank him for it. My memory may be deserting me, but I think of Professor Edwards as being in the Goldilocks Zone of Afro-American activists. Too angry to be an MLK disciple and too intellectual to be a Black Panther. I liked him a lot. He was not feeling well but he took the energy and time to talk to me as a student and a new friend. We lost touch immediately, of course, when he was discharged but I never forgot him.

The second surprise came when I was asked to see another young Black graduate student who had just returned to campus from his native Zimbabwe where he was visiting family. He had a cough and I explained I wasn't a doctor but if he wasn't running a fever or felt short of breath, he could be seen at the student clinic on campus in two days, this being Saturday. He held up a non-descript paper bag and asked me to look at its contents. Inside was a quart-sized mayonnaise jar and inside was a 15 inch worm.

'I coughed this up this morning and I thought someone should take a look.' I was impressed. I asked him to wait in the lab while I went to the library to check Kevin's texts on parasites. I found it. Ascaris lumbricoides. Usually asymptomatic and known to be a common human infestation, on occasion the mature worm would be coughed up since it resided in the lung tissue. I told the student that it wasn't dangerous or serious but rather common in Africa and he should report to the student clinic on Monday, and I would take his worm and bring it to the clinic myself and explain to the doctors there what had transpired. He thanked me as

I took his name and address with phone number and he left as I sat for a while keeping the Ascaris company. I have never met another American doctor who has had an experience like that. Close, but not like that.

I approached Senior Year calmly. I completed all the courses required to receive a degree in Psychology. I completed all the courses required by medical schools to apply. So, I could take any damn course I wanted as long as there was room which meant that I had to get cracking and enroll in some courses asap, not having done this before leaving for Israel. Medical school admissions would start to come by mail in the next 6-12 weeks and then continue over the course of the year. I had applied to eight med schools, each for a different reason and one was Cornell Med in NYC. The day I interviewed for Cornell Med I had influenza, a fever of 104 degrees, a blistering headache, total body pain and hallucinations due to fever and not drugs. I remember telling them that if they accepted me, I would need both scholarships and loans. I think they suggested I looked unwell. Did I mention there was a blizzard outside the interview room, which fortunately took place in Ithaca. I had trudged up the hill from Sage to be there on time. Anyway, I tried not to think of med school, but I found my mind focusing on the Edgar Allen Poe story, 'The Pit and the Pendulum'. Amazing where a fever of 104 degrees can take you. If you haven't read the story, perhaps you saw the movie starring Vincent Price. In my fantasy, I was strapped to a stone tablet in a dank, dark room with the only light coming from 4 lit torches attached to bases in each corner of this room and above me was a large razor-sharp scythe which swung back and forth and with each swing it would go lower until, inevitably, reach me. I did not know what would happen next, but I could guess.

137

I did consider a good feature of living at Sage Infirmary was trudging up the hill to campus (a very, very, steep hill) and I could feel my chest, and arms getting stronger each week, my breath coming more easily, and just maybe if the scythe sliced through my shirt and a bit of my chest I would be in good enough shape to escape...somewhere.

For some odd reason, as I was registering for my Fall semester courses senior year, I had an epiphany. Something deep in my Reptilian brain (thanks for that Dr. Lenneberg, for I think it was your spirit helping me along) told me that I had to take care of unfinished business. It's a good lesson for everybody, really. Taking care of unfinished business.

So, I walked over to a Registrar who was not otherwise occupied and asked her, "Do you think there is an opening in the Comparative Anatomy of Vertebrates course?" And just like that, I was enrolled. The course had changed a bit. It was harder in that it was now worth 6 credit hours for a one semester course and there were three labs and two lectures plus meetings with TA's and the Professor. But it was taking care of unfinished business. I asked myself, regardless of whether I get accepted to med school, would I really consider myself worthy of becoming a doctor if I didn't go back two years and change a decision which radically altered some of my college experience. Did I still feel cowed by that ginormous eel (that is a strange transposition of words, isn't it?) I didn't need to take the course. I wanted to take the course for a myriad of reasons. So let me share with you what happened because of my epiphany.

I loved the course. We dissected all kinds of vertebrates starting with eel like creatures and working up to cats. The reading and the lectures

139

and the TA's filled in so many of the holes. Kevin was great because he had learned most of this the previous year. The Professor kept two huge African condors (think huge vultures on speed) in a barn 30 miles outside of Ithaca and would occasionally bring one to our lab and let it flap around the room scaring the shit out of all of us until he fed it 5 or 6 large voles and returned it to a cage.

By the end of the semester, I was pulling an A+ in this course and A's in all my other courses.

Cornell had a unique system for final exams after the first semester of the year. You went home for the Christmas holidays, then you came back to campus for a two-week study period where you would prepare for your final exams or finish up your term papers, then would begin finals week when the actual testing happened. I didn't understand this, but there you have it. Looking at my courses, all the work had been finished before Christmas break, except for my final exam in Comparative Anatomy of Vertebrates. I did a back of the envelope calculation. And I concluded if I skipped the final exam, the worst I would get was a D in the course. During this prolonged period, the university excused Kevin and I from our work responsibilities at Sage. If I played this right, I could leave for Christmas break and not have to come back to campus until final exams were over in roughly 6 weeks. Now mind you, I had no exotic place to go, having seen the pothole numerous times, but I would find something. Maybe I would drive out to Wayne County and check out the fairgrounds.

I went over all the details again to make sure I hadn't forgotten anything. I checked in with Kevin and he agreed it could work. And then I went to speak with my professor of comparative anatomy. He listened thoughtfully and then this is what he said.

141

"Okay. I will make you a deal. If you take the final exam, I will give you an A+ in the course regardless of how you do in the final. If you skip the final exam and take the time to relax or visit friends and family, I will give you an A in the course." I was in shock. I'm still in shock writing this more than 50 years later. I had started not really understanding what college was all about. Achieved a relatively poor GPA freshman year. But each year grew and matured as a student, to that very moment when this thoughtful professor was going to reward me for no other reason than I had an epiphany that I needed to finish unfinished business (he knew my story.) The prof knew I had applied myself and learned the material as well as anybody and losing an A+ to get an A was a gift.

You know something else. Whether you are an eel or a pigeon or a cat or a horse or a man, and whether your skin is white or black or yellow or brown or red, when it comes to your insides, we are all pretty much the same. The following year, Gross Anatomy of Humans was a breeze.

As you may have suspected from the title of this memoir, now you know that I did get into a medical school. All the med schools that I applied to even though my GPA was not high enough in the graduation class of 1971 from the Cornell College of Arts and Sciences to qualify me for summa cum laude or even Phi Beta Kappa. But it was a comfortable 3.8 so I was competitive enough to be admitted several times over. Why was that? I don't really know but I will venture several guesses. I had mentioned the MCAT's, the standardized version of the medical school 'SAT's'. These were given in the Spring of my Junior year and as I remember there were four parts: Math, Science, Humanities and Current Events. They wanted to know if the applicant took the time to read the newspaper. As I am sure you know I did so-so in math, damn good in science which was heavily weighted on organic chemistry and biology of vertebrates, outstanding in humanities, but I achieved a perfect score in current events. I may have been the only applicant in the country that did that. I think the current events score had some deeper meaning to the admissions people, like this kid wanted to know what was happening in the world and that predicted his success in med school. Then I had an interesting set of experiences. Some undergrads went on polar expeditions or tagged great white sharks off the Great Barrier Reef of Australia but all that I did with my time must have impressed somebody at these schools. But the real reason I was accepted to med school was defined by a very nice, very proper psychology professor with a pronounced British accent who sat down with me while I was having a quick cup of coffee and asked if he could give me some advice. I had just declared psych as my Major and didn't know this professor. I was a lowly sophomore.

This is what he said: "when you get to med school, keep your focus on becoming a clinician, taking care of patients...they are going to try to make you into an academic and scholar working for a university med school where you will be writing grants, running labs, teaching and administering.... don't listen to them. Your great strength and your inner passion are for people. You will get the greatest satisfaction diagnosing their illness, curing them if you can and healing them regardless." Then he got up and left and I never spoke with him again. In fact, I never saw him again, which I thought a bit unusual. I never even knew his name. But I never forgot what he said that day. Funny thing, though, as he was walking away, he kind of faded into the milling student crowd, almost like he disappeared into a row of corn.

Try as I might, I can't remember any interesting anecdotes or stories from the rest of Senior Year. It was a great time and I enjoyed it, but we were still deeply entrenched in Vietnam, there were many states, we now call them 'Red States', which tried hard to enforce Jim Crow laws, and there were many groups across the country who felt disenfranchised for one reason or another. The country had experienced Woodstock and that was a reminder that Woodstock Nation still existed with hopes that one day the bombers would turn into butterflies above all nations. For a year or a bit longer Haight-Ashbury in San Francisco was a constant reminder of our counterculture. It was Hippie Central for that time. But Cornell was just for schmoozing, getting stoned, partying and waiting for life to happen if you were a Senior. Oh, I almost forgot, the Lacrosse team won the NCAA Division One championship, but more to my interest in sports, the Big Red Men's Ice Hockey Team won the NCAA Division One National Championship and did something that had never been accomplished before and never has since. They went undefeated, 27-0.

Chapter 5

Year One

"Well, I won't back down

No, I won't back down

You can stand me up at

   The gates of hell

But I won't back down

No, I'll stand my ground

Won't be turned around

And I'll keep this world from draggin' me down

Gonna stand my ground

Well I know what's right

I got just one life

In a world that keeps on   pushin' me around

But I'll stand my ground"

I Won't Back Down....Tom Petty and the Heartbreakers.....1989.....from the album Full Moon Fever

College was all about learning to be a student.

Medical school will turn out to be all about learning to be an adult.

In the early drafts of this memoir, I described events that should have helped to develop my sense of who I was becoming. My values, principles, integrity, morality were amorphous but beginning to become fixed in my mind. In writing this story, my hope was that readers would sense that I was changing as I 'grew up.' I intended to tell interesting and humorous anecdotes to reveal the process. And I wanted the tales to be self-deprecating, for one of my principles was to be humble. Or, if it was hard to be humble, avoid sounding arrogant or self-promoting with shades of hubris. I had not really understood the word narcissism yet. I had given no thought to what role my personal history with all its thorny stories had in shaping who I was becoming. I think that many of my friends, colleagues and countrymen don't give this much thought, certainly during the crystalline moments of their early twenties. And maybe never.

I am saddened by what I see as lip service being paid to mental illness in the news today. We are a violent society. Perhaps we always have been. After all, the roots of American Democracy grew deep enough to give birth to the Revolutionary War. Division over the morality of slavery resulted in the Civil War. Perhaps our tendency to turn so easily violent explains our cultural fascination with gun ownership and the use of guns. I'm not speaking of hunting, target shooting, or protection, but semi-automatic long guns with extended ammunition clips which are used so often for killing innocents at schools, malls, and theaters rather than their intended use as weapons of war; and often these mass shootings are inextricably linked to mental illness. I feel we should embark on campaigns similar to those initiated by the National Institutes of Health educating the country about the importance of normalizing blood pressure, reducing cholesterol, screening for breast, colon, skin and prostate cancer and treating diabetes.

Mental illness is so very common and has been severely aggravated by the Covid pandemic with its isolation and personal loss either actual or ambiguous for which no closure is apparent. Personally, I think there are other factors in our society that feed the prevalence of mental illness, chief amongst them being social media platforms, gaming, and ubiquitous screens. I hear a lot of stories, almost daily, about mass shooters and speculation followed by reporting about the shooter showing signs or being recognized as mentally ill or having emotional problems. While I hear the verbal connections, I don't see effort and money put behind a campaign to normalize these medical problems and offer obtainable and non-marginalizing approaches.

This isn't a book advocating for more psychotherapy. I didn't get my undergraduate degree in clinical psychology. I went to med school. And as a doctor, I see a huge block of the American public suffering and not being given an effective path to address their suffering. I am guilty of going off on a riff that is important to me. I tried very hard to direct my friends and patients to psychotherapy and other approaches simply for better self- understanding and coping strategies for difficult life issues. It was hard. Most of the time I failed. But it was always worth the effort. I am afraid that until we do something about the proliferation of guns, smooth the disparities in life and normalize the treatment of mental and emotional illness we won't heal as a culture. Healing will require both responsibility and accountability by all of us and I can't just see it yet.

I knew I didn't want to become a narcissist after observing my Major advisor as an undergraduate. I was a psych major but that didn't help me avoid

154

being narcissistic. I did know that narcissism reminded me of Dorothy peeking behind the curtain in Oz to find that the Wizard was only a little man, a loser, who had the need to project himself as all powerful and always right so he would be feared, and he could control without having the requisite accountability to do the job well. How do you like that metaphor?

Just as I travelled the paths of my college years with you, always honestly, with feeling, hopefully with occasional humor and not without my personal sense of integrity and occasional outrage; now I will try to do the same with the four years of med school. I can't promise you anything except an accounting of what I learned from year to year in a personal way that anybody can understand. And provide some thoughts about growth and maturity along the way.

MATURITY: Exhibiting the thinking, emotions and behavior of an adult.

That is Google's definition of maturity. I looked it up online just now. I Googled it. When I read that simple definition several times, it occurred to me how complex this simple idea can be. I am an adult at age 74, therefore I am expected to think about any issue deeply, have feelings about my thoughts, and behave in a way that betrays my thoughts and feelings to everyone else; as long as I filter them through a very complicated mechanism that alters them so they take into account the rules and laws of society; the personalities, sensitivities and prejudices of other people; and add their moral weight and importance to me.   Google's definition doesn't mention anything about all of that. You and I use filters constantly and often different filters simultaneously. Wasn't that true of your last cocktail or dinner party; business or Board meeting; family celebration or get together for Thanksgiving?

156

Okay. Too serious? I think we should start our journey through the early part of my medical school education. You already know a lot about me. Let's see what I do with it as I move into Olin Hall, the student dormitory at 69th and York Avenue in Manhattan, right across York from the entrance to Cornell University Medical College (CUMC). Most but not all of my classmates live in Olin which is a pretty standard dormitory. The ones that don't live there are mostly married and need an apartment, sometimes big enough to accommodate their young children. But they live close by.

As clear as my memories are of Cornell and the campus in Ithaca, my memories of the physical characteristics of CUMC are hazy, like I am looking through windows in my mind, but they are fogged or streaked with age. So, I'm not going to spend a lot of time describing CUMC except to

157

mention that all the changes in the Medical Profession of the last forty years have had some major impacts on the character of the medical school and its partner, New York Hospital. For one thing, it is no longer CUMC, but rather Weill Cornell Medicine. A patch embroidered on a fleece that I am wearing to ward off the early Spring chill reminds me. This is because a philanthropist in New York, Sanford Weill, donated $100 million dollars to the University to benefit the medical school. This is a wonderful and miraculous thing and if I knew Mr. Weill, I would have liked to thank him personally. It has also been a focus of philanthropy across the country. Not from Mr. Weill, he has many other interests to support with his wealth. Just yesterday I wandered around the campus of the Hospital of the University of Pennsylvania where I receive my medical care. This is the central campus in West Philadelphia and not the metastatic out-patient sites in Philadelphia, the collar counties and New Jersey. The level of care and the research that occurs in this west Philly campus is beyond imagining. I felt like I was on the bridge of the Starship Enterprise. Penn also was the beneficiary of large gifts as have many, many large, often University affiliated, health systems. I think the incredible thrust of growing medical knowledge and medical treatments have boosted this philanthropic support. All for the good.

The CUMC campus in 1971 when I started med school seemed like it had been crammed into a small abutment on the east side of New York's midtown along the East River. The medical school and New York Hospital merge together as a single structure. When you enter the med school, the library and stacks are just to your right and the hospital is straight ahead. The hospital has been greatly updated of course but the library has gone the way of IT library science which makes me sad. I used to study in a small cubby area in the stacks where I wouldn't be interrupted, and I could concentrate. So much of medical education is memorization and you never know when an obscure fact that you managed to squeeze into your brain can pop up and be critical for a diagnosis or treatment. When I felt my joints stiffening, I would get up and wander about the old volumes of medical journals from a hundred years earlier. Sometimes I would pull one out and leaf through it for a few minutes. I remember vividly a case report from 1856 in a journal called The Lancet, which is still published in England today. A man in London succumbed to constipation, not having had a bowel movement in ten years. I would return the volume and reclaim my cubby and think, 'gee, isn't it great that today in 1971, everything there is to know in the profession of medicine has been described and we don't have to worry about new diseases.'

Except Covid, Lyme Disease, Ebola, Legionnaire's Disease, and I could go on for quite a while.

Do you wonder about my naivete? Medicine is biology and it's important to remember that biology always changes, evolves and sometimes presents us with unexpected challenges. Covid presents our planet with a sterling example that is continuing to evolve. How do I feel about this insight? Frightened. Sometimes it's good to be frightened because it arouses us to action as we recently saw with the early and immediate scientific response to the initial Covid virus through the development of vaccines, a piece of scientific work that garnered two biologists with the Nobel Prize in Physiology and Medicine in record time.

And for me, Covid brings up a word that frightens me even more: extinction.

Eight million people died of Covid-19 globally, one million in the United States, but the numbers would have been much, much worse without vaccines. Hundreds of millions.

And if instead of a corona respiratory virus (SARS Cov-E 2; also known as Covid 19), the pandemic had been due to a new version of a simple virus from Central Africa that causes periodic localized outbreaks, and this pandemic virus was a novel transmissible respiratory virus evolved from a strain of Ebola....... extinction event.

And what have we learned to change our behavior? Not too much. There will be more pandemics, epidemics, infectious diseases, systemic diseases, immune system dysfunctions that we should be planning on combating even before they occur.

That requires investment in public health, epidemiology, in education regarding vaccines and other prophylactic treatments, and in combatting the ridiculous mis-information swirling around health-related topics propelled by the internet, social media and politicians which defy rational understanding.

Recidivism taking place culturally regarding women's control over their own bodies and health should infuriate us. Anger over the overturning of RoevWade would be a good thing. But I am old and sick and only one person without much power.

There are several other memories to mention on the other side of the smeared windows in my brain. In the dormitory, Olin Hall, just off to the left of the front door was a lunch counter run by Betty, called the Betty Bar. There were only a few offerings, 90% of which were hamburgers. Betty offered two options for her burgers: raw and very, very rare. And everybody ate them. During my first year a famous South African heart surgeon, Christiaan Barnard, visited CUMC and gave an evening lecture. He had done the first human to human heart transplant and was going to describe the procedure. Loads of faculty, residents (often referred to as house staff) and students grabbed a burger on their way to the lecture. Within a week, there was an outbreak of a mononucleosis like syndrome amongst several dozen members of the New York Hospital and CUMC staff. But here was the thing: none of them knew each other or lived near each other. They had the same clinical findings. This required an epidemiologic approach. They did have one thing in common. They had all eaten at the Betty Bar before Dr. Barnard's lecture. Betty was so busy that her burgers all came out raw. And the hamburger meat was infested with an organism called Toxoplasma gondii which was usually transmitted to humans from contaminated cat poop and caused a completely different set of symptoms if you had a cat in the house and got sick from it. So CUMC was able to describe a cluster of patients with a new syndrome caused by T. gondii and a novel mode of transmission. That bit of medical history was the good part because the paper that resulted was published in the Green Journal, a reputable but often ignored medical journal otherwise known as the American Journal of Medicine. T. gondii won that time. That was the unfortunate part. But everybody recovered in short order.

There was a gym in the basement of the dorm and every Friday night CUMC had a 'mixer', a dance with a DJ or band, and anybody could come and mix. These were very successful. My close friends and I would first go to Chinatown in the shadows created by The Tombs, NYC's jail at the time, and have dinner to get away from institutional food and eat on the cheap, then head back and mix. My filters won't let me say anymore.

There were other important hospitals on campus: The Hospital for Special Surgery immediately uptown from New York Hospital and

165

hanging over the East River Drive (a premier orthopedic hospital with the reputation of occasionally operating on special thoroughbred race horses whose owners wanted their leg fracture to heal so they could be put out to stud; these operations were performed in a basement OR;) Memorial Sloan Kettering Hospital for Cancer was catty corner from CUMC and took up an entire square block.

A private psychiatric hospital sat in front of the formal entrance to New York Hospital on the south side of the building. That was called Payne Whitney which also had a campus facility for psychiatric admissions in Westchester County where CUMC would have picnics and rugby games in the spring and fall on the beautiful multi-acre grounds. Rugby games with teams from other med schools were often played at these outings. You likely don't know this bit of trivia, but rugby is the sport of medical schools.

And just south of P-W was a small but famous research facility, Rockefeller University. Scientists there were said to have contributed greatly to the discovery of the double helix that describes our DNA. I seem to remember a sculpture of the double helix on the grounds of the facility. For me, Rockefeller's key attribute was having the best cafeteria on the campus which overlooked the heliport on the East River around 66th Street. There was romantic lighting for dinner so if you got there at the right time you could sit by the windows overlooking the river and watch the helicopters land and take off under subtle and subdued lighting which enhanced the experience.

There were 95 students in the Class of '75 and to my memory, perhaps six of them were women. Fifty years later, almost all medical schools have greater than fifty percent women in each class. I think there are likely many insights that can be drawn about American culture from this fact. In any event, I think this and many other changes to my profession are for the better. But there are a few glaring consequences of change which are not.

The first week, we got our white coats which is a rite of passage for med students. And our black bags, paid for by a pharmaceutical company though I have no idea which one. Maybe pharmaceutical companies' writ large all contributed. The white coats had the Cornell/New York Hospital patch embroidered on the left sleeve. And we also got name badges to pin on the left breast pocket. The recognizable patch on the left sleeve was circular with a likeness of the Good Samaritan ministering to an injured or sick person sitting under a tree holding onto a long stick he apparently had used as a crutch or cane. Around the border CUMC/New York Hospital was written but the letters were so small that it was hard to read. One ironic wit in my class who would become a suite mate and a good friend, Bob O'Connell, told us that written on the patch was the medical school's mantra: 'give us the stick and we will beat you with it.' Uh-huh.

We gathered in a traditional med school lecture hall which was much more modern but otherwise like the lecture hall where I stared at the gigantic eel drawn on the huge blackboard. While this was the first time our class sat in a lecture hall, it wasn't a lecture but rather an orientation session by the Dean of Students who for some reason I think was Dr. Daniel Alonso, a pathology professor, but I could be wrong. Sorry if I am, Dr. D. I remember nothing from this friendly lecture except one jarring bit of advice. The speaker stressed that it would be a good idea if we didn't 'shit where we ate.' He wasn't referring to the Betty Bar, or any of the cafeterias. I distinctly remember him stressing this advice which I went on to ignore for the next four years. I did go to Cornell undergrad, after all: No Limits.

My roommate that first year was a friend from undergrad days, Tom Delaney. We had separate bedrooms and a shared bath. Tom had been a championship swimmer and water polo player at Cornell who was known for being a big party guy at a jock fraternity. But now, he suddenly looked as beaten down and worried as the rest of us. Anyway, Tom has remained a close friend even today.

As classes started that week, several of the single men coalesced into what you might call a clique although, truly, all 95 of us were a mega-clique and I felt we each had the other's back. I had heard stories of medical schools where the students would back-stab each other continually over the entire four years with the goal of obtaining the best internship programs after graduation. Honestly, I never saw any of that at CUMC. Not in my class for sure and not in the upper classes or the subsequent entering classes.

We were proud to be there, and we were one organism committed to becoming good doctors.

I started to tell you about this clique of a few men who became quite friendly. I already mentioned Tom and Bob. Then there was Stu Fox who I bonded with because we were both great hockey fans and both lived and died with the New York Rangers. When the Blueshirts lost, we would be depressed together...and they lost a lot. He loved to talk, and I loved to listen to him. Stu may have been the brightest light in our class except for one habit he brought with him from college, and he went to Cornell undergrad although I don't think we ever met there. He waited for the last minute to study for exams. He couldn't shake that habit which didn't work well in med school. If it did, they would have graduated him after the first year. Brain wise, he was unstoppable. Oh, and he was a hell of a pool player. Steve Seidman was in the group, but I have noticed that in any group of friends like this there seems to be an inner core and an outer core, sort of like a thermonuclear bomb. Steve was there, but in the outer core. Then there was Wally Schlech, another outer core guy although he was capable of ping-ponging between the inner and outer core because I think he was such a unique person. And I can't tell you why. He just was. He played the bagpipes, often after midnight, in the halls of the residence. I didn't mind. I don't think anybody did. It relieved the tension. I have one lasting memory of Wally. All med students in the US must take a series of standardized tests that I guess were used to gauge our progress in learning the necessary things in becoming a doctor, the first exam being in the early days of the second year. This was an unknown and most of us were a little nervous about what it would be like. We did know that it lasted all day and was arduous. Wally showed up with two sixpacks of beer in a paper grocery bag at 7 in the morning and put it on the table next to his exam book. He then proceeded to drink all of it but slowly so that it lasted the entire day. For Wally, it was a calming remedy. No proctors interfered.

By contrast, sitting on the other side of me, was a classmate who I ran into in the men's room early in the test and found him vomiting from anxiety. Everyone handled their stress differently.

Just a story. I never saw any evidence that Walter Schlech was an alcoholic or abused any substance. He was the best rugby player in our class and knew more great rugby songs than anyone else.

Bill Powers was another outer core guy. He was a Dartmouth grad and so I was always pissed at him because Dartmouth always beat Cornell in football, and he always gave me a hard time about it. Of course, so did all the other teams in the Ivy league. Always. Cornell football had one claim to fame while I was an undergrad. Ed Marinaro, who was the runner-up for the Heisman Trophy his senior year. I don't think any other Ivy football team had a player that won the Heisman or even was in the running. Marinaro played a few years for the Vikings as a running back, then graduated to become a television star in Hill Street Blues. I always thought he should go into the food processing business and process a line of pasta sauces: Marinaro's Marinara. He did not go to med school. But he was a hell of a halfback.

Jean Pape was not in the clique at all and while everybody liked him, nobody seemed to know him or even see him outside of class. But he bears mentioning because he was one of the most interesting students in our class. He was Haitian-American and looked dangerous.

During third year, we all eventually had 'dog lab' at some point during our surgical rotations. They divided us into teams of four and we were each given a live dog and every week we had to perform an operation on the dog (take out a lung or a lobe of the thyroid, or the spleen), then take care of the dog post-op so it would be ready the following week for more surgery. I can't tell you how excruciating this was for me. The dog loved us. When I would make rounds on the dog post-op, it would be waiting, tail wagging, giving me all kinds of affection. The four of us rotated responsibilities in dog lab: anesthesiologist, surgeon, first assistant, circulating nurse. Jean was in our group. So was Bob O'Connell. I can't remember the fourth. Our dog survived all six surgeries. I think ours was the only one. Most dogs died after the second operation and that was the end of dog lab for those students. You didn't fail dog lab. It was just an experience they wanted you to have. So, after surviving all six operations, we had to euthanize the dog. They didn't give us any other options. We had to do it. That was my worst moment, almost, as a med student.

As I mentioned, Jean Pape was Haitian-American. He didn't play rugby, play the bagpipes, play pool, drink beer, go to Chinatown or mixers. He did two things that I know about: he studied medicine and he worked for the resistance movement that met weekly in Harlem to undermine the totalitarian corrupt regime of Papa Doc Duvalier, the dictator of Haiti. Always better to have Jean at your back. Fortunately, he was a nice guy, even funny, but not really that often.

Josh Nagin was a good friend of mine but was in the outer core because he was mostly involved with his girlfriend who he married. I spoke to Josh less than a year ago and they were still married and sounded happy. I remember he had an interesting career that involved getting educated early with computers in medicine. Chris Lynch was another outer core guy who always seemed to have a girlfriend. I liked Chris. He seemed to have a good grasp on things and was well balanced. Then there was Cle Landolt.

Cle was inner core while somehow keeping himself outer core. I don't know how to describe him. He was a Harvard grad and was largely very stereotypical of Harvard undergrads, but in a good way. He was tall, and big, and handsome, and outgoing, and smart (but not that smart.) He was the guy who would want to bird dog your girlfriend but wouldn't do it unless he asked your permission first and if you said no, he would keep his distance. He became a cardiac surgeon which totally fit his persona. And he died very early of a cardiomyopathy, ironically, which greatly saddened and shocked me since he was the type of person who I expected would live forever.

Dan Hanley was inner core but again, a bit like Cle, kept himself in touch with the outer core and the outer world. He did this by living on New York's West side in an apartment by himself, almost unheard of for a classmate. He became a well-respected neurologist at Johns Hopkins where he still is as far as I know. I couldn't tell you any characteristics of Dan's that would give you great insight, but he was the type of person who loved to tease people about their idiosyncrasies. Sometimes I thought this teasing would get close to crossing over some invisible line as if his filters needed changing, at least with me and I wondered about how he felt about Jews. But if you asked me today, I finally concluded that this was Dan's way of keeping the constant stress at bay and everyone relaxed. It worked. Thank you, Dan.

And then there was Stu Brogadir. A staunch outer core guy who everybody loved but about whom I have few memories other than I counted him a friend.

I apologize to anyone and everyone who I left out that should have been included. I wasn't dissing you. I used the list of our class on the last page of our yearbook which if you still have it and check, listed the members of our class in the smallest font possible and my vision leaves something to be desired. Unfortunately, we have lost a surprising number of classmates, and I didn't mention those that have died above except for Cle.

In invisible ink, at the very bottom of that last page, using diluted lemon juice, which is an old spy trick, I found a hidden message which said, 'CUMC, give us the stick and we will beat you with it.'

Chapter 6

Year One

"Moon shining down through the palms

Shadows moving on the sand

Somebody whispering the 23rd psalm

Dusty rifle in his trembling hands

Somebody trying just to stay alive

He got promises to keep

Over the ocean in America

Far away and fast asleep".......Long Road Out of Eden....Eagles.....2007 from the double album Long Road Out of Eden

(Maturity: thoughts, feelings, behaviors of an adult.)

When I started CUMC in September 1971, I was 22 years old and certainly not a fully formed adult. But I was ready, willing and able to be educated.

I hope to provide a sense of how I became more adult, a mature adult, without going into the details of med school class work. Still, I want to prepare you for my feelings about medical practice today by the end of the story. Hopefully, I will satisfy any curiosity you have about the education of a doctor. I will concentrate on the anecdotes and stories I experienced and observed which might prove much more entertaining and at the same time accomplish my goals.

Early in my first year, Tim Harris with his new girlfriend, came to visit me for a weekend in the city. Tim was now a first-year law student at Cornell living in the same house in Ithaca where he had spent the previous two years. It's often assumed that doctors and lawyers don't get along. That's simply not true, except when it is. Tim and I remained good friends throughout our lives.

Tim and I had many shared experiences throughout our lives that strengthened our friendship which began with an immediate bond forged by sharing that freshman suite in University Halls 4.

Despite majoring in psych, going to med school and considering myself an intuitive individual, I have always been struck by the immediate antipathy or the immediate friendship that can occur when two strangers meet. What drives that instant chemistry. It remains a mystery to me when it occurs.

Tim's girlfriend, whose name I can't remember, was also his classmate. So, I thought to myself, when it came to Cornell professional education what was good for the goose was not necessarily good for the gander. That is, the med students were periodically reminded not to shit where they ate. Apparently, the same was not recommended to the law school students. I know, because I took Tim aside and asked him. In fact, I had the impression that it was encouraged which says something about the legal

184

profession. I am not entirely sure what that would be. I felt this distinction, if it was true, was unfair but since I had no intention of paying any heed to the earnest advice of the CUMC Dean anyway, it hardly mattered. Tim and his girlfriend got married that year, but then divorced within a few months, so maybe they were doing a scholastic exercise in real time and hopefully learned from the experience. Maybe the med school Dean advised us from his personal experience. Tim ended up marrying a terrific woman and had four children. I wish they lived happily ever after, but Tim got sick. I was good for phone support but that wasn't enough. I miss our conversations and occasional visits.

Anyway, I want to share a story which occurred while Tim was visiting me in Manhattan with his law school girlfriend. It was the week of the Italian festival in New York. If you are or were a New Yorker, you know this was called the Feast of San Gennaro and occupied about two blocks of lower Manhattan where the Italian restaurant district was squeezed between Chinatown and SOHO. Even if you have never been to New York, you can picture the festival: kiosks lined both sides of the narrow streets selling all manner of Italian foods, desserts, specialty items and there were the usual palm readers and spiritualists. The streets were packed tighter than an anchovy tin with people going both ways at once. As I am now remembering it, the festival must have been cancelled during the pandemic because thousands would have gotten Covid.

It was very lively back in 1971 and I was talking to Tim as we slowly made our way through the crowded street, and he was looking at me when he walked directly into a young man going in the opposite direction. They both fell causing a minor disturbance in crowd flow. When they got up, I made sure both were all right, when...hey, Tim and this young guy knew each other. They were next door neighbors in Beverly Hills and had grown up together! How weird. It seems that Tim's friend was

186

in dental school in Boston and was only in New York to attend a symposium. He had just gotten off the subway and was making his way to Chinatown to meet some friends for dinner.

So I ask you, what are the chances that a Los Angeleno from Beverly Hills going to Cornell Law School in Ithaca, New York would be visiting his mate in Manhattan and decide to grab dinner at the Feast of San Gennaro along with 10,000 other people; and collide with his next door neighbor from LA who was living in Boston but had come to NYC to attend a symposium and was on his way to Chinatown to meet friends. Twelve inches either way and they would have passed each other not knowing. I have been wondering for a long time what cosmic shift occurred because that accident altered something about our universe.

I call this a small world story, as in 'isn't it a small world' or 'six degrees of separation'. These small world stories keep popping up in my life.

By far, the first year of med school was dominated by Gross Anatomy and, of course, many stupid jokes flowed from the name Gross Anatomy. The fact was that we were dissecting human beings who once lived, breathed, walked the earth, hopefully loved and were loved, and maybe had children. They deserved respect and our appreciation, at least I felt that way. Once they had been preserved with formalin and perhaps other chemicals to prevent potential problems like decay and microbial infestation, they were brought into a large room with 25 concrete tablets on pedestals which vaguely resembled autopsy tables. They would stay there for the entire course, which lasted about two thirds of the year. We spent every morning with our cadavers. Everybody gave their cadaver a name. Our guy became Alfred. I think that humanized the course a bit. The class was divided into groups of four, so four students per cadaver. The only classmate that I can remember from my team was a student named Will Yee from Honolulu who had gone to the University of Hawaii undergrad. I never got to know Will very well, but I remember him distinctly from that course because he was incredibly funny. If Will got tired of medicine, he could easily have been a successful comedian. And believe me, you need a funny guy during those long hours of tedious dissection.

The faculty of the Pathology Department seemed roughly divided into vaguely distinguishable groups and the docs who did most of the autopsies of expired hospital patients were selected to teach gross anatomy.

As students we were strongly encouraged to convince the grieving families to allow an autopsy to

189

be performed and CUMC/NYH was very successful referring deceased patients to what my friend Bob O'Connell referred to as the 'Coma Clinic'. That was supposed to be humorous but not accurate since the patients were way past coma and into 'The Dead Zone' to paraphrase Stephen King. I felt this poked fun at the pathologists and not the patients. That may have been a bit of denial on my part.

Anyway, a large group of pathologists became very skilled and even subspecialized in reviewing specimens from surgery. You can imagine the importance of getting tissue from a patient anesthetized in an OR and the diagnosis and subsequent surgical approach was dependent on the pathologist's knowledge, experience and skill, all combined in a matter of minutes. This was hard work, tense work and precise work and I often wondered how excellent tissue pathologists felt about coping with everything that depended on their expertise under pressure.

You might wonder why a physician would choose to teach medical students about the gross anatomy of patients that they would never meet unless there was a zombie apocalypse. I know I wondered. I think the general answer is that most if not all the faculty who supported our dissections and taught us anatomy walking from one cadaver group to another had PhD's without a medical degree or they were MD/PhD's and taught students because it tied in with their research grants or administrative tasks.

But there was one interesting exception who I will describe to you. I liked him and he was a good instructor. His name was Fakry Girgis MD.

Dr. Girgis according to the personal story he shared which has never been independently corroborated, was that he had been a successful general surgeon in private practice in Cairo, married with a family. He was living the good life. He and his family were Coptic Christians. As a result of his religious beliefs, in a predominantly Muslim country, for reasons that I could never quite figure out, Dr. Girgis emigrated with his family to New York City.

Trying to understand why Dr. Girgis felt compelled to leave Egypt, I have read a little bit of the complex history of Egypt at that time. This is a bit far afield from Medicine and my personal history; and even further from the more generalized sixties and seventies mantra of sex, drugs and rock and roll; but I felt the need to understand Dr. G., to have a better sense of what he felt was important and why.

As I understand it, Egypt was a Republic lead by a monarchic system until 1952 when General Gamal Abdul Nasser staged a successful coup, deposed the

King and began to make changes to the societal structure under martial law. This led to the first free election ever in Egypt in 1956, which was won by Nasser who then became the first freely elected President of Egypt. Of everyone who voted, 99.5% voted for Nasser. This sounds corrupt by modern standards, but it makes sense to me.

Under the King's rule for multiple generations, the division of wealth and power was unevenly distributed in Egypt even more than it currently is in the United States. And if you protested the unfairness of the Elite Class having all the perks with no opportunity for a typical Egyptian to rise in societal status, they shot you. Fortunately, we live in a Democracy, so we don't get shot in similar situations. We seem to shoot each other for no good reason instead.

Retrospectively, I believe that Nasser deserved all those votes because what he did for Egyptians over the next twenty years was incredible. Egypt became a model of a modern Middle Eastern state. Of course, things being what they are and were, politics and religion and foreign policy got really complicated and apparently things didn't go well for the Coptic Christians who represented a minority religion.

Nasser did have one blemish that reduced his regional esteem, the Six-Day War with Israel. Israeli intelligence expected an attack by the Arab League which included the countries surrounding Israel, and that included Egypt under pressure from her allies. The Israeli Air Force had been bolstered over the previous six months by the receipt of one or two hundred F4 Phantom Fighter Jets from the US allowing for a pre-emptive strike on the Egyptian and Syrian air forces, destroying them on the ground. That's why the war lasted only six days. One day of air warfare and five days of negotiating a truce and end to the war, I guess.

Turns out that the IAF attack occurred on June 5, 1967, my eighteenth birthday. You may remember that Robert Kennedy's assassination and death occurred on June 5, 1968, my nineteenth birthday. I haven't investigated this any further fearing some type of cosmic trend, but I tend to stay close to home on my birthdays ever since.

I have been fortunate enough to see the IAF in action. The pan-Arab mantra today should be, 'don't go to war with the Israelis', but instead it is 'sex and rock and roll.' No drugs. Of course, surreptitious alcohol is okay in Saudi Arabia. Nobody listens. It's just another day in paradise now and who knows how the Gulf States will evolve but a regional conflagration like we saw back then is hopefully less likely. Hopefully. Intifadas are allowed. Wholesale slaughter is frowned upon but does sneak up on civilians.

That was quite a riff, wasn't it. But it is all about Dr. Girgis. He spoke impeccable English with a British accent, sort of. That was great. He smoked unfiltered cigarettes continually in the anatomy lab. That was horrible. Even worse, when he would come over to see how our team was doing, he would flick his ciggie ashes into our dissection which was just plain mean. And disrespectful. I don't think he meant it to be mean. There were no ash trays.

When Dr. G. got to New York, he applied for a medical license. Even though he had all his credentials, and they were in perfect order, New York, nor any other state, would grant him a medical license, so he couldn't practice surgery or any form of medicine in the USA. I don't know if this makes any sense, but he needed to find work and teaching gross anatomy at an Ivy League Medical School and a fabulous hospital seemed like a good idea.

The only other teaching pathologist in the gross lab who I remember was the Chairman of the Department, Dr. Roy Swan who I understand has passed away. I wonder if he donated himself. I am sure he was a very nice and certainly smart pathologist and I know he was an MD but he may have had a PhD also. One thing is for certain, and I am not trying to be cute, he was a stiff. You just had to know him.

The gross anatomy course was a snap for me with a solid A or whatever they gave you since I don't think we got a record of our grades (thank you Comp Vertebrates.) You were going to have to die or commit a crime not to graduate whatever med school you were admitted to because so much energy and money had been poured into your education at this point. No students died. I don't want to tell tales out of school, but it is possible a crime was committed. Whether yes or no, everybody did graduate in 1975. I can't say the same about Cornell Law School. They graduated in 1974. That's because Law School is only three years. And you know how uptight those guys and gals are about billable hours.

I think most of what I know about our insides I learned from that college course on comparative anatomy, and they should consider something like that to be incorporated into the med school curriculum, particularly with the current cadaver shortage. The only other lasting memory I have of the first year is the smell of a cadaver, a kind of funky formalin smell that is hard to scrub away. But you get used to it. You can get used to anything.

Chapter 7

Year 2

"Why does love have to be so sad?"....Eric Clapton

"Some people never come clean

I think you know what I mean, oh

You're walking the wire, pain and desire

Looking for love in between

Tell me your secrets, I'll tell you mine

This ain't no time to be cool

And tell all your girlfriends

Your been around the world friends

That talk is for losers and fools

Victim of Love

I see a broken heart

I could be wrong but I'm not, no I'm not

Victim of Love

We're not so far apart

Show me what kind of love have you got."......Victim of Love....Eagles

I have been racking my brain trying to shake loose a clear picture of the summer break and the start of Year 2. But only fragments are appearing. I favor a stream of consciousness in telling a story so when the stream doesn't even meander but keeps drying up along the way only to re-appear, my writing can become choppy and nonsensical.

Ten years ago, I wrote a complete novel. It was a satire about a small American community dominated by a large hospital. I never showed it to anybody and never tried to have it published. I wanted to see if I could do it and what it would take to finish it. I had never taken a creative writing course, but I read some books on creative writing and was probably most influenced by the Stephen King book 'On Writing'. If anybody had good ideas about creative writing, it had to be King. If I condensed all that I learned from his book to the one lesson that helped me the most, it was not to worry about what you wanted to write on any given day, but rather, take one of your characters and begin to consider what they were doing that day and everything else would flow from that. It was a simple notion but for me it worked well. Of course, that book took almost three years to complete, and I went through 12 drafts. But there were multiple subplots that intertwined, and they all worked out by page 370. I haven't looked at that book in ten years, but I may read it when I finish this. This book is different. It is a memoir. It includes my memories of the long middle segment of my life. Perhaps I should call it a hemi-autobiography since I seem to be shaking my brain's cortex to see what falls out, the cortex being the newest portion of our brain and contains memories, thoughts, and all that stems from them. It's certainly no deep dive into my rather pedestrian life. I'm trying to use my memoir as the skeleton on which I can hang anecdotes that by the end will allow me to draw some conclusions. They probably won't be polished, finished conclusions because I already see that these things are always in a state of evolution and flux.

I don't remember exactly what I did that summer except I had to have a job to make money. I just don't know what it was. See what happens when you hit your seventies. (Not the Seventies, my seventies.) I can remember jobs I had in high school but not when I was in med school. But I can remember how the year started.........

..... it started for me in the New York Hospital employee cafeteria which was a typical hospital employee cafeteria but dull. I'm sure that today they have multiple dining facilities scattered over thousands of square feet catering to the healthy tastes of young America: organic foods both fresh and processed, farm fresh produce shipped from suburban farms, sugar free beverages without high fructose corn syrup or artificial sweeteners, more brands of yogurt than states in the union. Tell me, don't you really hate the taste of artificial sweeteners in Coca-Cola or tea or coffee? You use them because of your diabetes, or because you are trying to lose weight or just feel guilty about adding real sugar. And have you ever tried zero sugar Coke? Not lines of coke. The Coke that has been quenching Americans' thirst for well over a hundred years.

My father was a dentist and the most honest person I ever knew. His integrity titer was off the charts. When I was a young boy, he showed me a piece of varnished oak and on it, he poured two ounces of Coca-Cola from a bottle (no cans back then, just good old fashioned glass bottles.) The Coke took off the varnish in about two minutes. Then he said to me, 'what do you think that is going to do to your teeth?' The lesson never stuck. I have been drinking the original, from glass bottles if I can find them, my whole life and I still have all my teeth and they are in good shape.

I was having a healthy lunch (chicken salad with chips) chatting up some classmates. Uninterested in their discussion about the prior years' lectures, I was glancing around without any agenda or focus. The place was full of med students, residents, nurses and most of the people having lunch I recognized from last year except for the first-year med students. Across the eatery was a table with two women first year med students identifiable by their clean and new white coats with the Good Samaritan on the left sleeve and the standard name tag on the left breast pocket. I had ditched mine because I wasn't going anywhere near patients for the next three months. School was going to be all lectures and labs. No cadavers on the one hand and no planned visits to the nursing units on the other. A slave to fashion (I admit it), I was wearing khaki slacks, a blue oxford cloth buttoned down collared shirt, slightly frayed, preppy Cornell tie loosened at the neck and penny loafers. This is what I wore every day, changing only the tie which went from red on blue to blue on red. But I knew that I had the lean relaxed body habitus of an Armani model. All I needed was the money to go shopping at Bloomingdale's and Armani to grow up and start his haute couture career. Then Bergdorf Goodman here I come.

But I wasn't thinking about clothes at that moment. I was having a classic Reptilian brain reflex that I assumed men had universally. Our brains are incredible organs, but not particularly healthy appetizers as once suggested by Hannibal Lecter. Too much cholesterol. Perhaps we can discuss the brain another time. It's enough to know that one simple way of thinking about our brain is that we have the new part that allows us to memorize the three dimensional inside of our bodies or the starting line-up of the New York Yankees, and make various connections with other information. The earliest portion of our newer brain helps us develop feelings, emotions and value judgements. Then there is the old part which is sometimes referred to as the Reptilian brain because it parallels the structure and function of reptile brains. It's so cool that just a short paragraph and you understand the brain.

To expand just a bit, and I am going somewhere with these thoughts, the Reptilian brain is somewhat limited and rigid about what it controls: breathing, heart rate, body temperature, reaction time, balance, and physical attraction. I registered what I had spied across the cafeteria as an increase in my respiratory rate, heart rate, slight increase in body temperature controlled by sweating, immediately getting up from the table and almost tripping over my own feet. There was just something about one of the two women at that table across the cafeteria that had activated my Reptilian brain, completely overwhelming my newer brain. Before I could stop myself, I was on my way to her table, introducing myself and asking if I could join them. They said, 'please sit down. Join us.' Now it was up to my newer brain.

Let's back away for a second and consider maturity, and how well it fits this scenario. I haven't spoken much about my girlfriends because they were all great and I had no problem dating in high school or college, but something was missing. Not sex....it was the sixties after all. It was some poorly developed ideas in my newer brain when it came to relationships with women when there was the beginning of mutual attraction or what we now call chemistry. I guess this is a nuanced and different form of 'organic chemistry' fitting better with psychology than the 'hard' sciences. These poorly shaped ideas could be given labels: persistence, commitment, thoughtfulness, affection, longevity and love. What was love? I had no idea. Certainly, when I sat down at the table that day. And maybe even now at age 74. I had a little idea about the other labels. There were some labels that were already stamped into my behavior like honesty and integrity. And I certainly understood desire and attraction. Check that, I knew when I felt desire and attraction. But I had no idea what love meant, and I didn't even know enough to wonder about it and try to find out more.

You know, it reminds me of that interview I never mentioned way back at the beginning of this memoir. The one where the New York Times Science journalist was interviewing the two famous astrophysicists about what had been learned about the nature of the Universe. Their answer was that we had learned that we had been asking the wrong questions.

I hadn't learned that yet. I hadn't learned that I wasn't even thinking about the right questions, and I had to consider this before I could understand what the right questions were. Then I could learn the right answers and begin to understand love. Of course, none of this occurred to me as I sat there firing up a conversation with these smart, attractive first years. I wonder now how many of my male friends and school mates were as in the dark as I was and how many even thought about this...but I dismissed the whole conversation in my new brain. I had a simple goal in that moment and that was to arrange a dinner with Natasha because that was the name of the woman who had activated the Reptile in my head.

Chapter 8

Year 2

"Keep on, keeping on.." from 'Got to Get Better in A Little While'....Derek and the Dominos Live at the Fillmore and many blues and rock musicians going back forever.

So far so good. I had a date with Natasha for Saturday night. I planned on taking her to dinner at a new intimate French bistro that had opened on First Avenue just north of 73rd street. It was family owned and operated and was just a store front with soft lighting and perhaps six tables. I had no personal experience with real French cuisine, just French dressing in a bottle, but I knew the French were gourmet diners and this place had gotten a good review in the New Yorker. It had all my requirements. Walking distance; new, small and intimate; four stars and inexpensive. But first, classes started.

There was another pathology course that lasted three quarters of the second year, but the lasting fragrance of formalin was gone.

As an aside, whenever I listen to the Eric Clapton live version of his hit song 'Cocaine', I think of formalin because throughout the song he has a repeating rejoinder: 'that nasty cocaine'. That's how I think of formalin. That nasty formalin. That's a good mental connection for generation X-Y-Z to have when considering trying cocaine. Try cocaine, end up smelling like formalin to a bunch of first year med students. Particularly in LA and NYC.

This second year pathology course was rather academic and difficult if your vision was iffy and/or you suffered from headaches. It had to do with learning the microscopic aspects of anatomy or what we docs refer to as histology. First you learned what normal organs look like after being prepared so a thin slice could sit on a slide and be viewed through a $6000 binocular microscope. This allowed you to use both eyes to view the specimen. Take the spleen, for example. Take it out of your abdomen and it looks like a giant kidney bean. But under the lens of a scope, a totally different story emerges. Eventually we all got pretty good at identifying normal tissue microscopically.

Then you learned what our organs look like under the scope when they are afflicted by a seemingly endless universe of diseases. Take the lung. Two large spongy sacs. You know they're very important but they kind of look gross and unimpressive. Like something that might have been coughed up by a Bull shark. Never a Great White shark which is much less discerning when it comes to their diet and will digest anything. Great Whites, I'm told, will even eat a Volkswagen Beetle. And great white's are more voracious. You could ask Roy Scheider, if he was available, but he's gone on to a bigger boat. I pee'ed next to Roy at the opening of a Broadway show during intermission. He was a short but charismatic dude. I was going to ask him how he felt blowing up a fake great white shark, but I kept my powder dry and just nodded hello as we washed our hands.

By the time your familiarity with the microscopic characteristics of the lung in common disease states is complete, you had no brain space left for remembering the Yankees' starting lineup. And that was just the lung with common problems like emphysema, chronic bronchitis, cancer and pneumonia.

Fortunately, we had advanced tools in 1972 to help us identify what we were looking at under the magnification of a high-powered microscope. They were called books. With pictures, photographs taken through the microscope, drawings and text. Today, my imagination leaps to the inevitable conclusion that you just snap a computer through a USB port to the microscope and within 30 seconds the HP printer in the middle of your lab prints out a description of what is on the slide with a diagnosis, any possible alternative diagnoses, references in the scientific literature as current as last week and a discussion. And your computer printout is admissible in a court of law should you be called as a witness in a medical malpractice lawsuit. Tim would have reminded me of this, although he didn't do medical malpractice litigation. Pathologists who spend their time looking at fresh surgical specimens have a tough job and one's opinion is always open to criticism and disagreement, two factors always argued by plaintiff's counsel.

I think they may have changed this form of litigation to a less onerous name. Malpractice seems so harsh and accusatory, like a crime was committed. Now they call it medical negligence. Much more pleasant. Like you just forgot something, like a sponge or clamp in the operative wound; or an umbrella in the car door when a downpour was expected.

Don't worry, that almost never happens anymore because of Patient Safety Programs in hospitals. But back in the 70's, negligence occasionally occurred.

It was in the histology lab where we all took that nationally standardized first test for med school students. The one where Wally to my right took the test hydrating with Schlitz and the unnamed student to my left threw up. Maybe he had a GI virus. In those days, we hadn't identified the culpable virus for that nasty problem, so we called it 'winter vomiting disease'. Today, most cases of winter vomiting disease (often accompanied by copious diarrhea) occur in outbreaks and are usually caused by the Norovirus. There is good news and bad news if you are caught up in an outbreak of norovirus, like

219

on a cruise ship or a resort in the Caribbean during a hurricane. The good news is that it lasts about 36 hours, and you are better. The bad news is that you don't develop immunity so you can get it again and again, it has evaded attempts to make a vaccine, and it is unbelievably contagious.

It's hard for me to remember the various courses they threw at us that second year. I am not certain physiology was one of them although the more I think about it, maybe that was first year...it all blends together. Sticking with the lung, physiology would be the course where you learned the function of the lung and how that worked. We all knew it was necessary for breathing but what I hadn't really thought about was the mechanism for air to go in and out of these two large spongy sacs that connected to the heart in the middle. Turns out the lung is passive when it comes to air movement. Like most movement in humans, it requires muscular action and the muscle that was most important here was the muscle that separated the lungs from the belly: the diaphragm. I don't want to get too technical, but when the diaphragm actively contracts, it sucks air through your mouth and nose into your lung and when it relaxes, the air flows back out. There are some accessory muscles that help but most of the real work is done by the diaphragm. I will let you explore this interesting physiology in your own time and there will be a test at the end of the book.

The histology lab slowly faded into histopathology lab where we learned to identify the organs and the diseases that can afflict them and in physiology we learned how the organs worked when things were going smoothly.

For me, the hardest organ to understand was the kidney and the reason was math. The kidneys do so many things that control fluids and salts and acidity of the blood in such complicated ways. Believe me, it's not just about urination. And to understand it all, with real life consequences for taking care of patients, mind you, you had to apply mathematical formulas and understand them. Not my strong suit. And then if things went south and dialysis came into the picture...oy vayzmir. That was what physiology and histopathology were all about.

This squinting into microscopes and working out math formulas to achieve proper acid-base balance tires me out at my age. You can believe that those first two years required a lot of intense studying compared to college. And it's a good thing that we had learned how to study in college, or we would have been in trouble. Somehow, as we approached the end of the second year, all the coursework seemed to be coming together in a way that vastly improved our readiness for patient care. And I would add improved the capacity of our brains to think on our feet and remember minutia at the right time.

It was Saturday afternoon, and I was going to have dinner with Natasha and my attention was shifting to that encounter. We hadn't spoken since that day in the cafeteria except for a hello and goodbye passing in the halls of the dorm. But when we met in the lobby, she looked ravishing, dressed in jeans and a striped shirt, and smelling slightly sweet and sour due to the layering of Shalimar on formalin.

It turns out that she was from Delaware and had gone to Smith College to study Slavic languages. But she didn't like Smith. No boys to smooch in Croatian. But things were rapidly changing everywhere in those days as you will remember from the early part of this story and some previously all men's colleges were accepting women. Like Princeton. I've been to Princeton, so I understand how cautious they can be. Anyway, Natasha transferred to Princeton undoubtedly because of their strong language program. And their men. And she graduated with honors in 1971. We were the same age. Then she moved to Manhattan having lined up a job translating for a bank. Somewhere in there she had an epiphany, just as I had. Except hers was that she didn't want to spend her life translating Serbian for Chase Bank. Why not use her talents to become a doctor? Natasha was way ahead of her time in that regard. More and more women were going to med school. So, she applied and was accepted to CUMC providing. She didn't have all the necessary course work. Like organic chemistry. She spent a year taking night classes to finish her necessary college credits before matriculating at CUMC a year after I did. I really respected that. Work during the day, go to school at night with a sturdy goal in mind.

She shared with me that her days at Chase were unusual in that everybody worked hard until lunch. Then they all went out to lunch and drank martinis until quitting time. Then she went to Columbia for her course work. I respected her even more. I also moved my checking and savings accounts from Chase to Citibank.

As we ordered coffee and dessert, she shared with me that at Princeton she had taken a summer and backpacked around Europe with her boyfriend. Boyfriend? Yes, she had an ongoing relationship with a guy she met at Princeton who was in law school at the University of Michigan. Relationship? They only saw each other during holidays and the summer, and I should know that if we were going to be dating. Dating? She said it like it was a foregone conclusion.

We walked back to the dorm holding hands and entered the lobby at which point she looked up holding my eyes with hers and said, 'would you like us to go to your room or mine?'.

The next afternoon was still Sunday, and I was in the stacks studying although I was having a hard time concentrating. The Reptilian brain will control you like that sometimes, particularly when you are young. Sometimes when you are older as well, particularly at mid-life. I thought to myself, 'okay, you were hot for this girl, you didn't hesitate, things worked out beautifully for both of you, she was smart, interesting and decidedly and devastatingly sexy, and gorgeous. You were a Cornell grad with a wealth of experience behind you. What was it that felt different now?'

I decided that during our evening and night and morning together, some vague power dynamic had shifted between us. When we ordered the bouillabaisse, I felt like I usually did and part of that was, 'in control'. When she left my room to shower and start her day, she was 'in control'. I think that was what changed but even now, fifty years later, I'm not sure that 'control' had anything to do with it. Still there was that sense of a shifting power dynamic. I concluded that I hadn't gotten to that part of the histology and physiology courses yet.

Maturity: exhibiting the thoughts, feelings and behaviors of an adult. In the stacks that afternoon I asked myself where I was in the continuum of maturity. I concluded I wasn't that mature because of this vague control issue. It bothered me. I didn't understand it. I knew I liked Natasha. She was smart, funny and sexy. I had gone out with a fair number of women who were like that. I wanted to see Natasha again and as often as possible. So, I felt something for her that was more than just hanging out with her.

What was it? I didn't know. And about my behavior. I decided I had acted normally within the bounds of my experience. But then there were these issues hanging out in space that I knew nothing about: like boyfriend issues and relationship issues. And did I actively do anything to seduce Natasha, or had she seduced me? I didn't know. I wasn't sure that it mattered. I guessed that it was mutual and my experience with women to that point hadn't encountered as sophisticated and independent a woman as Natasha.

Feminism entered my mind. A bit. Hadn't I spent considerable time in conversations with co-ed friends in Ithaca about feminism and wasn't that supposed to level the playing field between men and women in all spheres: business, salary, socially, sexually? And didn't I accept that this was a good thing, anti-misogynistic and a mature man understood and behaved consistently with those ideals. But this was getting complicated because other thoughts and feelings were being generated that I hadn't experienced before to any degree, like jealousy,

228

inferiority and rejection. Yet these bad feelings were normal, I guessed, if you were out there looking for a relationship. That was it. Relationship issues. That was what confused me. I had lots of friends and what they now call friends with benefits, but I never got into relationship issues even with young women that I was dating for a long while. And when I dated the same gal for months, I never went out with anyone else. I guess that meant we had been exclusive. She had been my girlfriend. I had been her boyfriend. But somehow, I didn't picture all that as a relationship. To me it was having fun and doing what young people have always done.

So, there were no conversations about our relationship during those 'relationships'. And, as I have learned over my lifetime, having no conversations about new and confusing aspects of relationships can be a great way to destroy a relationship. Like sharing thoughts and feelings, intimacy, vulnerability, empathy and compassion. I knew I was always honest, and I had integrity but all these other things, I just hadn't felt them or discussed them in terms of a 'relationship'. And there was an enormous aspect of relationships that was too big to even try to think about while I was studying the spleen. Love. Had I ever loved anybody with whom I had a relationship. I didn't think so and I doubted that I ever would until I understood love much, much better. As crazy as I was about Natasha, I still felt it was in the moment, and what I was feeling couldn't be love. After all, it was only one date and one night.

I had a lot to think about in my spare time and not a lot of spare time to think about it. And a lot to learn about relationships and love.

I closed the door in my mind palace which led to the room where I was now keeping my thoughts about love and relationships and opened the door to histology. But the door in my mind palace that led to thoughts of love and relationships wouldn't stay closed. If you are a Sherlock Holmes fan, you will understand this.

I finally convinced myself that there was a lot of negative energy going on in my head in the stacks. I should simplify things. It seemed obvious that Natasha and I liked each other, were attracted to each other, enjoyed sex with each other, and wanted to continue to date each other. That was established fact, and we should just go with it. The boyfriend relationship that Natasha had been very clear about was external to our relationship and I wouldn't worry about it, enjoy the moment as it were, and if our dating intensified our relationship, the boyfriend would go away as an issue. And during the process, I would try to learn more about the deeper roots of long-term relationships, and even love, maybe. I went back to studying feeling much better. But as I climbed out of the stacks, once again there was a

231

vague sense of unease surrounding me that I was not used to and couldn't describe, like the smell of formalin on sheets that had been washed multiple times.

Academically, the first two years of med school were winding down towards their inevitable conclusion with the beginning of patient care responsibilities. We had either learned and remembered everything we needed to know, or we had learned how to find what we needed to know in the library. Today, you find what you need to know on your smartphone just outside your patient's room. And that's assuming that the computer in the patient's room didn't already tell you. Today, in many hospitals, the IT systems will tell you what to order for your patients based on real time data on the patient in the bed in front of you backed up by the latest published algorithms in reputable medical journals like The New England Journal of Medicine.

But when I was finishing up my second year at CUMC, there were no computers and those that existed required an entire building to house one of them and a bunch of weird punch cards to use them. I know. I saw them back in Ithaca. My class took a course on physical diagnosis where we learned the importance of taking a thorough history from the patient and sometimes from their family and friends; and doing a thorough if not exhaustive, physical examination on the patient...repeatedly if they were sick. We used tools like a stethoscope and a reflex hammer and a tuning fork, and ophthalmoscope. You may have heard about these tools but never actually have seen them. I'm sure they are in a museum somewhere.

While I was still early in my clinical career, I already knew that I was destined to become an internist and possibly subspecialize in a clinical field within internal medicine. It appealed to my intellect and my classmates who gravitated toward it were my friends and thought like I did. The surgeons or future surgeons I knew and were friendly with were just different. Not bad. Excellent physicians. But in ways that are hard to describe they had a 'different culture' from internal medicine. When I was in the early part of my training, I considered surgery rougher, less analytic, less intellectual. But that's not true. Surgical culture is determined by the environmental characteristics and limitations of their world and the need to be precise regarding decisions and actions. I respect them at the highest level.

My world was the world of internal medicine, and my hero was a man named William Osler who died many years before I was born. Sir William Osler was born a Canadian but with family in England where he eventually received a great deal of his medical training and started his vast contributions to the profession. He then moved to Philadelphia at which time he was married to the great-granddaughter of Paul Revere. He spent several years at what is now the Hospital of the University of Pennsylvania which included the Philadelphia General Hospital, a city hospital like Bellevue in NYC. I was fortunate enough when I was a resident in training at HUP to wander through the PGH which is no longer standing and find a small museum where there were items displayed that you could pick up and examine that had been used by Osler including his journals where he made copious notes about his patients. Unfortunately for Osler, he lived at a time when he strongly influenced the clinical approach to patient diagnosis but had few options to cure his patients and heal them after they recovered. As a result, many of them died. And Osler took this as an opportunity to do autopsies on his patients to better understand the disease process which had defeated them and him. His autopsy table and implements to perform autopsies were in that museum. Cool.

He didn't stay in Philadelphia. He was invited to Baltimore to help in the formation of a university with a medical school and teaching hospital that was to be called Johns Hopkins. It was at Hopkins that Osler wrote extensively regarding the emerging field of internal medicine, and this became the conclusion of his many contributions and why many consider him the father of modern internal (or adult) medicine. This is what I learned from Sir William Osler which has never left my thinking, even today, retired and ill.

Osler said on many occasions that 90% of the time, the diagnosis of his patient's disease could be made by taking a thorough history. He used to say that 'the patient will tell you his diagnosis.' And 95% of the time, the diagnosis could be made if you did a thorough physical examination as well. Once you had the diagnosis, you could use what you had available to cure the disease. And heal the patient. And heal the patient. This repetition is intentional. Osler believed that diagnosing and treating a patient's disease were critical but insufficient. Once cured, the patient had been wounded both physically and mentally and needed to recover from the shock and trauma of the disease process. The internist had the responsibility to recognize this and aid the patient's healing. Osler clearly believed this. I do as well. Which brings me back to my earlier discussion on psychotherapy which can be a marvelous helper to the physician in healing a patient.

I practiced medicine at a major nexus point for American medicine. I had my own practice for 25 years where I saw patients with arthritic and auto-immune diseases, and often by default, acted as their general internal medicine doctor. And I practiced using the basic philosophy and tactics of Osler because that was how CUMC taught me. Then I became the Chief Medical Officer of a healthcare system in Delaware where I helped this healthcare system rapidly advance into the age of modern and often computer driven medicine that we experience today. I cannot say that there has been a decline in the quality of care of patients. Quite the contrary, all the changes in my profession have brought enormous benefit to patients who previously could not be treated in any significant way because we just didn't have the tools. And I am astounded with how rapidly things have changed for the better.

But I am sad and dismayed. Because what has changed for the worse, in my opinion, is the doctor-patient relationship. That sacred bond of trust between two human beings is based on the knowledge and humanity of the physician and the vulnerability of the patient. When was the last time your doctor entered the examination room and sat down, relaxed, looked you in the eye and asked what brought you in today or what did you want to talk about? When was the last time the doctor entered the room ignoring your presence, sat down at the computer and immediately began click-clacking input on your case without even saying hello? The doctors today are just as good or better and smarter than we were at CUMC, I just don't think they know what they have lost personally by the changes they have been forced to adopt. They have been asking the wrong questions, just like the astrophysicists. Medicine has not changed that much. Only the technology, pharmacology, the economics and business of medicine has changed. And somewhere in there the doctor got lost, with only a vague sense of a shift in something indescribable, like I felt after that first evening with Natasha. To me, physicians are becoming avatars of insurance companies, corporations, venture capitalists and the government, inputting data, carrying out computer driven orders, pacing their time to some executive driven demands. Heuristic analysis has become a victim of all this.

Do you know what heuristic thinking is about? It's the part of your new brain that says my experience and my memory and my intuition tells me that what the data says I should do with my patient is wrong. I can smell it. I can taste it. And I am going to ignore what the boss wants because in the end I am only accountable to my patients; to diagnose their disease, cure it and heal them.

And do you know what all this change does to doctors that they don't understand? It takes the joy out of being a clinician. The surgeons still hold on to a lot of what I call joy. But even in the sanctity of the operating theatre there is intrusion. Have you had your hip replaced? Did you know it was likely that a non-physician marketing a brand of hip prostheses was in the OR while you were asleep advising the orthopedic surgeon?

I firmly believe in data driven, computer enhanced decision making aided by heuristic analysis in the practice of medicine. And I believe, and many colleagues of my age agree, that the personal and sacred joy is leaving the practice of medicine and that is a shame.

The second year ended on a down note. I told Natasha that I loved her even though I wasn't sure. The entire year went by, and we dated regularly but never discussed those hazy thoughts of mine in the stacks that afternoon after our very first date. I didn't understand relationships or love any better than I did at the beginning of the year. I told her I loved her, but it wasn't an honest declaration. I just didn't want 'us' to end and I felt helpless, so I tried throwing out a lifeline. She told me it didn't matter what I felt. She had warned me she would be going back to her boyfriend and that was what she planned on doing. And that's what she did. I was a victim of love. But I had an exciting summer planned and maybe that would lift my spirits.

Chapter 9

Summer, 1973

"Well, I've got to run to keep from hidin'

And I'm bound to keep on ridin'

And I've got one more silver dollar

But I'm not gonna let 'em catch me, no

Not gonna let 'em catch the midnight rider..."

Midnight Rider, Allman Brothers Band, performed at Summer Jam

Five of us from the inner core, signed up for an externship

245

program at Tompkins County Hospital for our summer break after Year 2.

It was not a requirement of med school and was not connected to CUMC. Let me explain. Ithaca, New York is in Tompkins County and Tompkins County Hospital was the acute care hospital for the region, a part of the southern tier of upstate New York known as the finger lakes. These were long narrow but large lakes originally gouged by glaciers thousands of years ago and fed by creeks and streams. Not so different from the Archbald pothole except they were horizontal rather than vertical.

Cornell's campus was on the top of a hill overlooking Ithaca's finger lake the name of which is Cayuga. That is why our alma mater begins, 'far above Cayuga's waters....'. On the far side of the lake was Tompkins County Hospital. I am of the impression that originally the hospital had been a tuberculosis sanatorium around 1900. You see, back then there had been a significant outbreak of tuberculosis in New York City, and without any scientifically proven treatment, patients were often sent upstate for the fresh air away from the overcrowded tenements in lower Manhattan. These patients were offered other unproven remedies, but the fresh air was the mainstay of treatment. By 1973 the hospital had evolved into an acute care facility with emergency rooms, ORs, and medical wards. There were plenty of medical staff. Ithaca was considered a great place to settle, and I couldn't agree more. And to their credit, the staff physicians wanted an opportunity to teach, to be exposed to current students from university hospitals and possibly entice a few to settle in Ithaca and work at Tompkins County Hospital.

There were also a few students in the externship program from Upstate Medical School in Syracuse, and from Albany and Rochester as well, but we were the core 5. We were given a schedule to rotate through different parts of the hospital with different physicians doing the tutoring. We had lectures which the community doctors had worked hard to prepare. But the culture of medicine there essentially called for an end to the workday at about 2 or 3 in the afternoon for the docs who then went to play golf, go boating and fishing, hike and just take advantage of the beautiful surroundings. The nurses kept working following medical staff approved orders as to what to do about problems that might arise. I admit to being surprised, rounding on patients in the ICU who had, let's say, a heart attack. After 3 pm, no physician was available immediately but there were orders that directed the ICU nurses to administer medications and other measures depending on the problems that they faced. And if a patient went code blue, the nurses did what they could. This was a jarring contrast to New York Hospital. But we weren't there to learn clinical medicine, we were there to observe a different medical culture. Of the five of us I think two were at Cornell undergrad and the two of us hung out a lot on campus. Tom Delaney was the other CU grad. It was proving to be a relaxing, interesting and enjoyable summer. Golf, softball, boating, bar hopping, flirting with townies and exploring the many parks and gorges that dotted the landscape. I had a great time.

We weren't paid any stipend and that was only fair since we didn't have any responsibilities. But we were given room and board which included as much food as we wanted and nice accommodation in the part of the hospital where I think the TB patients had stayed years earlier.

The only negative I remember was the pathologist most responsible for interpreting surgical specimens. I did tell you I considered this a tough job. But this doc was a mess. No. He was a dick. Excuse my language. He was a messy dick. I just didn't like him from the get-go. He was nasty and his lectures were stupid, although some of my friends thought they were hilarious. He liked to show us surgical specimens from mentally ill patients who had harmed themselves in various ways. Not for me.

And to make things worse, he immediately hated me which made us kind of even, so the two of us spent the summer insulting each other at every opportunity. Not that it mattered. You can't like everybody; he just didn't like being challenged. Thinking about it, he was exhibiting signs of extreme narcissism, a characteristic I was becoming increasingly familiar with hanging out with CUMC doctors back in New York.

I remember meeting a 94-year-old surgeon who was scrubbing into a hernia repair. He was assisting. The primary surgeon introduced him to me before we scrubbed. He was a gentleman, as you might expect. The younger surgeon, as he was introducing this nonagenarian, said 'can you believe it, 94, and still practicing.' To that the older surgeon looked at me with a smile and said, 'oh, no, I was practicing until I was about 63. Now I know what I am doing.' Tompkins County Hospital was a trip.

There was one more experience that I wanted to tell you about: Summer Jam.

Woodstock Music Festival had occurred several years earlier in upstate New York on the property of a farmer named Yazger. I don't care how young you are, I am sure you have heard about Woodstock Nation. Depending on what part of the country you lived in you might have imagined a huge group of bloodthirsty hippies gathering to have wild sex while taking mind bending drugs and listening to the Devil's own music. That wasn't Woodstock. They sold maybe 60,000 tickets. I would have to look it up. 500,000 people showed up. It was totally peaceful. There were hippies, and bankers and professors and farmers and families and all types of people who made the trip to Woodstock, NY and lay out on the land to listen to some of the best musicians of our time for several days. You can watch it if you have a DVD player or listen to it by downloading the digitalized CD's. I didn't go. I could have gone, and I am not sure why I made that decision, but I always regretted it. Scranton, which is where I was that summer, was only two hours away, although the traffic did eventually become a problem as you got closer to Yazgur's farm.

I mentioned that the Eagles are one of my favorite rock bands. On their last studio album from 2007 they have a song called Cloudy Days and there are a few lines that I sometimes sing to myself just because they appeal to me: 'I believe in second chances, I believe in angels too, I believe in new romances, baby I believe in you.' I hadn't had any new romances of note in Ithaca during the Tompkins County summer, but I had a second chance of sorts regarding Woodstock. There was a rock festival planned for Watkins Glen not far from Ithaca on July 28. It wasn't going to be as extravagant as Woodstock or as long, but it would prove to be the last giant rock music festival of the hippie era. It seems that these festivals have been replaced by stadium concerts. Later in my life, my wife Leslie and I took our high school freshman Michael to the Philadelphia baseball stadium to see the Rolling Stones. Despite the driving rain and wind, the Stones were awesome. I hope to go again with my now adult sons to celebrate my 75th birthday. We have tickets for the show which will be at Lincoln Financial Field, The Linc, where the Philadelphia Eagles play pro football. Mick Jagger will be 80 or 81.

The Watkins Glen rock festival producers were looking for medical volunteers and I signed up before the ink on the poster was dry.

The festival was called Summer Jam and it had only three super groups scheduled to play sets and then jam together for about 24 hours. The three groups were The Grateful Dead, The Band with Robbie Robertson and my favorite of the three, the Allman Brothers Band. There were many rumors, like the Stones were going to show up, but none of that happened. Here is what happened, and it leads to one of my favorite small world stories of all time.

I had to get there early so I was parked up close. The stage was something else and the speaker system was of new design, developed so that any delay in the music from one set of speakers closer to the stage to the next set of speakers further away would be compensated by electronics and it would all come off as one song without echoes which had been a problem at Woodstock. It worked great. I was a second-year medical student with no emergency medicine or clinical experience. The other volunteers were medical and surgical residents from Upstate Medical Center at Syracuse University and Albany Med School and nurses from their emergency departments. My inexperience prompted them to ask me to sit on the stage and triage anyone in the crowd who became injured or looked sick around to the back of the stage where there was a medical tent. Wow. That sounded perfect to me. And they had arranged for helicopters to transport any pregnant women who went into labor or acute surgical problems to Syracuse. Could any of that really happen? You would think that a woman who was about due would stay close to home. They had sold, I think, 50,000 tickets. More than 600,000 people showed up and some of them looked very pregnant to me. As far as attendance, we beat Woodstock.

I did my job, which wasn't hard, although we did transport about six women who went into labor. I remember that shortly after The Band started their set, there was a huge thunderstorm, which caused a delay and made the ground extremely muddy which in turn had most people dispense with their shoes and sandals. There was a fair amount of drug use by the Jam goers, but it appeared to be mostly weed and wine which meant a lot of broken glass on the ground. The other drug that made the rounds was what was called windowpane LSD. These were clear buttons stuck to strips of paper which you would lick off for your trip. Powerful stuff. Two enterprising fellows brought tanks of nitrous oxide and sold hits to concert goers for $2. Nitrous oxide, which dentists use to make you a bit anesthetized, is harmless. There was a police presence, supposedly, but I didn't see any police. None were needed, in any event.

After about 12 hours I was relieved from the stage having sat through The Band and the Allman Brothers sets and I went back to the medical tent for coffee and nourishment. This is where the story gets interesting.

The biggest problem in the medical tent were people who had cut or lacerated their hands, arms, feet and legs from slipping on the muddy ground which hid broken wine bottles. Boones Farm Apple mostly. One young guy came in and was seen by an exhausted resident from Syracuse. This kid had a nasty laceration on the palm of his right hand. He was seriously muddy. But he wasn't stoned, and he was very pleasant. The resident whispered to the nurse with whom he had been collaborating and the nurse brought this young guy over to me. He told me his problem and the nurse told me the resident wanted me to suture the laceration. I carefully examined the bad cut across his palm and checked to see if his pulses were present at his wrist and if he

257

could move all his fingers. So far so good. He hadn't cut any vital structures like nerves, tendons, muscles or arteries. But lacerations of the palm were tricky and risky because they could easily become infected and that could lead to all kinds of severe consequences for hand and arm function. I whispered to the nurse, 'I have never sutured a laceration.'

She asked me if I had ever practiced on an orange.

'Not even a tangerine.'

She whispered back, 'don't worry I'll talk you through it.' This was my first personal experience with the value of establishing a rapid and solid relationship with a nurse. The two of us carefully cleaned his hand, wrist and forearm to the elbow. I explained to him my biggest concern, especially given how muddy he was, that the hand could get infected. We prepped the laceration which was probably 3-4 inches long and deep. At this point I had watched surgeons suture operative wounds, but I had never spent any time in an ED. I suggested a type of needle I had seen surgeons ask for and suture material the name of which I vaguely remembered from somewhere and she kindly recommended an alternative.

'You're right, that makes great sense' I said. And I started to sew. It felt like it took me 4 hours, but I put in 6 sutures in twenty minutes. The nurse bandaged the hand while I stressed to the kid that he had to see his doctor or go to an emergency room as soon as possible after leaving Summer Jam to make sure there was no evidence for infection, and I told him his doctor may want to prescribe an antibiotic for a few days just to be on the safe side. He seemed confident even if I wasn't, so we said goodbye and he left.

After returning to Tompkins County Hospital, I slept for 24 straight hours, then slowly forgot about my patient in the medical tent and what might be happening to him.

I didn't forget Natasha, however. I would periodically let her enter my thoughts which would make me sad. I considered myself dumped. A victim. Possibly a victim of love. I considered myself used. A victim. How could she do that to me after all the time and fun we had together. While I didn't like to think about it, she had been honest from the beginning and I could understand how my own feelings, to the extent that I appreciated them, could have prevented me from consideration of the possibility that I could fail to win her from the distant boyfriend relationship. I even wrote trashy romantic poetry sitting on an outcropping overlooking Cayuga Lake at sunset just below the Cornell campus...and then burned it in a little funeral pyre as an offering to some unknown Greek god. When I got back to CUMC, I found I was angry at Natasha and had no other feelings. I wouldn't speak to her and ignored her even though I felt a softness from her towards me. That lasted a year. And then it was gone. My senior year, I just resumed a friendship with her. I wonder what she thought about that. We chatted and joked when we saw each other but we never dated or got together. Eventually she married a classmate of hers who became a rheumatologist, which I found to be ironic. He is a friend of mine, and I would see him at scientific meetings in different cities and we would talk about CUMC and old times and difficult cases. But I never saw or spoke with Natasha again. Fairly recently, he called me at home which I found a bit unusual because it was out of character for our relationship. But I finally concluded that he had missed seeing me at the meetings and he just wanted to touch base. He valued our friendship. I never found out what happened to the Michigan lawyer boyfriend from Princeton undergrad days, and I don't care to know. Chances are he felt like a victim as well but maybe not. After all, he went to Princeton, where narcissism goes for lunch.

Writing about this has opened a lot of memories which I will have to examine since I have the time. I am still trying to gauge my maturation into an adult. But I don't want to leave you hanging so I am going to finish by sharing the rest of the small world story that began at Summer Jam with my first and only opportunity to suture a hand laceration.

The next chapter will begin with Year three. There is a lot to tell you. But I am going to skip ahead to Christmas vacation that third year. Before the medical and nursing schools broke for Christmas break, there was a wild party in the nursing dorm at CUMC. I was dating a nursing student that year which I will tell you about in the next chapter and the party was in her friends' suite. I was on call for my team on the internal medicine service, what we called a sub-internship, which gave us a kind of increased status. But I wanted to stop in and say goodbye to everybody that would be going home for the holidays. I spied my girlfriend in a corner talking to several of her schoolmates. It was crowded but a young good-looking guy pushed his way over to our corner, came up to me, and asked, 'are you Jim Newman?' He didn't look familiar. I told him I was and had we met? Then he said this.

'You really helped me last summer' and he stuck out his right hand. 'Look, you can't even see the scars where the stitches were!' I looked at his hand and I looked at him, and asked, 'Summer Jam?'. And he said to me 'right on. You sewed up my cut and you were so concerned about infection that you scared the shit out of me, and I saw my family doctor the next day, but he said it looked great and, like you said, he gave me some penicillin and told me to come back in a week and he would take the sutures out. And it healed up fine and I have had no problems with the hand and wrist.'

'Where do you go to school?' I wanted to know. 'Southern California, USC, my father's alma mater. I'm home for the holiday break and my girlfriend goes to the nursing school here and he motioned to a nursing student I knew. When I found out that you were in school here, I had to meet you.'

'Well, I'm glad you introduced yourself and it's great to see your hand did fine so now I can stop worrying about it.' And he went off to join his girlfriend.

Now what are the chances that a New Yorker who was a college student at the University of Southern California, being home for the summer, would go to a rock festival where there were more than a half million concert goers, cut his hand at two in the morning, find the medical tent, end up with me as the guy who sewed up the cut and then seek me out at a crowded party in a nursing dorm on the East Side of Manhattan six months later to thank me. It boggles my mind. Was there a slight wrinkling in the force? Did space bend just an infinite fraction. I don't know. I just don't know.

Since I like these small world stories so much, I want to share another one that flows from 'the year of Natasha.' I have never really forgotten about that year.... obviously. From what I have written so far, it rarely entered my conscious thoughts. Until something odd happened when Leslie and I were in France in 1990. My mother-in-law Gert and my mom were taking care of Michael and Craig who were ten and six at the time we were away. My mom went back to Scranton before we returned and Gert with her manfriend Mike took the boys for a five-day weekend at a resort in the Catskills. This would break things up a bit for her. They were seated at a table that accommodated eight, and they always were seated with the same four other people. Guess who they ate with three times a day for five days. Natasha, her husband Steve, and their two daughters who were about my sons' ages. Of course, Steve wanted to chat with the boys about our friendship. I don't think Natasha said much since the boys couldn't remember her at all. But what are the chances that this woman, who influenced my thinking so much during my second year of med school, would be seated with her family and with my sons and their grandmother at a resort in upstate New York for a five-day weekend while my wife and I were in Paris. They came from NYC, my sons with their grandmother came from Wilmington, Delaware, on the same weekend and were seated at the same table. Again, time-space warps ever so slightly.

Chapter Ten

Year Three

'Two Out of Three Ain't Bad'...Meatloaf from the Bat Out of Hell album

Our third year at CUMC was a sea change from our prior education. We now dressed in fresh new white coats, white poplin hospital approved slacks, shirt and ties which rapidly disappeared and were replaced by surgical scrub shirts and stethoscopes draped around the back of our necks. The pockets of our white coats became overloaded with the paraphernalia of the intern for many of us would be sub-interns working with the teams responsible for shepherding sick patients through their hospitalizations. These teams would include real interns (now called first year residents), a second-year resident and sometimes, depending on the service, a third-year resident. The team would make work rounds on the patients early in the morning and then go about making sure the plans for each patient went smoothly. There would be a series of rounds and conferences, previously known as lectures, throughout the day, some of which we were expected to attend. We were the lowest on the pecking order but since everybody above us had been through the same experience, 98% of the time we were fully accepted by everyone else. Each team had an attending physician who had the responsibility of rounding with the team daily. These were experienced clinicians with excellent teaching skills who were in private practice and on the faculty of CUMC. The students did not go on these rounds but rather met with our own teaching attending, trained to teach third year students. There were four students per team, so that made for a nicely bonded group who watched each other's backs on these rounds. These teaching attendings were always on the lookout for potential young partners as the year progressed.

One note, and I apologize to anyone who is offended. Every medical school I have ever come across, and there were many, called these clinicians 'teaching attendings', save one. And that 'one' was Harvard medical school and its affiliated hospitals, the greatest of which is The Massachusetts General Hospital, or MGH. Now there is no question of the excellence in medicine represented by Harvard. I respect it. And as a resident myself a few years later, I had the opportunity to work with Harvard med school grads and Harvard trained physicians. The most important mentor in my career was a product of the MGH and I loved and revered the man.

But Harvard teaching hospitals called their teaching attendings, 'Visits.' To me this gave not just the teaching attendings, but the entire operation a kind of Ecclesiastic aura, as though it was more than a hospital but a shrine to an Everlasting Higher Power who, if truth be told, must be a Harvard

271

trained physician. This really pissed me off, because as far as I could see, Harvard trained docs had the same knowledge base, common sense, warts and peculiarities that every other doctor had.

But it taught me something. It taught me about the psychological aberration that infected all doctors to some degree. I have mentioned it before. And that aberration is called Narcissism, or if you prefer, refined arrogance. You could periodically throw in the term hubris as well.

I believe that a little smidgeon of this, appropriately applied, is a good thing for physicians and particularly surgeons. It is no small thing to take a very sharp sterile knife (scalpel) and slice into human flesh. And while not as dramatic, it is no small thing to trust the infinite weight of the pharmaceutical companies whose only God is called Profit and feed molecules designed to lower blood pressure, normalize blood sugar and shrink tumors to patients who would rather be eating pasta. Or to stabilize the depression of an adolescent. Or to deliver a fetus into an uncertain world. Or to stop a pandemic.

At the MGH, teaching attendings were called Visits, but what they did was the same as teaching attendings at CUMC. But Harvard had to be different. They may have had an inferiority complex. One friend of mine who came out of the Harvard University system told me a story about teaching rounds at the MGH. There was a particular strategy employed by the students and residents on these rounds. Usually, the Visits would ask questions about the patient being presented by a member of the team. If the team member knew the answer, the rounds proceeded normally. If the team member did not know the answer, and it was considered a sign of weakness and lack of preparedness not to know the answer, there was a tactic employed in which the

273

student or resident would begin an oral dissertation about a subject that he or she did know quite a lot about but had nothing to do with the question that had been asked. This would go on, sometimes for half an hour, until everyone had forgotten the initial question or time ran out on the team's rounds. This was called 'the Harvard Method.' And only Harvard doctors could employ it. They had it copyrighted. The 'Visits' were not stupid and understood what was going on. After all, most of them had gone to med school or trained at Harvard. They were fine with the strategy because they felt it was benign and avoided embarrassing the questioned presenter. It reminded me of a Ponzi scheme. No one wanted to upset what was happening lest the whole house of cards would fall and Harvard would drop off the US News and World Report top 10 medical school list.

It's not like Harvard or any school in Boston had rejected me. This was not about revenge. It was about integrity. I had never applied to schools in Boston. I hated the Boston Celtics, the Boston Bruins, the New England Patriots and especially the Boston Red Sox. Although I loved Fenway Park for it represented the old school baseball my dad taught me as a very young boy. And I like Boston Common for the history it represents.

I dislike the way the city is laid out, the lack of parking, the T, the Union Oyster House, Faneuil Hall, the Charles River, the television show Cheers. I don't know why but perhaps 'Visits' had something to do with it. It just seemed to me that all these iconic Boston things were saying, 'here lives the great Visit of Boston, swear fealty or die.'

Back to the third year at CUMC. That school year lasted 11 months. We all had a month off in August to recover before the fourth year began. There were 3 months of internal medicine, 3 months of surgery, 1 or 2 months of OB-GYN, a month of pediatrics, a month of psychiatry, a month of Neurology which is capitalized here because it deserves special attention. Internal Medicine was special to me, of course, and you rolled through three different teams, often in different locations. I spent two months at New York Hospital and one month at Memorial Sloan Kettering. An inner core friend spent two months at North Shore Hospital which was one of CUMC's community teaching hospitals on Long Island.

In Surgery, everybody did a month of general surgery at New York Hospital but then they offered some choice. I picked Urology only because the Urology Service at NYH had no interns, so the third-year students acted as interns, giving me a much greater degree of responsibility and independence. Then I picked cardio-thoracic surgery so I could observe directly how the engine of the body worked in concert with those two large spongy sacs in health and disease. The other rotations in other fields were

276

cut and dried. I will say that we learned an enormous amount in the third year. Everyone had special experiences that will stay with them forever. And forever will give them a chance to shape their thoughts on what they saw and what they did. And how they felt about it when things worked out well or when things went south. Finally, with all those opportunities to think and feel, our behaviors began to change: toward the patients, toward our colleagues, the profession in general, the public and societal institutions like the media, sports, art and culture, and especially toward ourselves.

MATURITY: thoughts, feelings and behaviors of an adult. We were maturing.

Unfortunately, maturing is not a linear process and not an easy one. There were so many opportunities to take bypasses that ended up leading you nowhere.

In one important way, unrelated to tapping on chest walls or listening carefully for heart murmurs, third year began the same way second year did.

I mentioned that I arrived back at CUMC angry at Natasha, which I didn't understand but reflecting on it, was probably a good defense mechanism whether it was mature or not. But something else happened that I didn't expect.

I was in the medical library looking up something, or more likely reading the current NEJM, or even more likely the New York Times which was an addiction for many years dating to senior year at Scranton Central High School. On my way out, my attention was drawn to the study table to the left of the librarian's kiosk. There were four nursing students sitting there whispering to each other. I didn't recognize them so they must have been just starting. CUMC nursing school required two years of college prior to matriculation, so these women were not fresh out of high school. By the way, this was an era when men didn't go to nursing school. That came later. Then one suddenly looked up and our eyes locked. My Reptilian brain went into overdrive. It had been dormant all summer. Now, all those brain chemicals that powered my transmission from deep below my mid-brain's amygdala were being released all at once. I walked over to the table, totally ignored the other three (very unlike me) and introduced myself. Her name was Linda.

I am going to step outside this history of my life, this memoir, to say that I have changed the names and some of the personal stories of all the people mentioned here except for my classmates, especially the inner core. The one exception was Linda. That was her real first name. I will spare you her last name lest you might know her. She was the purest light of this period of my life, and I only hope that I can give you a sense of what I learned and what I despaired from our relationship.

Linda grew up in one of those States in the Deep South where her dad was a famous academic surgeon. Her grandfather had been responsible for the creation of the Payne Whitney Psychiatric Institute on CUMC's campus. She had gone to a junior college in Boston in preparation for going to Cornell's nursing school. On the outside, she was every man's and any man's dream: one hundred percent drop dead beautiful. Blond, green-eyed, slim and graceful. On the inside she was even better. Smart, funny, engaging, dedicated to her profession, sensual, kind, empathic, intuitive and forgiving. This last attribute, forgiving, was the key that could have unlocked what might have been. I can only hope to explain. We went out that night and every night for almost the entire year. Things fell apart at the end because of my own selfishness and confusion...and her willingness to forgive me for inexcusable behavior until she no longer could and that extinguished our flame. Her school year ended normally in June, and she went to Europe to visit family. We exchanged letters for a while but that slowly faded and when she came back, it was to search for someone else. I have checked on her once the internet became a staple of life and found that she had married a CUMC graduate who became a surgeon and they lived in the town in which she had grown up. I knew and liked him. He was a few classes behind me. There is a song, again by Eagles, from the Long Road out of Eden double album, called 'Do Something'. It is a sad but hopeful song that tells of a young man who has been rejected by his love and is paralyzed by the loss. The song urges him to do something, because it is never too late. I wish I had known that song back in 1974, but Eagles were just entering their formative years and Don Henley or whoever collaborated on it were decades away from conceiving it. That is a great double album, their last studio album and I recommend it highly.

I will make one observation now, and it has to do with Natasha in contradistinction to Linda. I don't doubt that when I told Natasha I loved her, and it was the first and only time I told her that, I knew in my heart that I did not love her. I desired her. I certainly had strong feelings for her. But I told her that as a last-ditch effort to keep things going, because I saw everything fading away (for further context, listen on U-tube to another Eagles song, Waiting in the Weeds.) How many rock and roll ballads have verses something like 'don't fade away.' My favorite is Eric Clapton's 'Bell Bottom Blues'. This must be a classic adolescent's reaction to being rejected. But I was a second-year med student who wasn't an adolescent anymore. Or, at the very least, had been asking himself the wrong questions. I'm also confident that Natasha didn't love me in any way, and she knew that from the very beginning. And I am sure she felt she had told me that in no uncertain terms and, as a result, felt no guilt about breaking up. She liked me, enjoyed my company, learned from me and was attracted to me, but whatever love is, she never felt any of it. And I'm good with that...now.

In my mind's eye Natasha transforms into Meatloaf singing from the Bat Out of Hell album: 'I want you, I need you, but there ain't no way I'm ever gonna love you, now don't be sad 'cause two out of three ain't bad.' Knowing Natasha as I do, the image of her turning into Meatloaf must sting a bit. Sorry. For a guy who looked like a fat motorcycle bum who lived on a barstool, he had a sweet singing voice.

Telling Natasha that I loved her was the first time I was able to acknowledge feelings and state them plainly even if they were not totally true. You may disagree, but that is a very brave thing to do. It displays your vulnerability to another human who is

283

important to you in a very, very personal way. Especially when you know they feel differently. Especially when for an entire year you never had any conversations that touched on any of these feelings, which in my case, because I was afraid that any conversation about this would abruptly end our affair, for that is what it was, an affair. But also, because I didn't know about these conversations and how important they were.

The intersection of my life, my evolution, my maturation, Natasha and Linda seems cosmic to me. It's quite likely that it would seem trivial to everybody else. Shit happens. This may be one of the great lessons of psychotherapy. It's what you do with the shit that counts. Do you examine it and change in a positive, reflexive and responsible way or do you become jaded and tuck it away somewhere never to be seen again because it is too painful or too complicated. Sometimes, therapists refer to the first way as 'activation.' It's not a small world story. It is a clash of events that strikes me as dramatic. At least it was for me over a long period of time.

The tragedy of my relationship with Linda was that I never told her that I loved her, when I did. She was the obverse of Natasha. I think about this every now and then. In retrospect, I remember so much of our relationship and time together, which I have no intention of probing in this memoir. And through the perspective of time and experience I realize that there was true love in my heart for her. Yet we never talked about it. It wasn't fear of rejection that stopped me because I had no fear of rejection. Again, I turn to one of my rock and roll heroes, Tom Petty, for just the right inflection: 'it's alright if you love me, it's alright if you don't, I'm not afraid of you running away honey, I get the feeling you won't.' The song is 'Breakdown.' 'You see, there is no sense in pretending, Your eyes give you away,

Something inside you is feeling like I do, We've said all there is to say.'

I probably hadn't identified the feelings back then, but I think I was confident that Linda loved me as well. She never said it. I like to think we both saw the promise in each other that could grow into a powerful bond. But where Natasha was an alpha female in her psyche and a true feminist in my belief, Linda was much more traditional. She let me take the lead. If I knew enough to have these sensitive conversations with her, I am sure she would have been very receptive. I didn't know enough about myself or about the conversations you are supposed to have. I don't know why. So many things I never understood considering how smart I am thought to be. Since family of origin has so much to do with shaping who we become, maybe the loss of my father, the aloofness of my mother, the culture of Scranton bears some responsibility. Or maybe it's just the way of the world. As I write this, I am sorry that I never told Linda that I loved her and that I was in love with her because I was and if she reads this, consider it a heartfelt apology that can never be made more heartfelt. And if Linda was to read this and examine her memories and decide that I am wrong and she never loved me and could never love me, well, I am okay with that. At this point in my life, understanding what I honestly felt and feel and accepting it is the most important thing for me.

Graduation week, one year later, I sought Linda out in her dorm suite, and we did have a conversation about our relationship. We were both graduating in two days or so and I wanted to put an exclamation point on how things ended between us a year earlier. What I did was disgusting and I am ashamed of it even now. I was going to Philadelphia for my residency, and I remember asking her if we had stayed together, would she have come with me. And in her open and totally honest way, she said yes. And then I lied to her. It was a terrible thing to do and broke every principle I hold dear. I told her that I didn't think it would have worked out anyway. I don't even know why that came out of my mouth. It just did. It was defensive, misogynistic, bigoted, anti-feministic and not true. It was hurtful and it was a lie. I feel that I implied that our relationship was all a lie. It was incredible bullshit. I am so ashamed of saying that to her then. I close my eyes and I see my younger self playing out in that scene and I weep. My only hope is that it is a fantasy that didn't really happen.

If that is the way it played out, maybe the comment meant nothing to Linda. Maybe I was so far lost to her that she just didn't care what I said. But I will tell you it mattered to me and still matters. I loved the woman, I didn't understand what that meant, I never talked to her about it, I never said it to her even though I had said it somewhat corruptly to Natasha years before, and then I lied and told her our entire relationship ultimately was built on bullshit. Just to make myself feel better about what I knew in my heart I had lost. Do something. What I did was walk out of her dorm room. I didn't even kiss her goodbye. I was an idiot.

Chapter 11

Third Year: On the Nursing Units

"Oh yeah, alright,

Take it easy baby

Make it last all night

She was an American girl"....Tom Petty and the Heartbreakers: American Girl

The third year we were sent to the clinical services in New York Hospital, Memorial Sloan Kettering and a number of affiliated hospitals in New York and the other boroughs and surrounding suburbs. I can't remember where I started but I do remember that I did my 3 months of internal medicine toward the beginning and my 3 months of surgery towards the end. In between were the other major clinical specialties that I mentioned. Now we were 'third years', 'sub-interns' and 'medical clerks' (pronounced the way the Brits pronounce it, 'claarks'.) This was a grueling year, but it was made much easier for me because I had Linda to return to and comfort me whenever I finished the day's work. And I could comfort her.

I am going to relate anecdotes that I remember from that year in no particular order because they were fixed in my memory as events that challenged my thinking, aroused feelings I didn't know I had and eventually must have affected my behavior. I still wonder whether I matured or took a lot of bypasses that got me nowhere. Up until that point, a good portion of my life had been devoted to 40 km detours without the benefit of visiting Head Smashed in Buffalo Jump. You know, I don't think I told you about that buffalo jump. I will have to add it as an addendum.

One anecdote that stays with me always was an admission I worked up one evening when I was on-call and sleeping in the hospital paired with an excellent intern and second year resident. The admission was a young woman in her early forties, and she unfortunately had developed an aggressive breast cancer during the previous year. There was a limited and repetitive approach to treating breast

293

cancer then: radical mastectomy followed by a difficult course of primitive chemotherapy and radiation therapy to the cancerous side of the chest. Despite having survived her treatment, the cancer had progressed and now was metastatic, documented to have spread to her lungs, liver, spleen, bones and brain. She was admitted with fever and signs of pneumonia. Despite her pain and her anguish, she suffered through my Oslerian work-up and was very kind to me in the process. I then presented her to my intern and resident with plans to culture her blood, induce sputum with respiratory therapy, start broad spectrum antibiotics, re-stage her cancer, consult her oncologist and assess her pain control. Also, in addition to her cancer's invasion of her lungs, she had pneumonia and was finding herself short of breath just lying in bed, so oxygen supplementation seemed appropriate.

My team listened attentively and then told me they had some alternative suggestions that I should consider. The patient didn't have a living will, which was almost unheard of in those days. The team told me I had done an excellent work-up, and first we should attend to her pain with sufficient morphine intravenously so that she was resting comfortably. Second, they thought oxygen supplementation using nasal cannulas which were less intrusive than a facial mask to ease her shortness of breath was an excellent idea. Third, we should ask if she would like any family or friends or clergy to keep her company and we should check on her frequently through the night. No cultures, no antibiotics, no aggressive respiratory therapy, no consultation with her oncologist but maybe a phone call was in order to give him a status report.

'She will die tonight if we do that', I complained. And they said, rather gently as I remember, 'and don't you think that is the best outcome. Why should she continue to suffer when there is no hope'.

There it was, a lesson I had never even conceived of in Oslerian doctrine: diagnose, cure and heal. But wasn't there always hope. 'Yes, there is hope, but it is relative to the odds stacked against her. She has been overwhelmed by her disease that we simply don't have the means to improve, even a little bit. The quality of her life can't get better. Our job now shifts to easing the next phase of her life, which is her death.'

I wrote her new orders, and the intern signed them, and I went to my on-call room but I couldn't sleep. I kept thinking I was complicit in her death. Or I had done nothing to save her from death. I believe this is an experience every physician who cares for patients goes through at one time or another. My time was then. And I came to believe we had done the right thing by failing to intervene but given it serious thought based on science, clinical medicine, and our most deeply held feelings about life and death. In fact, doing nothing was a positive intervention. She died peacefully two hours later. I arranged an autopsy with her parents who were very grateful for her care.

I have a contrasting anecdote to that story, and it also involved a cancer patient I admitted while on-call for the medical service. This was a sprightly man in his fifties who was sitting in a chair in his hospital room with his wife. As I entered the room, a nurse pulled me out to tell me that the patient's hematologist -oncologist was on the phone and wanted to tell me about the case. This is what he said, 'listen, this gentleman has had a long course of large cell lymphoma and has done very well but now he is coming to the end, beginning to fail to respond to my continued treatments. I know him well and I would like you to make him comfortable and not do any investigative tests or intrusive treatments. Just let nature take its course. I'm out of town but will be back in a few days from now.' Like the woman with advanced breast cancer, the patient graciously accepted my extensive history and physical. Chatting with him and his wife, for they were both outgoing and loquacious, I learned of their recent adventures. They loved to travel and had just returned from Majorca and Spain. They had a wonderful time exploring, touring, sailing and deep-sea fishing. He didn't suggest to me a man on death's door. So why was he admitted?

He had been having headaches and neck pain with intermittent fever for about ten days which hadn't resolved with amoxicillin and Tylenol with codeine (or scotch). He did seem to have a stiff neck and his deep tendon reflexes (the ones you elicit with that reflex hammer) seemed increased to me, but I had to admit, he had no other findings. He was being treated with a moderate dose of prednisone and a chemo agent with which I wasn't familiar.

I presented his case to my intern and resident. Their advice was to follow the attending hematologist's recommendation. After all, he had known the patient for years and followed him closely. I considered what they said and thought about the woman with widely metastatic breast cancer. And said, 'I don't agree.'

'Listen, this man is very active and enjoying life. He just came back from what must have been a tiring trip to Spain. And he and his wife have more plans to travel. The symptoms he complains about are recent and since both his lymphoma and his therapy can impair his immune responses, maybe he has an atypical meningitis that we could cure.'

That was met by great skepticism by my teammates. I told them, 'We owe this guy a spinal tap.'

They told me if we did it, I was going to be the one to do it because in patients like this man, they were notoriously hard to perform and that made a lumbar puncture an invasive study, just what his private attending told me not to do. But I performed it easily. The results were encouraging showing increased protein, lymphocytes and mononuclear cells, but the treasure came from the microbiology lab where special stains showed cryptococcal organisms which easily grew on culture of the spinal fluid. He had fungal meningitis which patients with his problems were prone to get. Within ten days he was feeling much better and within three weeks he was cured and ready to travel. I asked them where they were going next.

'Patagonia, to see the penguins.'

The intern and resident did not eat crow. For them it was all in the game. And I thought they were proud of me that I stuck to my opinion and let them share in the glory of a proper diagnosis. And the attending was wonderful to talk with about the case. He told me that he had been wrong when he spoke to me. That I showed clinical skill, personal fortitude and courage that was rare for a third-year medical student in his experience, he was proud of me and if I ever wanted to consider hematology and oncology, I should let him know. I didn't consider it.

I will now jump to surgery. You know why I picked a Urology rotation, which really wasn't very popular even though it was considered one of the strongest urology programs in the US (probably because the sub-interns kept the patients out of trouble.) And that is what this story is about. Mid-way through the month-long rotation, which I remember was in May, I was in the Urology clinic seeing patients working with the Chief Resident. There was a mix of patients who didn't have private docs with privileges at New York Hospital. The patient we saw that afternoon had a painful, tender swelling in his right scrotum. He was a man in his forties. The Chief Resident became very excited because this appeared to be a varicocele, a fairly common benign problem in men of his age which internists get exercised about, probably because they know little about urology and were always worried about testicular cancer. This was an opportunity for him to educate me so I could deal with a swollen painful scrotum thoughtfully and not demand immediate attention from a urologist. He was an excellent teacher and he explained that a varicocele was in fact a varicose vein that developed along its course beside the vas deferens (a tube that carried sperm to the urethra for purposes of ejaculation and starting a family.) I always thought that this was the most appropriately named structure in human anatomy since it was the vast difference from Fallopian tubes in female reproductive anatomy.

After thoroughly examining the patient and making him very uncomfortable, I went to the library and read all about varicoceles and even copied a few articles to take home. This patient's surgery was scheduled for the next week, and I studied the material so I could impress the Chief Resident. The surgery approached and I wrote his admission orders, once again examining him thoroughly per the Oslerian tradition. By this time, I was having doubts that this was, in fact, a varicocele based on my reading and the patient's history and exam. Osler was looking over my shoulder and likely nodding. While we were scrubbing into the case, I questioned the Chief Resident as to what else this could be. There had to be what doctors call a differential diagnosis, which means other possibilities. He scowled and walked away.

The patient was anesthetized, and all the players were in position in the OR with the Chief Resident in the operator's chair. To his credit, and ahead of his time, he asked, 'does anyone have any concerns about this case of a varicocele in the right scrotum.' Being consistent with my personal philosophy and not really giving a damn about my urology reputation, I said, 'are you sure this is a varicocele and not something else, something that may alter your incision or surgical approach?'

I was ignored and the first incision was made. Oops. No varicocele. But rather the swelling in the man's scrotum was a loop of small bowel. Somehow it had managed to herniate through some variation of the normal anatomy into the scrotum. This was very bad because it could be difficult to push back into the abdominal cavity where it

304

belonged along with the rest of the small bowel and could conceivably get injured, like losing its blood supply, becoming gangrenous and requiring an ileostomy, one that could even become permanent. This would not be what the patient expected when he woke up. Try as he might, the Urology Chief Resident could not reduce the hernia. As a result, he had to call the general surgeons to scrub in with him to help. This proved to be very professionally embarrassing. It also prolonged a 30-minute procedure into a five-hour marathon with many sarcastic comments passed around the operating table none of which were directed at me. They even stopped the OR music which the urologists usually enjoyed while operating.

There were two good outcomes. The patient was told that the surgery was a bit more complicated than usual, but he was very happy with the results. Second, the Chief Resident corralled me the next day and told me this: if I kept my mouth shut and never showed up in one of his operating rooms again during my rotation, he would guarantee me an A in Urology. And he was good to his word. I spent the rest of the rotation working on my tan on the roof of the dormitory. It was May!

I later asked myself, after giving it some thought, about the two contrasting reactions to my questioning of a senior physician. Why did the Chief Resident (who didn't become Chief because he was slow on the draw) react to me one way, while the senior Heme-Onc attending react to me in a completely different way. I didn't know why but I did have some thoughts about it. The Chief Resident was being challenged twice, in front of his colleagues and nurses, by a lowly sub-intern, about what was a standard urology clinical diagnosis with a standard surgical approach. He didn't like it, so he brushed me off. I thought of the 'Visits' at the MGH and made a mental note to check and see where the Chief went to med school. Because it seemed to me that this was one variation of narcissistic behavior I had noted in my profession. Sometimes it was subtle and sometimes it was so obnoxious that it hit you over the head like a sledgehammer. And sometimes it was absent entirely and always, like with the heme-onc doc. And I felt that it all came down to an amalgamation of everything that made up the personality of the doctor. In this minor instance, he was the Chief, the ultimate Urology resident. And if he made me look a little bad, then reactively he looked better. Rather than using everything that happens as a teaching moment, he took my questioning personally and made himself look like a victim. It was silly, really. But there was an important take-away lesson. In medicine, there are never any bad questions. Everything can be a teaching moment.

Was I a narcissist? I didn't want to be, and I didn't think so. I thought I could be arrogant at times; but only when I deserved to be arrogant...which is itself an arrogant statement. 'Hot stuff' said Mick Jagger at the El Mocambo, a club in Toronto where the Stones love to perform. I'm told it's a small venue. Must be totally awesome. I told myself that when I'm feeling arrogant, I should think of Mick and 'Hot Stuff' and laugh at my own ridiculousness.

Seriously, the real question I had to ask myself, was whether this tendency toward narcissism and arrogance in medicine a threat to patients. The patient was the central figure here, not the doctor. I didn't know, but I suspected it could be troublesome in more severe cases because it denied the patient an open mind with a broader knowledge base and an ability to look beyond the data into the physician's own experiential world and rely at times on their intuition rather than what their 'teaching attending' taught them. Heuristic analysis. An invaluable part of being a clinician.

So where did the Heme doc fit in. He showed some arrogance when I spoke with him initially but inevitably it didn't get in the way of how he viewed the patient, me, and the long view of medical care. He had made a mistake which could have been serious. But it worked out well for everyone. And I think it revealed his confidence in the interdependence physicians have with each other and with nurses and other health professionals. What had really happened here in the case of the man with lymphoma and meningitis? He told me 'look, this patient is also my friend who I have cared about for a long time; please don't make him feel worse.' If I had made him sicker, I don't think the hematologist would have been angry, I just think he would have discussed the case with me from a different angle. Either situation, regardless of what I had chosen to do, impacted on his ego and self-confidence. Everything was a teaching opportunity. And that was a very valuable lesson.

There was a lot to learn from these anecdotes and I tried hard to learn what I had observed and inject it into my behavior in a way that seemed professionally correct and best for the patient. I was maturing. Or so I thought. At least in my practice of internal medicine. Not so much in my personal   life.

Chapter 12

Medical School

Ends

The
Hippocratic Oath

"Somewhere, somehow, somebody

Must have kicked you around some

Tell me why you wanna lay there

And revel in your abandon

Honey, it don't make no difference to me, baby

Everybody's had to fight to be free

You see, you don't have to live like a refugee

No baby, you don't have to live like a refugee".....Refugee by Tom Petty and the Heartbreakers...1979..........from the Damn the Torpedoes album

This should be a short chapter, even though it covers two critical years in the lives of my CUMC class. By comparison, which is not a fair exercise, the last two years of college played a much larger part in determining the arc of our lives.

Maybe that's not a correct assumption. The slope of college, at least for me, would determine if I was even accepted to med school and which school I chose assuming I had a choice. I used to have a recurring discussion with my wife about how much of an influence did the college you

315

attended have on your success in life and did your success in college affect your career choices, provide you with opportunities, and expand your interests culturally and intellectually. Since at the time we had two sons approaching college age, this was very much on our minds. Leslie had gone to college and grad school within the SUNY system which is excellent and is an extension of public education in New York State, rather than going to a private university or college. We were both progressive liberals politically and she felt it made no difference where you went to college if you took advantage of it. And coming out of that system, I can share with you that she has had an extraordinarily productive life in all facets, much more than mine I would think, and one that will echo through time long after she is gone.

While I thought the SUNY system was excellent and she had made the most of her years in it, elite colleges and universities gave their students an added advantage in starting their adult lives, their further education, their careers, their families. I felt that way since my entire education and training throughout my entire life took place in Ivy League schools, and I think I was biased and a bit arrogant in thinking that. Natasha accused me of being a Cornell chauvinist. But I also think I was right. Both my sons received excellent educations, and both have become very successful in different careers, but one went the Ivy League route and the other a very fine private university. In my opinion their lives are equally admirable. But when it came time for my older son to choose between an Ivy League school and a state university, my wife punted and supported the Ivy League. Interesting. She had very strong convictions but when it came to her own child, she abandoned them and signed on with his choice of Penn. I believe my younger son avoided applying to the Ivies even though I was totally confident that he would have been accepted to one of them, probably Cornell, because his scholastic record was good enough to be admitted there and he had the legacy issue helping him. I had two Cornell degrees and my brother had a Cornell PhD.

Not sure why he never applied. That is part of his story. Anyway, everything I have written in this chapter is conjecture since I haven't discussed it with anyone in the family since. The arc of my life had been determined long before the beginning of my third year in med school. If I have been successful in writing this memoir so far, you will understand that in my soul I was destined to be an internal medicine doctor whose primary commitment was to the long term care of patients and a supplemental commitment to teaching, a bit of research, and while I wasn't thinking about this in medical school, leadership and shaping the way health care was delivered as dictated by law and policy. Since sub-specialization was part of the Cornell educational culture, I felt it likely that I would sub-specialize depending on my experiences during my residency. That's what happened.

The first and second year of CUMC was devoted to applying the basic and clinical science you had acquired in college, while the third and fourth years of med school prepared you for the diagnosis, curing and healing of patients. Sound familiar? The third year you participated in the care of patients in major fields of medicine. The fourth year you could choose focused areas of medicine and take electives where all your time was spent in that area. So, an outer core friend, Paul Pellicci, had established an arc of his career a long time before, very similar to my experience, except he was destined in his soul to become an orthopedic surgeon. And he became a fine one. Most of my classmates were not ready to decide in their hearts and minds where their path would take them, but those two years allowed them to choose what field their internship would encompass, or at the very least would give them a little more time to work out what direction they were going. And sometimes, it took more than an internship year.

Let me create an example. As a medical student you may be attracted to surgery and be accepted into a general surgery internship. But as the year progressed, general surgery no longer held its appeal although sub-specialization in surgery became tantalizing. This led to conversations with your colleagues, perhaps several mentors, program directors at your hospital, your husband (or wife or partner.) So perhaps as you are thinking all this through it occurs to you that you like the crispness, drama, immediacy and sexiness of surgery but not the immediate accountability and the family's demands. All the time you were spending in and around the operating process, it dawns on you that there was another physician critical to the surgery, the anesthesiologist, and maybe that had all the pluses you liked but with less of the minuses you didn't. I'm just using this as an example as to how physicians shaped the arc and path of their careers.

I had another good friend in my CUMC class that I have mentioned, Josh Nagin, who evolved from internal medicine to emergency medicine (which was just emerging as its own specialty) and finally to medical informatics and IT. He was open to re-directing his career and followed his instincts, joyfully.

Since I was going to apply to an internal medicine residency which is a commitment of three years, rather than the one year of an internship, I took electives in my fourth year to gain experience where I felt I had some weakness or in areas which really attracted my intellect. The third and fourth year takes me back to the discussions with my wife about college and the importance (or lack of importance) of where you go to college.

I feel very funky carrying on about private colleges, public colleges, elite universities, the Ivy League. Stepping back, I feel like a bullshit artist and a narcissistic one at that. Which makes me feel stupid, arrogant, unlikable, conceited, egotistical and a whole bunch of other things which I find embarrassing. So, all I can say is Brilliant. Just Brilliant (stupid.)

I have been asking the wrong questions again, or maybe stressing the wrong points. The critical issue is the availability of higher education which means continuing education after high school in today's world. I feel this is the most elemental and critical next move in the growth of a citizen. Exactly where, what and how needs to be worked out on an individual basis. It is amazing that as I re-draft this chapter in late June, the Supreme Court has gutted the concept of affirmative action which has been the accepted standard in most but not all states and a method to make continuing education after high school possible for thousands of young people who otherwise may not have the opportunity.

And if you have been reading my memoir, you understand why I feel continuing education is so vital to growth, development and maturation. If I feel that strongly about college, or med school, or any professional school, or medical training; then why not shoot for the most stimulating educational environment that you can attain.

And this is likely why I felt as strongly as I did about attending an elite college or university. Taking your academic record and merging it with your personal attributes and, of course, what your professors thought of you in written comments, determined where you would go for residency training. At commencement, you swore the Hippocratic Oath and the President of Cornell bestowed on you the degree of Doctor of Medicine. At that point you were a graduate physician. Whew! That was a long haul. I was 26 years old. I had collected knowledge, wisdom and debt. And I hadn't even started my residency training yet.

I had taken the Hippocratic Oath which the profession of medicine takes very seriously. I had a framed copy of it hanging in my main examination room when I was in private practice, placed so my patients could read it while waiting for me. Osler provided me with a mantra, Hippocrates demanded I swear to always adhere to it. Primum non nocere. Above all, do no harm. When you enter your third year, you already know the Oath. As you continue to expand the bandwidth of the Hippocratic Oath going forward, it encompasses many alternate routes, 'bypasses', wider and deeper thoughts and feelings about your profession with the resultant benefit that for each patient you care for, you discover a moral UNESO World Heritage Site of a sort, like the wonderful 'Head Smashed in Buffalo Jump.' This is the second time I have referred to the buffalo jump but I don't think I explained it.

SLIGHT DETOUR

Leslie and I were on a vacation in western Canada and we were driving west across the Canadian plains towards the Canadian portion of Glacier National Park. The plains were flat and went on and on in every direction except the very straight road's destination which was a mountain range in the distance. I was driving and didn't see any cars the whole time. Suddenly, Leslie said, 'Stop! And back up a bit.'

'Can you read what that says?' she asked. I thought to myself, 'see what?' But then I saw it, a small placard held fast in the terrain and looking like a poster for a politician running for office, if the office was the jackrabbit or prairie dog school board. I got out of the car and walked over to the sign which said in small font, 'buffalo jump' 20 km and an arrow pointing at a rut in the plains grass which on closer inspection proved to be a one lane road.

'Let's go.' It had been a long boring drive from Calgary to this spot in the middle of nowhere and my wife wanted to add 40 km to see whatever a buffalo jump proved to be. I understood her point. It could be very cool and make the drive more interesting. On the other hand, it wouldn't get us any closer to the grizzly bears and the glaciers. But I knew Leslie when her mind was made up, so I turned onto the rut like road and headed north to the buffalo jump thinking this was going to go on my list of bypasses without any rewards.

On the way, all we saw was grass and a sickly prairie dog. It's a little-known fact, but prairie dogs are reservoirs for Yersinia pestis, a bacteria that caused plague, the infection that killed off 80% of the population of Europe in the Middle Ages.

Finally, we came to a small paved parking lot with a stone path leading around a slight rise in the grass. At the end of the path was an entrance to a structure carved into the earth and a sign over the door that said 'Welcome to Head Caved-in Buffalo Jump.' A bronze plaque attached to the door frame said that this was a Unesco World Heritage Site. Inside we found we were in a museum dedicated to the Plains Indians of Western Canada. It was a small museum but it had excellent exhibits, was chock full of interesting information about life for the various tribes that lived there for hundreds of years and told the adventurous, exciting, but ultimately tragic story of two Native Canadian teenagers who did things that any teenagers from any age might do.

You see, Native Canadian tribes were 100% dependent on buffalo for every part of their life: food, clothing, shelter, medicines, tools, religious ceremonies. Everything. Fortunately, at that time, the North American plains were replete with huge herds of buffalo. Hundreds of thousands of them.

And it turned out that the 'flat' plains of North America weren't exactly flat. They had arbitrary drops scattered here and there as steep as 2 or 3 hundred feet. But because everything was covered with plains grass, it looked totally flat. Had me fooled. So the tribe would spend several months creating a runway of sorts, several miles in length, and bordered by fieldstones collected by the Native Canadians. The runway became more and more narrow until it ran into the lip of a drop-off.

Now the tribes had horses and they knew how to herd cattle. They also knew that the sociology of buffalo was such that there was always one buffalo in the herd, usually a female, that was a kind of leader. Just like in a wolf pack. So, when everything was in place, the tribe would rile up the herd of buffalo and its leader who would start stampeding down the runway, eventually smack dab onto the lip of the drop off where they would fall several hundred feet to their death.

.

At this Unesco site, there was a small cave under the lip of the drop-off just big enough for two adventurous 16-year-olds to hide and have a front row seat to a waterfall of hundreds of gigantic bison. They called this exercise a buffalo jump. This one was so successful that the animals piled up all the way to the lip, with the teenagers looking over into the 'catch' that day and got their skulls stoved in for their trouble. Forever, the site became 'Head Smashed In Buffalo Jump.'

329

They had a very nice restaurant in the museum. Leslie and I had bison burgers and fries with ketchup and cokes, then headed back down the rutted road to the straight boring highway that would take us to Glacier National Park, the Canadian portion, where the next day, while on a short hike from the center of the small town I spied several hundred yards away a grizzly bear. I bet you thought it was going to be a buffalo. Nope. We turned around and headed back into town.

On the way back to Calgary, I asked Leslie if she wanted to stop at the Unesco World Heritage Site for lunch but she wasn't hungry. We made it back in time to explore the Calgary Stampede which is sort of like a city-wide extravaganza every summer but no real stampede. I felt the western Canadians had learned their lesson regarding stampeding buffalo. There was a murder in the motel room next to ours while we were driving back; someone shot and killed someone else, which seemed a much more contemporary death than homicide by buffalo jump.

END OF DETOUR

Excuse my slightly jarring leap into my story, but allowing that young woman with breast cancer consuming her body to end her life naturally and with maximal comfort, you didn't have to approach the Oath with Kevorkian's methodology or philosophy, you could individualize it in small subtle ways of which there are countless examples.

There was no question in my mind that where you trained during internal medicine residency would determine how your life would proceed after those three residency years. For some graduates, that

331

meant employment, for others it meant private practice, still others wanted wealth and social status, but many just wanted patients to diagnose, cure and heal.

Except.

Except the process at this point was completely different from any prior process that we had experienced as students. And I believe that to some degree, it was corrupt.

Like the unfortunate professor at Cornell who had the administrative task of being a pre-med advisor for every undergraduate who wanted to apply to medical school in the middle of a war for which medical school was an exemption; at CUMC we had internship advisors. There were a number of such advisors, and each advisor had a small number of students to advise about the application process and to which programs the students should consider applying. I am reaching way back, but I think my internship advisor was an Infectious Disease specialist named Warren Johnson. Whether that was his name or not, he was a hell of a nice guy and we had very helpful discussions. I remember our last conversation.

You see, the national powers that were overseeing this process of matching graduate physicians with residency training programs had created computer programs that matched applicants wanting to train at a list of about 7 programs with a list of programs that wanted to train applicants coming out of specific med schools. They called this program 'The Match' and on 'Match Day', CUMC handed out envelopes to each of us and we would open them to find out where we were moving, just like the NFL Draft. And this whole process was done digitally by primitive computers, probably in Philadelphia or Washington.

What could be corrupt about the Match? Today, the word match brings up visions of Match.com or Wimbledon.

Well, each residency program ranked themselves against their competitors. You have read about echoes of this program published in popular magazines for years (US News and World Report has made a fortune on this interesting idea), paid for by the programs and their hospitals and their universities to prop up their reputations. And part of their reputation was created by the medical schools from which their residents had come. Being judgmental or maybe narcissistic, ten internal medicine interns coming from Harvard looked a lot better than ten coming from Ole Miss. I know I'm not being fair to the University of Mississippi. It reflects my bias and I apologize.

My last meeting with my residency advisor went something like this: 'Jim, not everybody is aware of some of the aberrancies in the Match program.'

Aberrancies?

'Well, you know that there is a national computer-based matching of graduates and programs. But sometimes we make both exceptions and alterations.'

Exceptions and alterations? Was Match Day engineered by a bunch of tailors?

'It's in Cornell's interest to make sure our top students go to the top programs, if the program is one that our students want to go to, of course. And it is in Cornell's interest that we match with the best students from medical schools with similar reputations and rankings. So, Cornell divides all the residency programs in all the different fields and ranks them in terms of their reputation based on our internal assessment. And we do the same thing for your class. We divide your class into ten groups and our advice to each student is based on stacking up how their position in the class matches with the programs we think they should apply to. So, you are in the top ten graduating this year and that's why you are AOA (med school Phi Beta Kappa) and have won some distinguished honors.

Cutting to the chase, we have had conversations with Moffitt Hospital, which, as you know, is the main teaching hospital at the University of California in San Francisco. If you rank them first on your list, they will rank you first and you will have the good fortune of training there. You win, they win, we win. And who wouldn't want to live in San Francisco?'

Moffitt was one of the most sought-after internal medicine programs in the country. What he was telling me was that I could take the chance out of the match, all I had to do was put them at the top of my list. I hadn't even interviewed there. Maybe this was great for me, but Cornell won by placing a graduate at UCSF and probably UCSF had won by placing a graduate at New York Hospital. And my advisor had put the lie to the integrity of the Match program. The fix was in. It was an impossible choice for someone as naïve and young as I was. I said 'fine, okay'. And forgot about the whole business of Match Day as soon as I walked out of his office. I think I went to a bar on First Avenue and drank Maker's Mark one shot after another. That was the first-time alcohol had passed my lips in four years since alcohol always gave me migraine headaches and this time it was a whopper. But the enormity, at least to me, of what I had done made me feel like a young idealistic George Clooney playing the part of the young med student in a coming-of-age movie (except back then it would have been Robert Redford.)

Here's the thing, I opened my envelope on Match Day in what promised to be the most anti-climactic act of my life and looked at the letter. It said The Hospital of the University of Pennsylvania. HUP. Where Dr. Osler had toiled for several years about a century earlier. And when I turned, I saw Dr. Johnson walking toward me. I gave him the old question mark look. 'What happened?' He just shrugged. Later I found out that one of my classmates who was in the bottom quartile of my class had been accepted at Moffitt in the internal medicine residency and none from UCSF had been accepted at CUMC. The entire experience was bizarre and somehow ironic. The student who went to Moffitt was the son of a biochemistry professor at UCSF. Politics. No matter who you are or what you do, you are never free from politics. My guess is that my classmate spent three quarters of his time taking care of patients with a new and poorly understood epidemic which destroyed the patient's immune system and was caused by a virus dubbed the human immunodeficiency virus or HIV and the disease it caused was called the Acquired Immune Deficiency Syndrome or AIDS. San Francisco was the epicenter of this new threat to humankind. His care of those patients at Moffitt and what we learned from the patients was a much bigger contribution to the history of medicine than my modest efforts describing and treating Lyme Disease when I was a Fellow after residency at Penn.

Fate had laid down a marker and it had a joker on it. The next three years at HUP proved to be the best three years of my life, professionally and personally. I met my wife to be when I was a Senior

339

Resident, I made some of the best friends I ever had, I developed a fantastic relationship with a mentor, I was taught by some of the most skillful clinicians in the country, I saw fantastic diagnostic problems and I lived, worked and partied in Philadelphia during the Bi-Centennial which was awesome.

Chapter 13

HUP Residency

"I used to be a rolling stone, you know,

If a cause was right

I'd leave, to find the answer on the road

I used to be a heart beatin' for someone

But the times have changed

The less I say, the more my work gets done

'Cause I live and breathe this Philadelphia freedom'....Elton John..Philadelphia Freedom, released 1977

At the Hospital of the University of Pennsylvania from 1975 until 1978, as an internal medicine resident, your life became synonymous with the pace and rhythm of the hospital campus where you rotated through three experiences: HUP, which was a top university teaching and research hospital; the West Philadelphia Veterans Administration Hospital (which we affectionately called the VAH-spa); and

343

the Philadelphia General Hospital which I was fortunate enough to spend a month at when I was a first year resident but the PGH was soon thereafter shuttered by the City of Philadelphia because it was an overwhelming fiscal calamity. I was happy to see it go because the level of care at a once proud teaching hospital had sunk to the level of the Washington swamp before they drained it and built Capitol Hill and the White House. Dolly Madison, had she toured the hospital in 1976, would have, well, melted out of sheer embarrassment.

The richness of our experience was a product, first, of the patient populations at all three hospitals, with each quite different. Secondly, the upper-level residents most of all, but also the faculty and leadership made indelible impressions on all of us. And thirdly, the administrative operations of the hospitals, which would be unrecognizable for today's residents at the futuristic HUP of 2023 where I was a patient, provided an incredible segue from a bygone era when the treatment of heart failure required the house officers go out to the various arboretums that dotted the Philadelphia exurbs and find a plant called foxglove, bring it back to the pharmacy laboratory so that the newly minted pharmacists there could extract digitalis, a significant advance in the treatment of heart failure in the 1800's.

Before I get too maudlin about the evolution of internal medicine since the days when Osler performed autopsies on his patients in the PGH, let me describe the differences between the three hospitals. Briefly.

We spent most of our time rotating through the different nursing units at HUP, which by far was the most advanced in terms of technology, administration, nursing and teaching. It was also the largest hospital with one small caveat and that was the Receiving Ward. The PGH remained supreme when it came to the sheer physical size and the lack of efficiency in their ED. Until it closed. You will excuse me as I take a moment to gnash my teeth at the consequences for HUP when the PGH closed, an event with which I was personally engaged. More to follow.

Meanwhile, we were betrayed by Dr. Relman during our third year of residency when he left HUP to become the Editor in Chief of The New England Journal of Medicine. Really, who could blame him. It would be analogous to my high school English teacher being asked to become the Secretary of State under President Kennedy. Dr. Relman was replaced by a respected but somewhat off-putting doctor named Lawrence Early who I believe did a good job, but I never got to know him. He was in a no-win position, sort of like any human replacing Derek Jeter as Yankee shortstop.

346

So, my class of residents walked into a hospital system that was just settling into a brand-new culture under Bud Relman's leadership. And we were perfect for it. No Limits. That was the motto a few of us claimed at Cornell six or seven years earlier. And that was how we felt now. Dr. Relman was remaking Penn and we were going to remake Dr. Relman into an iconic Chair of Internal Medicine. We were his Legionnaires! Now that I think about it, that may have been a poor choice of words, since the Legionnaire's Disease epidemic started about the same time we did.

Speaking of words, just a few about the other two hospitals that we staffed sometimes. The PGH was the City Hospital that closed during my second year, and I may devote some time to give you a sense of the issues there. It served the city's poor, downtrodden, sick and those trashed by the PPD (the cops working under Chief Frank Rizzo) and anyone else that was unlucky enough to walk into its ED. During the month I spent there taking care of very interesting patients, I had more than a dozen very sick patients who had been released from other hospitals in town because they had no money or resources to pay for their care. Fortunately, this is now illegal thanks to a federal statute called EMTALA which forbids a hospital ED, public or private; profit or non-profit; to kick anybody out because they can't pay.

Then there was the VAH-spa which didn't have an emergency room. That's the right idea, have regular hours, like a bank and no intrusive department like an emergency room. I'm not joking. Penn shared the VA Hospital with another teaching program that was part of the Medical College of Pennsylvania (MCP). An interesting group of residents and attendings, both of which were much lower on the quality listings of US News and World

348

Report. They took care of more than their share of patients thanks to one of my best friends who came to Penn via Tufts med school and Yale college. I won't give you his name because I still think the FBI has a warrant out on him on account of the grand jury indictment. Just kidding. Admissions to the VAH were based on a veteran's social security number. Penn would get the patients with SS#'s ending in odd numbers and MCP would get the patients ending with even numbers. My enterprising friend with Yale genes would go down to the admission office and make up new SS#'s for patients being admitted. If you ended with an odd number, unknowingly, you now had an even number and as a result you were admitted to the MCP residents. The yearly outcome of this practice was MCP got about 75% of the admissions; and many unsuspecting veterans, and these were men and a few women who had served their country proudly and well and some of whom had grievous injuries like PTSD, poisoning from Agent Orange, absent extremities, ostomies of

349

various types and eventually cancers from living too close to toxic burn pits. My only hope, and I tried to facilitate this with limited success, was to change the SS#s back so that their federal admin history wasn't too screwed up. I do know my close friend did worry about this for those he couldn't return to their prior social security status.

Despite all these administrative, clinical, socio-economic and legal differences, in my opinion, the single area that distinguished the three hospitals was the emergency department. The Veteran's Hospital didn't have one, although that didn't stop Vets from showing up at the front door at 3 am. It was a hospital, for goodness' sake! And many veterans depended on the VAH for their healthcare. How were they supposed to know there was no ED. The PGH had a big one, but it resembled an eighteenth-century sanatorium for the insane more than an ED. That's not quite right. You would have to take that image I just created and cross it with a

MASH unit as portrayed in the television series. If you came in, or were brought in by an ambulance, friends or family, or most likely, the cops, the first thing they did was strip you and throw you in a large pool that had been dug in the middle of the place where an antiseptic solution was supposed to rid you of the lice which the nurses felt you undoubtedly had. Not even so much as a BP taken yet. Vital signs could be in the toilet while you were in the lice dip. The idea of going home to your children with a louse infestation was greatly feared especially since these were very hardy Philly lice who were resistant to the usual measures. Then you were rinsed off and put in a hospital gown on a gurney in a narrow space that could be made private by hospital drapes that looked like shower curtains. There you would stay until a nurse got around to checking your vital signs. They were understaffed due to being underbudgeted, so this took a while. Finally, a single physician would enter the place around midnight, go into his office, drink coffee and read the sports pages for about an hour before he made rounds on the patients who hadn't left under their own power and against medical advice from the nurses. The station where the patients lay on their gurneys was called a Bay. I used to think about that and what came to mind was 'a port in any storm.' Having finished his (always male gender) coffee and read the Philadelphia Enquirer, the physician would make rounds consisting of reading the vital signs chart, a few nursing observations and doing a foot of the gurney exam so as not to get too close to the patient. There may have been twenty bays full of patients and it was now about 2 am. We called this clinician the Comp Doc. I don't know why. But I did know that he would walk from Bay to Bay without wasting much time while he was trailed by the head nurse and at each Bay he would stop for a moment and say, "Admit", "Admit", "Discharge", then three admits in a row, two discharges, six admits in a row, and so on. There did not seem to be any correlation between an admit or discharge order from the Comp Doc. Or for that matter, what was wrong with the patient or even what his, rarely her, vital signs and complaints were or if the patient looked ill enough to be in a hospital. Then the Comp Doc returned to his newspaper or maybe an Ellery Queen mystery.

This had large consequences for the interns on call upstairs that night. After the nursing administrative admissions work and similar activities in the admissions office, I would get a call always after 3 am, that there were 5 admissions for me in the ED. Not 1, not 2, not a diagnosis, not a list of meds, not a medical chart from prior admissions. Just 'you have 5 admissions.' And I was covering 24 patients already in the hospital. And don't forget that walk rounds with your team start at 7 am. To me that meant five essentially blank human avatars had to be worked up, orders written, patients tucked into beds, and you have achieved some basic knowledge of why they were there and what you had planned for them today, all by 7 am.

Now you won't believe this but there was real value here. You were exhausted, filthy, hungry and you were being asked to work under huge time constraints to buff up (read 'improve the clinical status') of five previously unknown patients with God knows what illnesses who would likely give you, your partner and your children lice.

With some slight modifications, most notably computers, there are important parallels with what practicing physicians are asked to do today.

Back then, you achieved some type of equanimity and accomplished what needed to be done and you were alert and ready to go at 6:45 am, coffee in hand.

Sometimes things happened that made life a bit easier. The team would round on all the patients on this large single ward with forty beds, all full, and you would come to a patient who was clearly deceased; rigor mortis had started so the death had occurred the prior evening. Yet, the nurse caring for this patient on night shift had carefully recorded vital signs every hour all through the night up until and including 45 minutes earlier. Okay. Shit happens. The nurses had a real challenge.

On one occasion, one of those 5 patient admissions was a man who looked to be in his early fifties. He had been found naked in the middle of a street in North Philadelphia and he was mute and possibly deaf as well. There was no medical record. It was mid-December.

There were no lice. I examined him and found his exam to be normal. I sent off admission blood

355

studies and they came back normal. What I just wrote is all I could tell my team when we saw him at 7:20 that morning. I asked for advice. They had none. But three days later, one of the nurses pulled me aside and told me that she had been following the movement of this deaf, mute patient since admission and he hadn't urinated. Not once. OMG, I had missed kidney failure. He was surely uremic (poisoned by a back up of the toxic substances normally excreted by the kidney.) I immediately drew kidney function blood tests and ran them down to the lab. They performed the tests 'stat'. I don't think they had ever actually seen an intern or resident before. The tests were completely normal.

I was getting suspicious. Was the nurse trying to make me look like an idiot? No. She was a very good nurse. So, I started to track his movements around the ward myself, carefully, and using every bit of tradecraft I had learned from James Bond movies. As a result, I discovered the diagnosis. Osler was cheering me on. This man had been drinking his urine. Every drop. Very surreptitiously. He was sort of a self-contained autobot. And he was now psychiatry's problem. It was a win-win, for me, for the patient, for my resident, whose name was Irv Herling and who became a cardiologist, who was on my case about this guy. But maybe not so much for the psychiatrist. But, hey, he had a choice. He chose to become a psychiatrist.

My residency core mates want me to tell one more story from the PGH to expand the bandwidth of patient care problems. Okay.

It was another 3 am admission, but much different clinical circumstances. I applied my Oslerian assessment, knowing his spirit could be close by. Remember, he worked at the PGH before 1900. The patient was male and about sixty with a fever of 104 degrees and he was approaching obtundation (a coma like state). At the very least, he was confused. I've had a fever of a 104 degrees as an adult and it does confuse you especially when you are sixty and homeless. The patient was sixty and homeless. I was 71 and, in my home, then the ambulance, then the hospital. Skipping over all the critical history and examination bits and pieces that could point to a diagnosis for this patient, I was concerned that this man had bacterial meningitis. I had to find out quickly because time is of the essence, and he could die very soon. I called for a lumbar puncture tray stat!

'Sorry, doc, no sterile lumbar puncture trays available.' Most hospitals at this point had disposable LP trays but, like I said, PGH had financial problems.

'Okay, sterilize one asap.'

Thirty minutes later an orderly shows up with a sealed tray. With nurses helping me, happy to see my interest, we positioned the patient on his side and held him steady. I donned sterile gloves and opened the tray while I was prepping the likely location that I needed to insert the needle. The lumbar puncture needle! It was there. It was sterile. Halfway down its length it had a right angle bend. 90 degrees precisely.

'Any other spinal needles?' I asked hopefully.

A chorus of voices answered, 'Nope.' And in three part harmony.

I attempted to straighten this long needle overcoming the bend, at which time the needle broke into two pieces.

'Okay, how about a 16 angiocath,' which is a long and large intravenous catheter. Nobody I knew had ever attempted a spinal tap with an angiocath but I figured it was worth a shot. Didn't work.

So, we empirically treated him with antibiotics that would kill the most likely bacteria responsible for bacterial meningitis, pneumonia, sinusitis, cellulitis or whatever 'itis' infection(s) he was cooking. By morning he was in shock and by lunch he was dead. Extremely unsatisfying conclusion. I filled out the death certificate and as cause of death, I wrote 'hospital insufficiency.'

I know I mentioned that I was on service at the PGH in December. The Philly PD were kind enough to bring many sad cases to the hospital for admission so they could get cleaned up, have some good meals, get clean clothes and Christmas presents. One of my admissions was again mute or so

I thought. He was a huge man and while he was not violent, the nurses insisted he be restrained in bed. Once we did that, he became violent, forcing me to treat him with massive doses of valium, the original benzodiazepine, intravenously. The PGH had plenty of Valium for intravenous use. After exhausting our supply of Valium, this barrel-chested fellow fell asleep and didn't move for three days. Now it was Christmas day and the hospital had arranged for an employee dressed as Santa Claus to make rounds in the wards and hand out presents to the patients. Everyone was grateful. When Santa reached the bed of the behemoth who hadn't moved in 3 days, Santa let out a loud, 'Ho, Ho, Ho, Merry Christmas.'

Now our patient suddenly and unexpectedly tried to sit up. The knotted muscles of his neck strained with the effort. His arms were like pistons of a locomotive, but he couldn't break through the restraints. His lips curled back from his remaining yellowish, crooked teeth and his eyes opened wider

361

than a Philadelphia hooker's hips. With a bellow that reminded me of a charging rhinoceros, he screamed, staring directly at our red-suited Santa, "Fuck Christmas!", following which he fell back onto the bed once again fast asleep. The next day, I rotated off the PGH service and said goodbye for the last time to the patients and staff.

Chapter 14

The HUP Receiving Ward

"Don't think I ain't thought about it

But it sure makes my shackles rise

And cold blooded murder

Make me want to draw the line

Well you're crazy mama

With your ball and chain

Plain psychotic

Plain insane

If you don't think I'm gonna do it

Just wait for the thud of the bullet

You're crazy mama, ah yeah"......Crazy Mama....Rolling Stones from the Live at the El

365

Mocambo album, originally released on the Black and Blue album, 1976

When I started my internship year at HUP, it did not have a true Emergency Department. This would have to be considered unusual for a large University hospital in a major metropolitan area. Nor did it have a residency program devoted to what would become the specialty of Emergency Medicine. What it did have was the last vestige of the pre-Bud Relman hospital. The Receiving Ward.

There was a joke amongst the residents at that time. Not a very healthy joke but one that seemed applicable. The joke was a simple statement:

every morning before dawn the house staff (the HUP name for the residents) that had been working in the Receiving Ward that night would go outside the entrance where patients were delivered for assessment of their problems and turn the bodies around so they faced the entrance, thus giving the appearance that they were headed into our 'emergency department' when they collapsed, never making it to the safety and care of our Receiving Ward. Like most jokes, there was no truth to the story, but it did point out that HUP really didn't have an emergency setting that could fully evaluate patients with emergent problems. We do now. One of the finest emergency departments in the world, where trauma, cardiac and neurologic catastrophic emergencies, gunshot wounds, ruptured aneurysms were all taken care of efficiently and successfully with the same ease of care devoted to appendicitis and uncomplicated wrist fractures.

The idea behind the Receiving Ward was that the wealthy patients living on Philadelphia's Main Line and cared for by Penn's private doctors would be delivered to a 'receiving ward' rather than an emergency room without concern that they would contract lice. HUP's Receiving Ward was the Le Bec Fin of emergency rooms (Le Bec Fin being the centuries old world-famous gourmet French restaurant in Center City Philadelphia).

You may think that I am being sarcastic about the wealthy class of Philadelphians who resided on the Main Line. That they were all jaded bigots who feared contracting diseases from those Philadelphians that were beneath them on the social ladder. I am being sarcastic. And I am being unfair, because those people brought into the HUP Receiving Ward had the same problems, medical, physical and mental that all Philadelphians had. And thanks to cable news, all of America knows that Philadelphia and the counties that surround it always vote Democratic because Philadelphians are progressive liberals by and large. Fortunately, by the time I began my residency, this whole idea of Main Liners was fading rapidly aided by the egalitarianism of the Bi-Centennial celebration.

Some of you may never have been to Philadelphia. It is above all the cradle of liberty, where America first came into focus. It is here that you will find the Liberty Bell, Constitution Hall, the home where Betsy Ross sewed the first American flag and many other sites dedicated to our freedoms. You will also find a great sports city with undying love and appreciation, no matter how large the disappointment, for their professional and college teams. You will discover a rich cultural mecca with the Philadelphia Museum of Art and its iconic statue of Rocky at the top of the front stairs, the new Barnes collection museum on the Ben Franklin Parkway, and you will find some of the finest dining in the world, particularly since the Bi-Centennial. And as a bonus, the best cheese steaks you have ever tasted.

And as far as the Main Line is concerned, it is a railroad connecting the central city with its suburbs.

The first time I went down to the Receiving Ward to collect my patient for admission, I immediately thought of the Eagles song 'Hotel California' with its famous last verse:

"Relax, said the night man,

We are programmed to receive,

You can check out any time you like,

But you can never leave."

Sends chills up my spine. We weren't in California, thank goodness, and it was my job and the job of my residency mates to make sure that my first RW admission left with a diagnosis that I cured and started to help heal.

The Receiving Ward was not Le Bec Fin. It was a cramped series of about 8 bays with a central nursing and resident center and in the back a tiny conference room for the residents. The paint on the walls was an institutional fading yellowish gray and the tile on the floor hadn't been waxed since Ben Franklin hobbled in to have his gout treated. There were no attending physicians to help with tough decisions.

The RW was run by second year residents: one from internal medicine and one from general surgery and they were the only ones with the power to overturn the wishes of the accountable private doc at home eating his roast pheasant. These two residents also had the authority to respond to the needs of the admitting teams upstairs. If the admission was iffy, they could send the patient home with instructions regarding follow up with their private doc, and if the patient might be sick, they could ignore the complaints of the admitting team upstairs that they were too busy and the RW resident was being a wimp. The RW was the last center of excellence to be impacted by the 'Relman doctrine' and it had several curious effects on patient care. First, it empowered the residents and provided a place where surgeons and internists became co-dependent and worked together to assess patients. Second, it gave residents the ability to make admission decisions from which, in the old days, they had been excluded. Finally, the residents could treat the patients in the

RW and give the patients time to improve to avoid admission. The only person who liked the idea of being an admission was the patient because they felt miserable and were frightened. Understandable. Of course this was before Covid. Certainly, the admitting residents upstairs didn't think there was an illness bad enough or a patient sick enough that admission was warranted. To them, it was more work and as the night grew longer, their resistance stiffened. The same was true of the attending physicians except their logic was different, because their concern was divided into worry about their patient and worry about their patient's attorney. Philadelphia County was known nationally for having juries hand out the largest malpractice awards in the country. This last factor was almost eliminated by the changes brought about by Relman because all patients were HUP patients and all doctors were employees of HUP, so any lawsuits had to deal with a giant beloved university health system and not a weak and isolated doctor.

One final observation regarding the practice of emergency medicine as the RW began to evolve into an emergency department. The residents in charge in the RW would on occasion get into a stand-off with either the admitting team upstairs or the attending physician at home. Usually, negotiation ended with the resident in the RW winning but on occasion, decision making was tough, on the razor's edge, so to speak. In that situation, the resident in the RW could call in a mediator to sway the decision one way or another. The Chief of Cardiology for example or even Relman himself. Nobody ever got huffy with these intrusions, and they were always very informative...good teaching moments. But that was the last word in terms of what would happen. Everyone accepted and mostly liked the compromise that the mediator proposed.

I should explain who this guy Relman was and why he was so important. Arnold 'Call me Bud' Relman MD was a product of Harvard and the

MGH. He was a well-respected scholar, researcher, administrator, clinician and leader. Several years before I got there, he came to Philly to become the Chairman of the Internal Medicine Department. He totally changed the institution. He basically kicked all the private practitioners from the Philadelphia area who had admitting privileges off the staff. He simultaneously hired employed academic physicians, all outstanding from various medical schools to replace them. As a result, a patient admitted to HUP, when I got there, had layers of excellent physicians caring for them. If their problem was cardiac, they would be admitted to the service of an employed cardiologist. And they would be admitted to a member of the house staff who had a separate employed attending physician rounding with the team on the cardiologist's patient. If the kidneys were going south, a staff nephrologist might be called to see the patient. There were exceptions to this structure. HUP had some older and world-famous internal medicine sub-specialists, and their status offered them a chance to remain under Relman's reign as Chair. And so, they did. Relman also identified a small group of internists, some of which specialized in certain areas without any formal training but were senior enough that they were recognized for this experiential knowledge base. Sylvan Eisman MD and Fred Goldwein MD come to mind. They were internists but also hematology-oncology doctors. These doctors formed a group practice, now employed by HUP, which operated outside the structure that Relman had set up because they had powerful connections to physicians in the communities served by HUP for many years. This guaranteed plentiful referrals into the internal medicine service. The residents referred to this small bastion of old world civility as 'The Gold Coast.'

I need to make a statement about slang, so you won't be confused. You already know that the term intern was slowly being replaced by first year resident. Second year residents were called JAR's which translated into Junior Residents suggesting some superiority over interns. And third year residents were called SAR's or Senior Residents which meant, well, you know what it meant.

I am going to conclude this chapter with a strong statement. In reading this you should have a sense of the HUP that I came to in July, 1975. But I haven't made one thing clear. The Medicine residents admitted and cared for all the patients. They were our patients. Not the attending 'visit', not the consulting nephrologist, not the cardiologist whose name was on the face sheet of the chart, not the residency program director Larry Beck MD and not Arnold Relman. They were our patients. And we controlled their hospitalization. The patients knew it and were glad for it. We knew it. The staff attendings knew it. The residency program director Larry Beck knew it. And Bud Relman knew it...and he loved it. He created the greatest internal medicine program in the country. Our patients. My patients. Osler's patients.

Chapter 15

Stories and Lessons on   the HUP Nursing Units

"Take your place on, the Great Mandella

As it moves through your brief moment of time

Win or lose now, you must choose now

And if you lose, you're only losing your life."....
Peter, Paul and Mary from the Great Mandella (The
Wheel of Life)

As I mentioned, all three years of
residency are mixed together as I hopefully share
with you the experiences that I and others had taking
care of patients at HUP. For that was our life for
three years, and as I mentioned, it was the best three
years of my life to that point. You will meet the
residents, the attending physicians, the anecdotes, the
experiences but not the patients for sake of privacy
even though what the patients experienced will be
shared.

And in the entire mix you will
understand how this joyful experience provided the

nutrients and water in which we grew our thinking processes, our feelings and in time (sometimes a very long time) the increasingly mature behaviors of those in my class of residents. We had been slowly becoming adult physicians, but now we were on the Express. I stressed how my class in med school had each other's back and that was true, but it paled in comparison to how strongly, how cohesively we had each other's backs during residency. I can honestly say that there was nothing I wouldn't do for those I shared that experience with, maybe on occasion with some grumbling under my breath. There was also a bond with the upper-class residents as well but the bond within my specific class was special and I hold each and every physician in my heart wherever they are now.

Excuse me, I think I said how the joyful experiences of residency provided the nutrients and water necessary for my class to expand their thoughts, feelings and those things led to a quantum leap in our maturity. Let me just say that while I will let that statement stand, I think there must be some allowance for variability when it gets to the maturity part. There were a few notable exceptions.

But let's begin with a story about a very mature resident named Eric Neilson MD. Eric was quiet and reserved and he stood outside our inner core because he was married and at that time, childless. If I graduated in the top ten students in my CUMC class, Eric outshone my clinical and academic prowess by a power of ten thousand, just as he outshone every other resident in my class all of whom graduated from the top of their med school classes. Eric was special in that way, even more so because he was so reserved. He kept his brilliance bridled and in check. Then, at the right moment, it shone outward like a beacon guiding us to key insights. If you ever feel the need to be reassured by what an Oslerian Penn trained physician should be in the finest sense, Google Eric Neilson MD. I would place him in the top ten graduates of all the medical schools on the planet of all time.

During our first year as resident interns, Eric and I were paired to work in the Medical Intensive Care Unit or MICU. This small unit of eleven bays and central nursing station was kind of a duplicate of the Receiving Ward but with more stuff and looked much nicer. The sickest of the sick came to us and the most frequent diagnosis was unstable angina or coronary artery disease that was on the brink of damaging the heart muscle or causing a fatal heart rhythm. There were no dedicated intensive care units for these patients as there are today. Modern cardiac care was in its infancy. Today a patient in the early stages of a heart attack is often treated by EMT's in the ambulance on their way to the ED while in communication with cardiologists by radio or cellphone.

As interns in the MICU, the two of us accepted all admissions from 8 am one day until noon the next day. The next partial day was the responsibility of our JAR paired with a sub-intern who was always an excellent Penn student given the responsibility of caring for the sickest of the sick while being mentored by the JAR. Eric and I finished our day while the second team took the admissions. We made continual rounds stabilizing any problems before signing out to the JAR and going home for a few hours' sleep. Then we would return to do it again every other day for a month. Every other night taking admissions, 70% of the 48 hour stretch. It was exhilarating for me. The ghost of Osler had come to inhabit my soul. I am not sure everyone felt that way since it was exhausting. I, at least, had no other life. No wife, no girlfriend, no dog, no cat, no errands, nothing. Just me and Sir Bill Osler. For me it was all about learning. No limits.

There was a small room adjacent to the MICU with two beds across from each other and a shower. If there was a moment's peace, you might catch some sleep or spend time discussing cases with your partner. It was in that tiny room that I asked Eric one night where he had gone to med school. I didn't know.

His face was expressionless as usual. Sometimes I wondered if he was going into the encephalitic stage of an Ebola infection. 'University of Alabama, Birmingham.'

That surprised me. In my ignorance, I didn't know there was a medical school there. And that was even though I had dated and been in love with Linda for an entire year at CUMC, who was from Birmingham and whose father was head of transplant medicine at the med school. So, I asked him what seemed the next logical question, 'Why did you go there?'

'Best medical school in the country.'

There was no movement, no twitch, no beginning of a smile at the corners of his mouth. In that moment, I knew with absolute certainty that the University of Alabama at Birmingham was the best medical school in the United States. Otherwise, Eric Neilson would have gone somewhere else.

'So how is it that you wound up at Penn for Internal Medicine?'

'Best medicine residency in the country by far.' Again, this was said softly and directly. He could have given me the launch codes for a nuclear strike.

'What about the Mass General's program,' considered by many to be the crème de la crème of residency programs in internal medicine.

'Inferior. Way below the experience here.'

Okay. From Eric's lips to God's ears. Bud Relman would have been dancing on his toes.

I looked at Eric for a long second. There was no facial twitch at all. I slapped him on the knee and said, 'c'mon, let's do some work.'

I learned something else that night. Something about medicine that would stay with me my entire career. At that time, women were not supposed to get coronary artery disease until after their menopause, presumably protected by their estrogens. As a result, many, many women with chest pain or angina like symptoms were discharged from emergency rooms, doctors' offices, and other havens of medical care. But that night, a 40-year-old woman, still menstruating regularly, without a hint of menopause, came into the HUP RW with intense pain under her breast bone that took her breath away, and had all the cardinal features of an acute heart attack, or what we physicians call a myocardial infarction. She was admitted to me in the MICU.

It was a routine admission other than she wasn't supposed to have the problem she obviously had. Her chest pain had gone away, and she was comfortable and amazingly calm. I worked her up and did all the right things. I put an EKG on her and ran a rhythm strip to see if she was having any atypical beats. Eric and I watched as her heart would throw in an extra beat called either a VPC or PVC (both meaning the exact same thing) every fourth or fifth normal beat. We watched this pattern for about five minutes when Eric tapped me on the shoulder and whispered, ('can I talk to you outside'.)

Of course, Eric.

'Did you know that every time she has a PVC you say "oops"?

No, I didn't know, and I told him.

'It may be better if you stop doing that.'

Right, Eric. And I stopped and never did it again. His understated point was that you should avoid saying things in front of patients that might upset them or cause undue worry. A valid point.

But that wasn't the lesson here. The lesson that women before menopause were perfectly capable of developing coronary artery disease and could have heart attacks just like men and only God knows how many women had been ignored when their complaint was chest pain because of some academic misconception spread by an unknowing Professor of Medicine who had been asking the wrong questions. Coronary disease is a result of multiple risk factors and while the pre-menopausal state may be protective, it can be overwhelmed by other factors.

Let me give you two examples from my own private practice that occurred later in my career that proved the value of the lesson that night.

Thursday mornings we had medical grand rounds at Christiana Care Health System's flagship hospital halfway between Wilmington and Newark, DE.

Medical grand rounds is the most important conference of the week. I hated to miss it and would start my office hours later than usual on Thursdays. I walked into the office that morning where I expected to see an empty waiting room. And it was almost empty, save for a single woman standing against a wall which she repeatedly banged with her right fist. I treated this woman for mild rheumatoid arthritis, and I knew she could be a bit off-beat at times. I looked at my secretary who just shrugged. So, I went over to the patient and asked if she would accompany me to an exam room, which she did. Turns out that she had gone to her family physician, who I knew well and considered a solid doctor, because she was having substernal chest pain identical to the pain described by the woman I admitted to the HUP MICU years earlier. Her family physician's secretary gave her an appointment to come back in three weeks which was the first opening with her doctor. But the chest pain wouldn't go away and was severe. I examined her and asked my nurse to get an EKG done asap.

Oops.

She was having a heart attack. We got her as quickly as we could to an emergency room with her EKG so they would believe her, and I spoke with one of the docs there. She did very well after bypass surgery. And she did not sue her family physician because I convinced her that suing her doctor would accomplish nothing but increase her stress level and probably cause another heart attack. She was just off-beat enough to find this argument convincing.

Afterward, thinking about the case, I wondered whether I had done the right thing in reasoning her out of a lawsuit against her primary care physician. There could have been many clerical reasons why that office didn't see her that day. I made up all manner of excuses for her doctor. In the end, it came down to exactly what I told her. Lawsuits are unbelievably stressful. Certainly, for the doctor but also for the patient plaintiff and their family. And I had discussed with her family physician what happened, and I was convinced the physician had learned a lesson that day. I was okay with my decision and just chalked the whole affair up to another day in medical practice.

There was another lesson in the case of the wall banging patient, but a small one. Nobody thanked me. Not for attending to the patient's chest pain. Not for arranging immediate treatment. Not for taking over for the deficient family physician. And not for preventing a medical malpractice suit. Just all in a day's work. A thank you would have been nice. I didn't send anyone a bill for my time.

And one final story that puts a point on the larger lesson and the need to consider the contrariness of patients at times. I had a patient with more severe rheumatoid arthritis than the wall-banger who had refused to see a rheumatologist and had to be carried horizontally (I swear this is literally true) by her daughter and husband into my office, screaming and kicking, so we could have our first consultation. This happened exactly as I just described. I don't know what she was thinking. Let's skip the psychotherapy portion of our relationship. She finally decided I was okay and submitted to my recommended treatment which radically quieted her active rheumatoid arthritis. Things had been going well when she turned up in my office on a Monday without an appointment, walking slowly, wheezing, and complaining of shortness of breath. My nurse, familiar with my patients and their occasional peculiarities and whims, immediately took her into an exam room, found me eating a brisket sandwich, and said, 'better check the lady in room 3.'

What I found was my patient in florid congestive heart failure. I had nothing with which to treat her though I considered using syringes and needles normally there for draining fluid from swollen joints as Southey tubes. But that was even too retro for me, so we called an ambulance and while we were waiting, I asked her what had happened. The previous week she had made plans to go to Atlantic City for a weekend of gambling at the casinos there. She loved to gamble. But on Thursday, she had suffered a bout of prolonged indigestion. Thinking nothing of it, she continued with her plans. Except that as the weekend progressed, she started to experience a new symptom, shortness of breath, especially when she lay down. She figured that was good news since it wouldn't interfere with her time at the blackjack table. Time enough to deal with it when she got back home on Monday (and immediately came to my office.) She had an internist and a cardiologist (!) but she came to my office. You just never knew what could happen to these patients and how they made decisions. Guess she thought it was her rheumatoid arthritis or a complication of my treatment. To make a long story shorter, she had suffered a heart attack when she thought she was having indigestion and had slowly gone into heart failure. When she got to the right physician, she did fine. I was glad of course and her rheumatoid arthritis never flared up during the entire episode.

For those of you wondering what Southey tubes are, they were part of the armamentarium of doctors in the 1800's for symptomatic heart failure which led to fluid retention (as it still does) and this extra fluid often collected in the most dependent part of the patient (the legs). Doctors would use hollow tubes possibly collected from bamboo or large reeds which had been sharpened at one end and stuck into the swollen legs of the patient resulting in the extra fluid draining onto the bed and floor. While this was going on, the pharmacists would be grinding up foxglove for its digitalis that was ingested by the patient and acted as a turbo for the heart muscle assuming it didn't kill the patient since correct dosing was critical with digitalis.

See, there is an interesting bit of medical history shared with you by a rheumatologist and not a cardiologist.

Women get cardiac problems, too, and they can get them before menopause. Today, it's been studied and published and we know it.

Back in the MICU in 1975, I am still toiling away and enjoying every second, really. Working with Eric was continually educational. I remember a patient who was a truck driver who was on his way home at 3 in the morning when he suffered severe chest pain underneath his breastbone, a symptom with which you should be familiar by this time, and which was very troubling to him. He hesitated, being a typical male truck driver, and then turned around (I think he was in front of the Philadelphia Zoo at the time) and headed for HUP. He was seen in the RW and sent straight up to Eric with a large anterior wall myocardial infarct. This is not good. He may have clotted off his left main anterior descending coronary artery, the one they call the Widow Maker. Eric spoke with the cardiology attending attached to the MICU that month and given the fact that the patient's blood pressure was rapidly falling, they decided to insert an intra-aortic counter-pulsation balloon to support his circulation until we could transfer him to the OR. The balloon was a rather new intervention used in extreme cases although it had been used during cardiac surgery for a while. This balloon was inserted through the femoral artery which provides major circulation to the leg and is just anterior or above the hip joint. You can feel the pulse by placing your hand over your groin.

Had he not turned his truck around; he would have been dead. But thanks to Eric and the teamwork of the cardiac surgeons at HUP, he survived with bypass surgery and was discharged with just one small complication. The emergency insertion of the counter-pulsation balloon under difficult circumstances had caused an aneurysm of the femoral artery which in and of itself the patient could live with. It was considered too difficult to fix surgically, so the patient was left with some claudication in his right leg, that is he limped at times because of slow blood flow to the right leg muscles.

And what did this man do? He employed a Philadelphia lawyer and sued both Eric and HUP for causing him a permanent injury to his right leg. Never mind that he was alive, and his life had been saved by Eric and HUP staff. He was going to punish them for his loss in right leg function. I don't know the circumstances of the lawsuit, and I don't understand the thinking behind it. Doctors and hospitals take lawsuits personally. It is an attack on their very being. It is like saying, you are incompetent, and you will pay me for that minus the forty percent the attorneys take.

Medicine is a risky business. Hospital medicine is especially risky. Every decision hangs on balancing risk and reward, pros and cons, benefits and consequences. The Patient Safety movement starting in 1999 taught us that repeatedly and is still teaching us. I was the first Patient Safety Officer at Christiana Care and therefore the first such doctor taking this responsibility in Delaware. I watched the whole business evolve. I know. And I am a rheumatologist.... but also an Oslerian.

I am probably looking at this the wrong way. It is just regular business as practiced in the US of A. Nothing personal. Just about money changing hands. Deep pockets, and all that. And maybe the patient was permanently disabled, couldn't work and needed some income. Who knows?

So let me tell you about my lawsuit, a process that Sir William Osler never could have imagined at the PGH or Hopkins or in England or Canada. I only had one lawsuit, but it is an interesting story. And   here   is   that   story.

Chapter 16

My first and only medical negligence suit

"They came this mornin' with a dog on a chain

They came and took my little brother away

His generation never even got a name

404

My mama was a rocker way back in '53

Buys them old records that they sell on tv

I know Chuck Berry wasn't singin' that to me

Mama

That's all right, it's your world

Hey, this is my life

She's my girl

My life / your world"....Tom Petty and the Heartbreakers...1987 from the album Let Me Up (I've had enough)

I need to jump ahead of my residency days to recount this story. After residency, we had a short interlude for fellowship, where I became super sophisticated in the diagnosis and treatment of rheumatic disease disorders and auto-immune disease. It was during this fellowship training that I made my one contribution to the history of medicine. I did this by collecting the data from a clinic caring for over 200 patients with Lyme Disease and with my supervisor, Dr. Allan Steere, convinced some truly expert biostatisticians at Yale that treating these patients for relatively short periods with common antibiotics, cured them of what was undoubtedly a bacterial infection even though the entire bioscience world disagreed. We turned out to be right. It's good to be right.

Now I was ready to enter the world of private practice and I chose to work for an established rheumatologist in Wilmington, DE. My reasoning here was that health care in Delaware seemed poised to undergo rapid growth attracting superior physicians and providing modern technology. Right again. I wanted a location where there weren't enough rheumatologists to treat patients and I was aware that new treatments were soon to be coming down the pike. Right again. And finally, I wanted to practice in a community where neither the patients nor the doctors knew fuck-all about the current state of rheumatology. Bingo. And I had a hook to immediately ensure my relevancy beyond the fact that I was so well trained at Cornell/Penn/Yale. Where you trained or schooled means nothing to a practicing physician. You must prove to them that you deserve their respect and their trust. And this is as it should be. My hook was Lyme Disease. Nobody knew anything about it. Lyme Disease was present along the New England and Mid-Atlantic coast and scared the population to distraction. I lectured at Medical Grand Rounds. I lectured at Pediatric Grand Rounds. I gave so many lectures on Lyme Disease that I was dreaming about ticks. And so were the docs who went to my lectures. I wrote a historical retrospective review for the Delaware Medical Journal. A bunch of state medical journals around the country asked to reprint it. These journals were educational but not peer reviewed, it was no big deal to have your name in their ink. I did everything to be a rock star except learn to play the guitar.

And my practice began to grow as referring doctors and curious patients made appointments. But not fast enough for my boss, the senior rheumatologist. Nine years my senior, trained and experienced, but I didn't like him. That wasn't important in the short run. What was important was whether I trusted him not to screw up my patients when he was covering because I wasn't available. I did trust him. His name was Russ.

Russ was the doctor who concerned himself with our practice income and he had a vested interest in seeing my practice income grow, first to help cover the extra costs I was creating for the practice, and second, to make money from my addition to his practice for himself. While this may seem odd, it was common in Delaware amongst doctors and lawyers and for all I knew it was the way business was done everywhere. I didn't have much of a head for business. I don't think he intended to be greedy about this, but he didn't discuss it with me either. They say medical partnerships are like marriages, so I guess the conversations I never had with Natasha and Linda, I didn't had with Russell either. Anyway, he took measures to fill out my schedule so I was always busy and thus billing for income that would come into his practice. He owned the practice. I did not. I was an employee, like a nurse, or a secretary, or a janitor. But not like his accountant. After three years, we had an agreement that I would become an equal partner and we would own the practice together. I was willing to see how that played out.

Now in my first year in private practice, I would see patients that Russ had scheduled who were referred by the State of Delaware Board overseeing requests for supplemental disability income. This happened initially about five times per week. I would

409

do a history and physical examination, review x-rays and labs, dictate a report of my findings and for roughly two hours of work, the practice would be paid $60. I was not expected to give an opinion about whether the patient deserved a bump up in his or her disability payments.

Every month, I had a resident from our hospital do an elective with me and it was very popular since they were seeing clinical problems that they had little experience with during medical school or residency. And I had a resident with me the day I saw the gentleman who sued me. His was typical of a case referred by the **DDS** (Delaware Disability Service). A man who had served in the military and resented what they had done to him which included a rather bizarre story about being tied to a chair in a room and bombarded with radioactive rays for two hours. After his discharge he did mostly manual labor. Now he was in his fifties and he complained of severe knee and back pain that prevented him from working at all and he wanted more disability income. Sounded reasonable to me after I examined him, but to be complete, I needed to review his most recent x-rays which had been taken at the VA Hospital in Stroudsburg, PA, which is in the Poconos. Could he get them and bring them to me? Maybe.

I never heard from him.

A bit less than two years later I received a letter from the attorney who was helping him fight with the State of Delaware over his disability payments. This attorney was famous for his skill in medical malpractice cases, but that was not what the letter was about. The lawyer wrote to tell me that his client had complained that I had injured his knees during my physical examination done for the Delaware Board on Disability and the lawyer had investigated this complaint but could find no evidence that I had committed any form of negligence and he had advised his client as much. But the lawyer warned me in a post-script: 'I don't think he will take no for an answer.'

What did that mean?

The statute of limitations in Delaware for medical malpractice is two years. On the second anniversary of my evaluation of this man for the State of Delaware, I was served with my first and only Superior Court subpoena by the Sherriff's office of New Castle County. I accepted the document rather shakily and took it into my private consultation room to read. The first thing I noticed was a peculiarity. It was written out in long hand with many errors of punctuation, grammar, and spelling and it was signed by the man with the knee and back pain. At the bottom there was stamped a receipt that the secretary at Superior Court had received $100 due for making a complaint like this. I was at a loss.

I called the Medical Society of Delaware, from whom I had purchased my malpractice insurance and asked them what I should do. They told me that the lawsuit had been filed in Superior Court without the benefit of an attorney, most likely because he couldn't find one that would take his case. This had a name, it was filed pro se. Now I had to report the situation to my malpractice insurer who would assign an attorney to represent me, and it would be this attorney who would be required to do the legal work for the guy suing me since he didn't have his own lawyer.

Really?

Apparently, this falls under legal ethics, two words which should never be used in the same sentence. All you must do is pick up today's paper and read about Justice Clarence Thomas and his most recent

413

crossing of the vague ethical lines for Supreme Court Justices.

I found myself on the phone with a feisty young woman who was to represent me while doing the work of my opponent. Legal ethics. And all this was paid for by me. Actually, my malpractice insurance premium was paid by Russ' corporation where I was an employee. I wasn't sure about the attitude I was getting from my attorney. She sounded like she considered me guilty until proven innocent. Maybe she was dyslexic. She proved to be a pit bull and fearless in the court system and years later became my patient, so the lesson here was don't go with first impressions. This may be more true for attorneys than others in society.

Her first move was to obtain the x-rays from the Stroudsburg VAH. No dice. He kept thwarting her every attempt. The whole business was becoming tiresome. Doctors take medical negligence suits very seriously, but it was getting harder to do that with this one.

Then we found out that he had a tumor of the fourth ventricle in his brain. Don't worry about the specifics. It wasn't thought to be causing him any problems. But maybe that story about the radioactive ray bombardment had some merit. No, too hard to believe. Finally, she appealed to the court and the judge assigned to the case, Judge Vincent Poppitti, ordered a meeting with the man with the bad knees and my attorney. I got to know Judge Poppitti because he dated my wife's best friend. He was a hell of a nice guy. He spent a good deal of his tenure as a judge in Family Court where he helped many people.

Everybody showed up for the meeting. I didn't have to be there. Afterward I got an excited phone call from my attorney. 'He pulled a weapon. He pulled a weapon in judge's chambers.' I didn't know if this was a common occurrence and whether it was good or bad. So, I asked her if she was frightened. She said no. She was watching how the Judge was having difficulty picking up his eyeballs which had popped out at the sight of the man threatening my 70-pound lawyer with a nasty blackjack and get them back into their correct eye sockets. This was her attempt at humor to diffuse her fright over the experience. Judge Poppitti did use his knee to press a button on the right inside of his desk and two bailiffs instantly appeared and hauled my nemesis to lock-up for several hours and from which he eventually spent 4 days in the state mental hospital before being remanded to prison for a short stay. Then she told me the judge used some Latin words which I didn't quite get to dismiss the case without any possibility of his coming back and suing me again. And so ended the saga of my one and only medical negligence lawsuit. Almost......

I was no longer part of the story, but I will finish it for you. The knee pain man now felt that my attorney was stalking him, and he made a complaint out to the Bar of the State of Delaware regarding her conduct. How did I know this? Delaware is a small state, both in population and square mileage. The knee pain guy went to a very good family physician who had a nurse of long standing who happened to have rheumatoid arthritis and happened to be my patient. Because of her medication, she made regular visits to see me, and she kept me up to date with how this gentleman was doing. So let me summarize it for you.

Uno. He won his supplemental disability income claim and that made me happy since I thought the severity of his degenerative arthritis really did limit his ability to work and the quality of his life.

Dos. A year later, he developed some type of lymphoma which I may have told you already is a cancer of the lymph cells. Between the tumor in his brain and the lymphoma, I began to wonder again whether the story about the Army irradiating him had some truth.

Tres. He died. I really wasn't very sad at the time. We all die. But he didn't have a very happy life and for that, I was sad. And he never knew that part of his legacy was my willingness to tell the story of my one medical malpractice suit many times at dinner parties and cocktail affairs to everyone's interest except for the lawyers who were there.

I did have several other encounters with the legal system in my role as treating physician, mostly giving expert testimony about one of my patients who was suing somebody else's patient. But there was one interesting encounter that I will highlight for you.

I mentioned that I started late on Thursdays so I could attend medical grand rounds in the morning. It was late fall and getting dark early. And it was heavily cloudy and damp adding to the gloom. I walked into my home around 5:30 to find it dark and empty. This was unusual since my wife and two-year-old son were usually home at that time. I went into my study to drop off my briefcase when I noticed a fat envelope on my desk which had been opened. The document turned out to be from Family Court and the document was a request that I show up at Family Court on an hour of a given day with five years of income tax returns so the Court could determine how much support I should pay for the care of my 8-year-old daughter. I did a double take. Could I have a daughter I didn't know about? The letter was addressed to me. No doubt about it. And given the address of the child in question, I suspected that the child was Black. You would think I would remember an affair with an African American woman resulting in a child being born nine years earlier. Let's see, nine years earlier I would have been a second-year medical student. That was the year of Natasha. The only Black woman that I had dated was a Panamanian-American nurse who worked at New York Hospital. That was in my senior year and things hadn't gone that far. As usual, I wasn't sure what to make of this. Then I wondered whether Leslie read the letter, packed a bag, took Michael and left. But she didn't. She had just gone to the supermarket. She had assumed the letter had to do with my practice since she had already seen the weird things that happened. I called a friend who was an estate lawyer. I had no experience with family law.

My friend, the lawyer, thought he had a sense of humor. He told me that he would send someone around to my office the next day to pick up the documents and I should go to a local department store to pick out a number of nice dresses for my daughter. Very funny.

My friend enlisted his partner who was an expert in family law. It turned out that there were two James Newmans in the City of Wilmington. The court had sent the letter to the wrong one. I thought they would tear up the letter and correct the mistake. Nope. Legal ethics.

They had to go through a procedure in which my letter was sealed in a court file and placed somewhere for a hundred years in case they needed it again. Then they could track down the other James Newman. That ended up costing me $600 for the family lawyer. There was a lesson here. Some lawyers make cheap friends. But then, it was just business as usual.

There is a post-script. The other James Newman ended up being shot to death in a drug deal gone wrong. Wilmington turns out to be on the I-95 corridor from New York to Washington, along which much illegal drug trafficking occurs. He was probably trying to get some money to provide for his daughter. I felt bad for her and him. Shit happens.

Chapter 17

More Stories from the HUP Residency

"Into the great wide open

Under them skies of blue

Out in the great wide open

A rebel without a clue".........Into the Great Wide Open....Tom Petty and the Heartbreakers....from the album of the same name

I'm sorry. I jumped ahead during the last several chapters to highlight some stories that were informative about my life as a physician. But I also wanted to avoid a jumble so let's return to the years following CUMC and my move to Philadelphia. I came to the City of Brotherly Love with no wife, no girlfriend, no pets, a small suitcase containing my clothes and toiletries, and a Datsun 240Z which was a present from my Uncle Danny who continued to be somewhat of a surrogate father when it came to automobiles. My first task was to find an apartment.

I wanted to live in Center City, that portion of central Philly that sat between the Schuylkill River to the west and the Delaware River to the east. To the west was less expensive and much closer to HUP so that was where I would look. It was an old residential neighborhood with a few hoagie shops, a dry cleaner and little else. The renters were 70% male and then there were women. Just about everybody was single. I soon discovered that many of the men were gay. Philadelphia, at least in Center City, was becoming a heavily gay community of men who had come out in the 70's. That was fine with me. The women were mostly straight which made things less confusing and stacked the competition in my favor. This was also fine with me. I lived there for one year and managed to have affairs with almost every woman who lived in my brownstone. By my count, that would be two straight women. Also, I was at HUP almost all the time, so I tried to make the most of the little time that I was at home.

That didn't work too well. Many a morning I found myself waking alone in yesterday's clothes on my fold out bed next to my cold dinner with the small TV flickering in front of me. I had fallen asleep eating Chinese food on my fold-out couch and stood up my date who lived two floors up in the process. That's fatigue at a level I had never experienced. Some HUP residents, mostly surgeons, lived in the suburbs and a few fell asleep at the wheel of their car driving down one of Philly's endless bypass roads. Nobody died but a few spent a month in a hospital bed rather than attending to a patient. I felt sad and lucky simultaneously.

I would put my feet on the floor, push my bed back into being my couch, grab a coffee, quick shower, change into another pair of hospital scrubs back from the Chinese laundry and off to HUP.

In those days, HUP was a Frankenstein hospital in that several separate hospital buildings had been patched together to create the greater hospital structure. In the aesthetic sense, New York Hospital had it all over HUP which sort of looked like Boris Karloff after a rough night out. There was the Moloney Building which I think contained the Pepper Ward where some of our most exciting rotations took place. That was also the site of the "private practice" Dr. Relman had created to augment referrals into the department of medicine. The so called 'Gold Coast.' Moloney had an entrance on Spruce Street just past 34th street. The formal address of HUP was 'Spruce and 34th Street'. And it may not have changed even though I now think of HUP as an ocean liner in the center of a sea of modernistic interlocking buildings sailing toward a never-ending medical nirvana. If you have ever been

428

to the newest iteration of HUP, you would understand my description. 34th and Spruce may have been an iconic address, too historic to change. Of course, HUP is way beyond Spruce and 34th street in today's West Philadelphia medical campus. In fact, the Children's Hospital of Philadelphia (CHOP) had to move across the Schuylkill River to Center City. It's also brand new.

Back in those days, there were no cell phones (how did we survive?) and we all carried pagers. When there was a code blue, the universal alarm for a patient who had a cardiac arrest, our pagers all went off simultaneously and the location would blare over the loudspeaker system. The immediate problem was to figure out the shortest route from wherever you were in the hospital to where the patient was. This is even a bigger problem in the newest HUP. That usually meant traversing various sets of stairs but sometimes it meant taking a short elevator ride. Since the buildings and floors of my HUP weren't always graded evenly, the occasional elevator stop would be two feet above the floor you were going to resulting in some nasty falls, strained knees, sprained ankles and a lot of cursing. Somehow enough doctors and nurses were close enough that they could begin the job of resuscitating the patient while twenty others observed, ready to jump in if needed.

Recently I found myself wandering around the current HUP, renamed Penn Medicine to be inclusive of all that is Penn in and around southeastern Pennsylvania. Ravdin and Moloney were still there. Otherwise, I felt like I was wandering around the Starship Enterprise. The underground garages alone must have encompassed 5 square miles. I sent a text message to my residency mate, friend and personal doctor marveling at all the changes but asking him what would happen if a visitor or employee coded in an unlikely place such as the fourth underground parking level of the Emergency Department garage. The short reply came back immediately, "Dead". David was being facetious. I think.

My class of residents divided up into a kind of inner core and outer core just like at CUMC but there were differences. For one thing, there were many more of us who were married or co-habiting. We were spending so much of our waking hours working, that marriage seemed to me to be superfluous and the wives, because my class was largely men, must have been long suffering although many of them had children already or their own careers and new jobs in Philly. Offhand, I can think of two women in our class and they were married to residents who were in our class as well (one of those two was married to a very funny surgeon.)

The inner core revolved around the sun, like a planetary system. And in our case the sun was named Tim Crowley. Tim was a brilliant doctor and an even more brilliant instigator. Also agitator. He got himself and the rest of us into more trouble than I thought possible. I think he set the modern record for time spent in Dr. Relman's office being reminded that he was a HUP physician and should act like one. He has since reminded me that he wasn't called on the carpet in Relman's office that often. Sometimes he was called on the carpet in Larry Beck's office, or Marty Goldberg's, or a half dozen other senior department physicians. But he always remained unscathed and ready to go again. I think Bud Relman was amused by all of it. Recently, Tim and I were having an email exchange about this and he told me, 'Listen, some of us, like you and Henry, live by your principles, but some of us live by a code.' He didn't take that comment any further but I knew exactly what he meant.

The inner core included me as the quiet voice of reason; and a wonderful doc named Ken Osnoss who was married and rambunctious. Then there was

Vickie Kusiak, another brilliant clinician who was married to the crazy surgical resident named Joe. My close friend David Henry was central to the inner core since he lent an air of gravitas to our shenanigans. Also, David had been in the Air Force so he could fly in an F-14 trainer jet. In the back seat. And Eric Neilson was there to provide data. Rich London helped round out the inner core providing energy and lame excuses for the rest of us. Arnie Cohen was also in that inner core, as was 'smilin' Art Greenburg. I really don't have to describe 'smilin' Art because his name says it all. Art sublet my apartment when we were SARs because I had moved in with Leslie. And Arnie had an incredible sense of humor which Harvard had not been able to destroy. All these people were at the top of their classes so it's dumb to keep repeating myself, but I do remember one thing about Arnie. He was from Brooklyn and went to Hobart college and Harvard med school and can verify everything I have said in this memoir regarding Harvard except when he says it, it is much

433

more snarky. Arnie didn't know how to swim. For me, being the former senior lifeguard at the Scranton downtown Holiday Inn pool, this was a huge deficit in Arnie's growth and development so during our senior residency year, our SAR year, I taught Arnie how to swim in the Penn pool. I wonder if he remembers I did that or if he can still swim. He and his family live out in Washington State now. Spokane, I think. Finally, I have to add a neurology resident (I never told you the neurology story) named Francisco Gonzalez just because he belonged to us.

There were a few residents who were just too reasonable and too pleasant (and likely too mature) to be in the inner core but they sometimes breached it: Gene Lugano, Haig Donabedian, Bill Lee, Stu Brogadir, and Taylor Cope. The rest of the class were just too nice and too good to get into trouble instigated by Crowley. However, if I forgot anybody, I am truly sorry and please email me so I can correct my error in the next printing.

Readers may remember an occasional reference to Chief Residents.... like from my med school Urology story. These were doctors who had completed their internal medicine residency and were excellent clinically, had strong interpersonal skills, and leadership potential. They served as a kind of buffer between residents and the bureaucratic layers above them: attending staff physicians, Departmental Chiefs, Residency Program Directors and, of course, Relman. This was especially useful when these faculty doctors were pissed off at a resident or the residents as a group, which happened more often than you might think. There were times that I thought of my class of residents as attending a camp. You know, a summer camp devoted to baseball, field hockey, archery; except our camp was dedicated to patients.

There were Chief Residents for HUP and for the VAH-spa. It's hard to remember names and associate them with their year in the sun but they were wonderful teachers and guidance counselors. One I remember is Malcolm Cox who had a strange idiosyncrasy in that he feigned a fake British accent. Mark Kelly, Mike Karpf, I guess there was a total of six for the three years. Oh yeah, Henry Sawin was our HUP Chief Resident when we were SAR's. His nickname was 'Half-time' for excellent reasons. Don't think old Henry took his responsibilities too seriously. Crowley loved him. I played a lot of golf that year with Dr. Sawin.

While those three years are really jumbled together in my brain, my intention is to relate stories or anecdotes of general interest because they are, well, interesting, but also because they highlight observations and experiences which expanded our thinking, our feelings and, believe it or not based on my comments so far in this chapter, our behavior. Okay, at least my thoughts, feelings and behavior.

To get it out of the way, after spending my first year of residency in a studio apartment on Spruce Street in Center City, I felt the need to expand my non-hospital living space, so I moved to a spot in a garden apartment complex that was across the street from Germantown Friends School: Blythewood apartments. A lot of young people lived there and as a bonus they had a pool. This will all become important in my SAR year but, at least, you now know where I am when I'm not at HUP. Also, it was a quick drive past the zoo into West Philadelphia and the HUP staff parking lot. Right past the MOVE house, a tragic part of Philadelphia's history.

So, I have spent time in earlier chapters describing the rise of Black political and/or radical movements because of impatience with the growth of personal freedom and political power on the Cornell University campus. And I am sure you are aware that these activities at Cornell were just a small part of integrated national efforts to peacefully (MLK, Jr.) or through violence (the Black Panthers) get rid of Jim Crow laws, secure voting rights and basically create an equal, just, integrated society. One of the left leaning, more violent movements in Philly was called MOVE and they purchased and occupied a house in the Cobbs Creek section of Philadelphia on Osage Avenue, not far from HUP. At one point, I guess there may have been 25 men, women and children living in the MOVE house. I drove by it at least once a day and there were always members sitting in front of the home.

During the Bi-Centennial celebration, the Police Commissioner of Philadelphia was a cop named Frank Rizzo. Rizzo's hard-nosed philosophy was one of the reasons that Philadelphia was a safe city, and the Bi-Centennial celebration was so

438

successful. I was at HUP when he was the police chief and I would see evidence of his orders to his troops in our Receiving Ward. Remember, the PGH had closed my JAR year, so when somebody was arrested, they were accustomed to complaining that they were sick and official policy was to take them to a hospital emergency department and that turned out to be our hospital's Receiving Ward, in the absence of the PGH. We would check them out, confirm that nothing was wrong and discharge them. But the Philly cops would be waiting outside the RW doors. Two hours later the same miscreants would be back having had the shit beat out of them. Ahh, no value judgement, just life in Philadelphia, City of Brotherly Love.

In 1978, I left HUP for my next period of medical training at Yale. And Frank Rizzo, running on his success as police commissioner, became the Mayor of the City. Now as the head cop, Rizzo had developed a feud with the MOVE people which festered and worsened as Mayor. By 1985, Rizzo had been replaced by Wilson Goode as the new mayor who had to deal with the MOVE house which was becoming a danger to the Cobbs Creek community. For some reason that I do not understand, he decided to drop two bombs on the MOVE house from a police helicopter on May 13 of his first year as Mayor. Like I already said, there were still 20-30 men, women and children living in the house. Two days before the bombing, the police force advised neighbors to leave their homes the next day and make plans to return after the execution of the plan. The bombs destroyed the MOVE house and ignited a fire which the Philadelphia Fire Department allowed to burn out of control destroying two entire city blocks of residential properties leaving something close to 260 people homeless and killing about 8, several of whom were children. As I write this in May, 2023, the final lawsuits were settled and the Cobbs Creek neighborhood has been restored to some degree of normality. As far as MOVE is concerned, I think it's gone. But not its place in history or my memory.

Meanwhile my residency class had been caring for patients at HUP and the VAH. Sometimes we would save lives, sometimes we provided a kind of respite care for 'Gold Coast' patients. What do I mean? I can remember a Gold Coast physician who would admit patients for an invasive procedure like a barium enema (think about your last colonoscopy, prepared for at home and done as an out-patient in a doctor owned facility ten miles from the nearest hospital.) Or perhaps admitted for a starvation diet to assess a failure to thrive at home accompanied by multiple physical complaints for which there were no obvious physical findings. If you think about that compared with today's standards when you must be in shock and septic to be admitted to a hospital and your discharge planning was generally finalized before they even started the first IV, it gives you pause. Residents hated these Gold Coast admissions unless they were from Sylvan Eisman or Fred Goldwein. Sylvan and Fred only admitted legitimately sick patients with interesting problems and each knew what he was about. Plus, one had a great first name. Sylvan. Like a wooded glade occupied by elves.

Whenever there was an egregious admission by a Gold Coast doctor, my residency class would react with an egregious response. For example, we devised a contest to see who could transfer a patient the furthest from Philadelphia for the next portion of their medical care. The first attempt was to pay for a taxi to take a patient well known to the VAH-spa for recurring admissions to the Chelsea Old Sailors' Home in Boston. We thought that settled the issue until Crowley transferred a patient from HUP to the Denver Jewish Hospital for Lung Disease because the patient had resistant atypical tuberculosis. Now we were sure that Crowley had won but a resident, who subsequently

442

left our program to return to Harvard where he could learn to be a better narcissist, found a patient at the PGH talking to herself in Russian. He stole the administrative records on this patient, took a train to Washington, DC, went to the State Department and found that the patient was in the US illegally and actually had the patient sent back to Minsk (which is in Belarus), her hometown. That settled the winner, who as I mentioned, returned to Harvard since that is where he belonged. The Gold Coast was temporarily intimidated enough that they quieted down and admitted stuff like sinus infections and migraine headaches.

There were patients who we all knew because they were chronically ill and would require repeated admissions for acute flare-ups of their complicated medical problems and their total lack of personal resources to deal with them. We are not talking about financial resources. Money was not the issue. Stabilizing the patient somewhere that didn't result in their bouncing back into an acute HUP hospital bed was, except such a place didn't (and often doesn't) exist.

Sometimes, a patient's story has an unexpected ending for all of us.

At the Philadelphia General Hospital, where I had dawdled for hours reading Osler's journals, the internal medicine service was consulted to see a patient at the Mills Building. The PGH was an entire city block square and besides the medical and surgical wards, which were large open wards, there was a jail, a tuberculosis unit, the Osler museum that I have described, and a rehabilitation unit called the Mills Building. Except I don't think anybody ever got rehabbed there. This was not drug rehab. This was for patients with strokes, spinal cord injuries, various dementias who were supposed to be getting physical and occupational therapy so they could improve to be returned to from wherever they came. It was staffed by several doctors training to become physiatrists who specialize in this kind of medicine. But one doc noted in the chart that one of the patients in the Mills Building had an abnormal lab test. These patients had standing orders to have labs drawn at regular intervals, perhaps monthly. This was in lieu of actually examining them. The abnormal lab value was the hemoglobin and hematocrit which can be indicators of anemia. They are part of a complete blood count. What this doctor noticed were changes in the blood count that caused him to worry about anemia. He did further tests which suggested to him that the patient was deficient in iron, likely because of dietary deficiency but other causes might be in play like bleeding from the gastrointestinal tract. He thought a reasonable approach to the problem was to begin supplementing the patient with iron tablets by mouth. This makes people terribly constipated but in this patient, it also caused a progressive dementia and reduced her already minimal activities of daily living (referred to as ADL.) He called us to help. After finding the Mills Building and evaluating the patient and reviewing the medical record, we discovered something totally awesome and immediately accepted the patient on our service on the medical ward.

The portion of the blood count called the hematocrit which reflects the concentration of red blood cells was 92. Anything north of 45 in a non-menstruating female is extremely abnormal. This lady's hematocrit was out there orbiting Pluto. Well, Neptune. And, as described, she was iron deficient by the usual blood assays. I was sure that she had unrecognized and undiagnosed Polycythemia rubra vera or P. Vera for short. Her bone marrow was manufacturing too many red blood cells. These cells appeared to be iron deficient because there wasn't enough iron in her system to go around. As a result her fluid blood was turning into a kind of cellular sludge. And this was probably causing her dementia which had bought her a bed in the Mills Building. Giving her iron supplements was further driving the production of red blood cells which appeared to be iron deficient and this was worsening her dementia. The physiatrists were filling her tank with super unleaded iron and her bone marrow engines were revving. The treatment was simple as nature itself. Bleed her slowly. We drew off a unit of blood every five days. Three weeks into this, she woke up. Four weeks in, she started to talk. And she had a memory and knew all kinds of things. Two months into drawing off blood her hematocrit was 43 and she was starting to walk and we were able to transfer her to a more modern rehab unit.

What a save.

The lesson here was to treat every patient as a tabla rasa. A blank slate. Someone that comes to you with a problem that everybody else has evaluated and they are carrying ten thick binders of medical records recorded by a regiment of doctors and specialists, should be a tabla rasa to you, his or her new doc. You start at the beginning, sometimes over the patient's objections, and take the history and be thorough. Then a complete physical exam. Once you have formulated your initial impression, you take time to review all those records. Now you are ready to diagnose and cure your patient and heal them if they will let you. You won't make much money and you won't please your corporate bosses, but you will be practicing medicine. And that is one of the greatest honors society can bestow.

I can remember a consultation I did for a middle-aged woman from New England who somehow found her way to my office in Wilmington, DE. She was a ten-binder patient. She had self-diagnosed herself as having chronic Lyme Disease which was causing her terrible arthritis. She had started with rheumatologists and infectious disease specialists in her hometown and then slowly worked her way south seeing doctors in Boston, Rhode Island, New Haven, Manhattan, New Jersey, Pennsylvania and finally Delaware. She told me that I was her last chance, and she knew of my history studying Lyme Disease. I told her she would be a tabla rasa; I would start at the beginning and review everything before rendering an opinion. Which I did.

When I finished late into the day, I concluded what every other doctor had concluded. She had classic rheumatoid arthritis. All the features by history, exam, lab and x-ray. And she had never, not once, been treated for it although many doctors had recommended excellent treatment regimens. A few doctors, for reasons that were unclear, had given her long courses of antibiotics which she claimed made her feel better until they were stopped, at which point she reverted to her horrible stiffness and pain. Wasn't this proof that she had chronic Lyme

Disease? Would I start her back on intravenous antibiotics?

I sat down with the patient and her husband. Studied them for a while and then gave them my most erstwhile and honest feelings regarding her situation. I told her that she unquestionably had very bad rheumatoid arthritis and desperately needed treatment. Furthermore, it was certainly possible for her to have severe rheumatoid arthritis and had contracted Lyme Disease. I couldn't tell from her medical records whether at one time she did have Lyme Disease, which was endemic and common where she lived, but chronic Lyme Disease was not causing her symptoms and it would be unprofessional for me to say otherwise. But she seemed to have a need to have Lyme Disease, and I thought a need to deny that she had rheumatoid arthritis, and I didn't know why that was but I knew I couldn't help her because it was impractical...she lived too far away and because she didn't seem to want anybody to help her. Her husband sighed. She became enraged. She shared with me that I was just another incompetent physician, but I shouldn't worry because she had another appointment the following week in Washington, DC, at George Washington University Hospital with another rheumatologist and the week after that, an appointment at a Lyme Disease Clinic in Lynchburg, VA. She had made those appointments even before she had seen me.

Human nature, like time and space, can be warped and bent slightly. While it is unlikely that William Osler ever sat down over a fine cognac in Vienna and discussed the nexus of human nature and general relativity with Albert Einstein, if he had, then I wish I had been sipping with them.

Chapter 18

HUP   REDUX

"Well ain't it a shame

That our short little memories

Never seem to learn

The lessons of history

We keep makin' the same mistakes

Over and over and over and over again

453

And then we wonder why

We're in the shape we're in

Frail grasp on the big picture

You keep on rubbin' that, you're gonna get a blister

It's a frail grasp on the big picture

I've seen it all before...."

Eagles: Frail Grasp on the Big Picture from the Long Road Out of Eden album. 2007

One afternoon during that first year at HUP, I remember the team rounding later than usual while on service in the Moloney Building. One of our

454

patients was a young man with acute hepatitis which had turned him a bright yellow. He needed careful watching, diet and treatment lest his liver go into acute failure. In particular, he had to limit his protein intake. The door to his room was closed as the team approached. The attending knocked softly and swung the door open to an unexpected sight: two naked men performing oral sex on each other, one a bright yellow. The attending rapidly closed the door and we moved away, uncertain as to what we should do next.

This was the mid-seventies and homosexuality was still largely closeted nationwide but things were rapidly changing, as we had just seen. And for some reason, Philadelphia, perhaps because of the Bi-Centennial, had become a center for gay folks to enter the mainstream. Not that having sex in your hospital bed was appropriate behavior. I had several thoughts a bit later in the day after rounds were finished. My first thought was whether the patient's partner was at risk for developing hepatitis, in which case we needed to have a discussion with the patient. My second thought was how the severity of the patient's illness did not seem to blunt his hormones. I would have to look up what happens to testosterone in patients with severe liver inflammation. My final thought was about HIV and how did this new pathogen fit into this situation. One way or another, homosexuality was becoming a large part of our thinking in medicine as it became a normal part of the greater society. It had to be part of our assessment of the patients' complaints.

During residency, each of us considered whether we should become general internists and be primary care doctors for adults or whether we should continue training in a 'sub-specialty', knowledgeable in general internal medicine but almost all-knowing when it came to cardiac problems, gastrointestinal disease, or whatever peaked our intellect. The factors that played into this kind of decision included intellectual attraction, personal or family experience with a disease, income potential, lifestyle especially time off from work, and relationships with senior doctors. This last factor included mentors, physicians who silently steered you towards their specialty because they sensed that you would be particularly suited to become a sub-specialist in their area of expertise. This was a major factor for me.

One of the faculty physicians brought by Relman to HUP was the new Chief of the Rheumatology Division, Alan Myers MD. Alan was from Baltimore originally and he would have fit naturally into our inner core had he been my age. A Mass General product, he had the cachet for academic medicine, and he liked it, but he was an atypical scholar. There were atypical mycobacteria (TB germs) and there were atypical scholarly academicians as well, although I am not conflating the two.

My generation of residents knew less about rheumatology than maybe any other area of internal medicine in large part because it was an out-patient specialty. But it did have its sick patients and those patients usually had auto-immune disease. Alan and I bonded early, and he taught me a great deal and not necessarily only about rheumatology. The first thing he taught me was about the hospital being a battle zone where sub-specialists were competing for patient care. Not for the money. For prestige. For reputation. For the honor. For the ego. That appealed to something deep inside me that I couldn't identify and maybe still can't. I think that one of the greatest honors a physician can experience is to be respected and loved by his or her peers for being a 'doctor's doctor.' That comes closest to my feelings on the matter. Alan taught me that you did anything you needed to do to get an inside track on seeing the tough cases and making or helping to make the diagnosis and find the right cure. When Alan got to HUP, they had no experience with this kind of physician, but it didn't take long for them to appreciate what Alan brought to the care of sick patients. And it didn't take me long to integrate his style and make it my own.

When I did a rheumatology elective with him and even when I was doing something else, I made it a practice to attend the sign out rounds that took place in the Receiving Ward around 6 am every day. That way I had a leg up on each day's admissions to the internal medicine services. My next stop would be the units where the new admissions had gone, to talk with the JARS about the cases and ask them for a consult so the rheumatology service could evaluate the patient. This was a new experience for JARS, a SAR showing up at 7 am before they had early morning walk rounds to ask for a consult on a new patient not even presented to the team yet.

'Okay. Sure. If you want one, okay with us. All we ask in return is for you to teach us.' Rheumatology got a reputation as a super teaching service, and this was especially appreciated when there was a patient in the ICU with some God-awful multi-organ fiasco and nobody knew what was happening or what to do. We knew. Alan knew. I knew.

Unfortunately, there is always a fly in the ointment and in this case, there were flies: Alan's faculty. Except for Barry Schimmer, also from the Massive, the other rheum faculty were narrowly focused on things of little interest to house staff. Perhaps the one exception was Sergio Jimenez MD, an expert on two things: collagen biosynthesis which was mostly of pediatric interest and scleroderma, a potentially fatal auto-immune disease for which we had little treatment and only a few approaches to its complications. Sergio was very smart and had a lot to teach if you poked him. Barry was an older version of me but much nicer.

There was one other faculty member in Alan's Rheumatology Department to whom honor and respect was due. That was Joseph Hollander MD who still skittered around the hospital despite approaching ninety. Dr. Hollander was one of the fathers of American Rheumatology as a sub-specialty and the first Editor of the major textbook in the field. Rheumatology began as a specialty in England and most physicians thought that had something to do with the climate over there. It didn't. It had more to do with the influence of Sir William Osler. Anyway, here is a little-known fact for all of you. The first prospective, placebo controlled, blinded study was conducted by the Empire Rheumatism Council in Great Britain around 1950. This type of study with various modifications has become the model for all studies of efficacy of treatment ever since. The study asked the question: did gold salt injections weekly help patients with rheumatoid arthritis as opposed to placebo injections with sugar water. Both were given weekly over a six-month period. Neither the patient nor the treating rheumatologist knew who got what. The answer was a definitive yes and interestingly enough, both treatment groups showed efficacy during the first three months of the study but the placebo sugar water injections had lost any efficacy after six months while the gold salts continued to show statistical benefit. This study, then, also showed the reality and power of a placebo effect which would need to be accounted for in future studies.

How did they know that gold salt injections might be helpful for rheumatoid arthritis? Remember I told you about Tompkins County Hospital in Ithaca, New York where some of my CUMC classmates and I spent the summer between year 2 and 3 of CUMC doing an externship and enjoying upstate New York. That's the summer I worked at Summer Jam Rock Festival. You may not remember that we stayed in lodgings at the hospital that at one time provided beds for TB patients from lower Manhattan at the turn of the century when tuberculosis was rampant in the city. One of the treatments used at that time for TB was the injection of salts of various metals including gold. And the report from that experience was that the gold salt injections did not help tuberculosis, but it seemed to cure patients with rheumatoid arthritis. A sort of small world observation that led to a very important study in Great Britain.

One of the pleasurable things SARS got to do was help host a visiting professor at HUP roughly twice yearly. The visit I remember was by Dr. William Kelley. Now this requires some background information. Dr. Kelley was, in some ways, a rheumatologist, but I don't think he would own up to that. He became famous for his research while a faculty member at the University of North Carolina where he discovered the enzyme deficiency that resulted in a very rare inherited disorder of males from birth that caused amongst other problems, severe early gouty arthritis: hypoxanthine guanine phosphoribosyl transferase deficiency. What a mouthful, although it did have a nice rhythm to it. This work landed him advancement as he became the Chairman of Internal Medicine at the University of Michigan which was a very prestigious position. Now he was visiting us. As SARS, our job was to take him to dinner and arrangements were made to have dinner in a private room at Chef Tell Erhardt's restaurant in Chestnut Hill, a suburb of Philadelphia. Chef Tell was famous nationally as a chef and culinary educator and a celebrity in the Philadelphia area where he owned four restaurants and ran a cookware business and had published a few cookbooks. Chef Tell was present to preside over our dinner that night. I remember that Dr. Kelley seemed reserved and was quiet, not participating in our SAR gossip. As the evening progressed, and I

464

have to say the food was delicious, my classmate SARS got absolutely plastered. Alcohol is a trigger for me because of a predisposition to migraine headaches so I pretended to drink the wine but remained quite sober. The lush rubber plant placed behind my chair fared poorly. As dinner ended, my mates decided that it would be a good idea to take the single rose sitting in a delicate vase in front of each place setting home to their wife, girlfriend or whoever. This did not compart with Chef Tell's notion of the conclusion of a good dinner party at his restaurant. He objected. We told him to fuck off. Dr. Kelley remained reserved. Chef Tell pushed Osnoss and grabbed at his rose. Crowley pushed back at the Chef and rescued the rose for Osnoss. Taylor Cope grabbed 5 or 6 vases with roses in them and ran into the street. Waiters poured out the door and a melee ensued. Somebody punched Chef Tell in his large nose enhanced by years of wine tastings. Blood sprayed over Dr. Kelley's starched white, white shirt and club tie (U of M). Somebody may have called

465

the police but by then we had all scrammed and were headed home. There was no fallout the next day or even the next week.

There is a postscript, however. Dr. Kelley became the Founder and CEO of the new University of Pennsylvania Health System where he remained until time passed after the publishing of an editorial in the New England Journal of Medicine written by Dr. Kelley on his plan to make Penn Medicine the largest and greatest health system in the history of the world. It was a rather grandiose statement to be published in a Massachusetts journal read worldwide but perhaps the new Editor in Chief, Bud Relman, was flexing his muscles. I am not privy to exactly what happened next. I believe Dr. Kelley is still employed by Penn Medicine in an executive capacity, but I do know that there was a famous, somewhat heated falling out with Judith Rodin, at that time the first woman President of the University of Pennsylvania following which Dr. Kelley was relieved of his CEO responsibilities. I think Dr. Kelley would have fit in nicely with our resident class. Sort of a partner for Eric Neilson but with less common sense.

Hanging on the wall all by itself on the third floor of the nexus of two ultra-modern buildings, Perelman and Abramson, at the vast Penn Medicine complex is a portrait of Dr. John Glick, looking somewhat older than when I last saw him. Quite a good likeness, I think. John was a young turk in the Heme-Onc Department at HUP during my residency. The use of the word turk in medical circles indicates a young physician who, because of raw intellect, clinical acumen, analytic capacity, research and publishing macho, and sheer guts is likely to be successful in the rarified air of academic medicine. That was certainly true of John. I have had no personal experience with John save for one observation when he intruded on late day rounds with his Fellow in tow. I was standing in the back of the crowded conference room somewhere in the Ravdin building leaning against the wall trying to fall asleep if just for a few minutes (it can work miracles). John was looking for a fight. Without apologizing for his intrusion, saying hello, asking if he could have a minute to discuss a mutual patient, John practically screamed, 'Did anyone check the serum copper level on patient XYZ and why is that critical?' It wasn't my patient, and I didn't know the details, but I can tell you I have never ordered a serum copper level on a patient before that incident and never ordered one since. One might as well order a serum porcelain or limestone level for what good it would do other than confuse the chemistry laboratory technicians. Nobody said a word. With that, John picked up a tray brought from the cafeteria loaded with cups, plates, half eaten sandwiches, cookies, and, I believe, a partially consumed birthday cake and threw the entire thing against a wall making an awful mess, and stormed out of the conference room. That was John Glick. A young turk. Gutsy.

BTW, Wilson's Disease is a very rare inherited disorder of copper metabolism resulting in copper deposition in multiple organs and causing various problems if not diagnosed. It does influence hematologic function. You go, Glick.

Chapter 19

SAR YEAR

"In this dirty old part of the city

Where the sun refused to shine

Please tell me there ain't no use in tryin'

Watch my daddy in bed a-dyin'

Watched his hair been turnin' grey

He's been workin' and slavin' his life away, oh yes
I know it. And you know it, too.

We gotta get out of this place

If it's the last thing we ever do

We gotta get out of this place

'Cause girl, there's a better life for me and
you"....'We gotta get out of this place'...Eric Burdon
and The Animals, from Animal Tracks. 1965

I started my last year at HUP with my life being
somewhat unsettled. As usual. Towards the end of

JAR year, I found that I had more time for myself and for my personal life. I started to date...a lot. Nurses, nursing students, social workers, hospital staff, medical students, doctors. But each date always ended as a one-off. I wasn't finding anybody who was likely to enrich my life. There was no Natasha. There was no Linda. I found that I wanted a relationship more than I wanted a date. I looked around me and started to think that maybe I should divide relationships in terms of two groups: those women that worked in medicine and would have a natural understanding of me and my life, and those that worked outside of medicine and could broaden the scope of my life at the risk of never really understanding me.

Then I had to make plans for the following year and whether to do a fellowship. I was 99 percent committed to subspecializing in rheumatology using the Alan Myers model of clinical practice seeking out the most challenging cases with teaching and even some research as struts to keep me upright. I had eliminated the possibility of being a full-time academic doctor. Too much bureaucracy. Too much politics. I didn't have the stomach to be a young turk in the Glick mode. Alan had promised me a fellowship with him at HUP and that sounded perfect to me. Fellowship was a 2 or 3 year commitment depending on the department program and the source of funding for the position. The third year was always a research commitment with the expectation that you would produce publishable work and a basis for grant applications. It was the secure route to an academic career. But, of course, no guarantees.

Then a thunderclap. Dr. Relman would be leaving sometime that year to become the Editor in Chief of the New England Journal of Medicine, a position from which he would gain enormous power and authority to direct careers, alter national policies and focus research agendas. No Bud Relman at the helm and his replacement unknown. That changed things.

Then another thunderclap, even louder followed by a virtual monsoon. Alan Myers was leaving. And with that fact, Sergio Jimenez left for Jefferson Medical College in Center City and Barry Schimmer set up shop at Pennsylvania Hospital, a historic hospital close by the historic east end of downtown. The entire mass of the Section of Rheumatology at HUP that I was counting on gone in a flash. Who was left? Some tightly wound rheumatologists and Joe Hollander MD, age 91. Alan guaranteed me that I still had a place as a fellow at Penn but that was a non-starter.

I huddled with Alan who was now my close friend as well as my mentor. Alan was a Mass

General product, and he well knew that he was fortunate to be the Chief of a Section under Relman. Why? I thought he was great at it. Academic careers required outstanding teaching and he was par excellence; phenomenal political skills and again he was outstanding; recruitment of fellows and faculty where he was very good; and funded grants for continuing research either to him or his faculty and by extension published research. Like me, this was not what floated Alan's boat. He had written chapters in textbooks and monographs devoted to a single disease entity and had his name on case reports and opinion papers, but he wasn't a research rock star. I didn't give a shit. Nobody gave a shit. Alan Myers should have been a fixture at Penn Medicine that never left. And he was loyal. He told me that he wouldn't rest until he found me a suitable fellowship and saw me on my way.

If nobody cared, why was he leaving. For the answer, I must share with you some of the internal

476

politics of great and famous medical schools. Just as I was becoming a SAR, the faculty senate of Penn Medicine was grappling with what to do with physicians like Alan. And the reason was tenure. The Bylaws or whatever governed faculty contracts was no different for medical faculty than the faculty of Arts and Sciences or The Wharton School. After so many years, averaging seven, the University either honored the faculty member with a position guaranteed for life or they cut bait. Penn didn't want to have to deal with that reality, so they were debating some compromise. A perfect example was the Cardiology Chief. He was exactly in Alan's position. Penn didn't want to cut bait for either of these men but these docs didn't meet the usual requirements for tenure, especially around research and grant funding.

So here was the compromise. They created two tenure tracks. A traditional track no different from what Penn had been doing since Ben Franklin's day and a clinical track that eliminated things like published research in reputable journals, multiple grants, active laboratories, national prominence. The stuff that remained was all the things in which Alan excelled as did the Cardiology Chief who agreed immediately to take the clinical tenure offer. Alan accepting clinical tenure was important because it normalized the compromise, made it an acceptable alternative to the traditional tenure.

But that wasn't good enough for Alan. Alan was a Mass General trained physician and the clinical track sounded like second class citizenship. When future, unforeseen decisions needed to be made, would the clinically tenured physicians have an equal say to the traditionally tenured doctors. And, in day-to-day life, would the clinical track people be treated differently.

I would have jumped on the clinical track and ridden it all the way to retirement. Alan was having no part of it. To him, they were offering a lower status that he didn't feel he deserved. I could see his point. He was old school enough to feel that he should be counted as a young turk while I was young enough to redefine a young turk to my liking and my needs. I hated his decision, but I respected it and supported him. So now, where was I going for my rheumatology fellowship?

Alan sent me to several programs to interview. The University of Connecticut, the University of South Carolina. Both reputable programs located in nasty places and led by autocratic Chiefs working off of shit grants but publishing big literature. All very nice but on the way out the door the Fellows would grab me and say, 'don't come here, this place sucks.' Not a ringing endorsement from those that should know.

Then I interviewed at Yale. I liked the location, I liked the medical school and I really liked the faculty and fellows. Best of all, I would be able to spend almost all my research time working with a faculty member named Allan Steere who was doing great work puzzling out a mysterious outbreak in Old Lyme, CT, of seemingly unrelated clinical manifestations, laboratory manifestations, epidemiology and potential treatments of a newly recognized disease. This local epidemic in eastern Connecticut around the small and charming towns of Lyme and Old Lyme initially was impacting children and their families along a tertiary road, but soon enough it was causing hysteria along the I-95 corridor. My job, outside of the usual fellow responsibilities, was to care for patients who came to our Lyme Disease Clinic at Yale-New Haven Hospital, all 200 plus of them, and carefully collect data. Lots of data. My research was new, ground-breaking, and totally encompassed the role of an

480

Oslerian physician. Love it, love it, love it. But to be honest, this was Allen Steere's research. I was just a tool and he was fortunate to have me. This is the minor bit of narcissism that all physicians are due on occasion.

So besides taking care of the Lyme disease patients, what was the life of a Fellow like me. I like to think that I brought the Alan Myers model to Yale and for the better. There were two Fellows each year except for the occasional third research Fellow. The two second year Fellows wanted to finish and go home to practice medicine. They had no illusions of wanting to be young turks. One of them told me a story that I found hard to believe. He had taken a course on how to set up your solo private practice. One piece of instruction was to cut two inches off the front legs of the chairs patients sat in while with the doctor in the exam room, thus giving them the sense that they were always falling forward out of the chair and thus were more likely to get up and leave as quickly as possible. Osler would have disapproved.

My partner was a doc named David Widman MD. A nicer man you would never meet and very smart out of NYU which had a bang-up rheumatology department unfortunately chaired by a historic schmuck. I only knew that by his national reputation. David had only one idiosyncrasy that I found irritating. But he was such a good guy that it was never a problem between us. The thing that would get me going was his inability to come to a decision clinically. This was apparent on rheum rounds and as he presented a case he had seen and come to the part where he shared his differential diagnosis and/or treatment, he wavered like a sapling in a hurricane. Usually, after about ten minutes, I would explode on him in front of everybody and say something innocuous like, 'so what the fuck do you think is wrong with this patient?' And you know, I would apologize later but he honestly was never mad.

He would just go through his thinking again, unable to really commit and feeling that this was good enough. It sometimes isn't good enough. But he didn't get that. On this decision making inability and the fact he wouldn't get angry with me when I would call him out on it, I would say to myself, 'Dave, you need some psychotherapy.'

So, when I got to Yale, my first day, I was on service for a month and that meant that I saw all the consults in the hospital for rheumatology and presented them to my attending on rounds which included any residents or students doing rheumatology electives. David Widman, and sometimes the second year Fellows would tag along. Do you know the Tom Petty song called 'Spike'. It's from his Southern Accents album. About a teenage boy who wears a dog collar down in Gainesville, Florida where Petty grew up. I know I've mentioned it before in this memoir because I like it. Tom and his guitarist Mike Campbell are sitting in this bar called The Cypress Lounge, despite being told never to go into The Cypress Lounge, when Spike walks in and Tom turns to Mike and says, 'Mike, this is going to be good...'

Sorry for that little bypass, but that was when the second year Fellows came with us on rounds. Because they knew the case that was going to be discussed, and like Spike in the Cypress Lounge, they knew, 'this was going to be good...'

I was chatting with the long running secretary of the department and asked her how many consultations might I see that first day.

'Oh, one may come in this week if we're lucky.'

And I said, 'WHAT??? Do you have a census of all the consults seen by us over the last 3 months?'

She did. She was very efficient and very helpful as well. The section of rheumatology was averaging six consults a month. Time to put on my mask, pull out my six shooters and put the pedal to the metal. I was very fortunate that month because there was one resident on elective and his name was Dan Rahn MD. Dan had Yale blue running through his veins: prep school, college, med school, and residency. Now he was the Chief Resident and we bonded very fast. Also, my attending that month was John Hardin MD, a great guy if ever there was one. Clinically good and interested but his heart was in his laboratory and, see, he went on to become a Chair of Medicine whereas Dan became something like the Emperor of one of the southern states, not Florida or Alabama, but still plenty prestigious.

The next thing I did was to discover their emergency department. They had one. If you are familiar with New Haven, you would understand why they needed a good ED. And, like HUP, they had a sign out session around 6:30 each morning. The next day I was there, meetin' and greetin' the Yale residents and taking down names and locations of admissions. My thinking was that anyone admitted to a hospital must have a rheumatic disease problem, diagnosed or undiagnosed, that could be a focus for teaching and learning. Dan and John agreed but my enthusiasm and aggressiveness was kind of new to them. With Dan at my side, as the Chief Resident, we had no problem securing about twelve consults that first day. When I told Hardin later that we had 12 consults to see, he almost fell out of his chair. I had doubled in one day the number of consults seen by the rheum section in a typical month. And these patients had real rheum problems which were either being ignored or mistreated.

Now, when you are a 'clinical' young turk like me, you know that when you start at a new hospital, you are not going to be accepted immediately. Particularly at a place like Yale where the house staff had a 'Harvard complex'. The Yale house staff were like 'Cornell?, Penn?, Pshaw!' But all it takes is to show up the locals once to be brought inside the tent. One of those patients I saw that first day was a woman who was very sick with a distinctive rash on her hands. There was no diagnosis so far but the team was waiting for Irwin Braverman MD to see her. Dr. Braverman was the best clinical dermatologist I ever met and he wrote one of the best textbooks of clinical medicine I ever read, Skin Signs of Systemic Disease. I understood the house staff's angst with this sick patient with fever and rash, but I had already written my consult which was on her chart. They were gathered around her bed and trying to be re-assuring, when I stepped into the room with Dan and John and David and introduced myself to the entire team, and then said, "I think this is very typical of toxic shock syndrome." A moment later, timed perfectly, Dr. Braverman walked in and glancing at the patient's hands said, "Oh, I see you have a case of toxic shock syndrome."

Bingo. I'm in the tent. And my written consult is already on the chart way before Dr. Braverman even knew about the patient.

The patient got better with antibiotics. I showed up every day for the ER sign-out at 6:30 am and that first month we had 92 consults including a few from the ER at midnight. Hardin was falling asleep at his bench (the insider's name for research lab.) Dan was thinking about a rheumatology fellowship which he ended up doing. And our Chief of the Yale Rheumatology Section, Steve Malawista MD, may his memory be a blessing, wanted to know what the hell was going on.

And I said, 'Steve, this is going to be good....'

Chapter 20

The Pool at Blythewood

"Well, I will provide for you

And I'll stand by your side

You'll need a good companion now

491

For this part of the ride

Yeah, leave behind your sorrows

Let this day be the last

Well, tomorrow they'll be sunshine

And all this darkness past

Well, big wheels roll through fields where sunlight streams

O' meet me in a land of hope and dreams"....Land of Hope and Dreams...Bruce Springsteen and the E Street Band from the Live in New York City album. 2001

I got way ahead of myself. I was beginning my SAR year at HUP and dating again as my personal time increased. As I said, not finding much luck with the women I went out with until the new interns started at HUP and there was a young woman from Brown Medical School who could almost have been a dead ringer for Natasha. Bad choice of words there, sorry. Of course, she had a boyfriend back at Brown University who she was sort of committed to and I had seen this story unfold once before and was reluctant for it to have another showing. Still, she was bright, funny and game for anything. I can remember that she came with me on a group outing with 2 or 3 of my co-SARS on a canoe trip down the Delaware Water Gap. Kind of a throwback from my high school days. That was too much for her given her schedule and I think she slept 24 straight hours upon returning. I remember her practically collapsing in my living room and my carrying her into the bedroom and tucking her in to sleep before retreating to the couch.

While she was working, I was relaxing and enjoying a SAR's life. I remember it being very hot that summer of 1977 which is why I was so happy Blythewood Garden Apartments had a pool of which I made almost daily use. This one day, aside from a young gal my age, the only people at the pool were an older couple and I soon realized that they were my pool partner's parents, visiting from West Hempstead, New York. She was quite attractive, and she didn't flinch at the sight of me in a bathing suit which was a must if I was going to ask her out on a date. The next night, I remember walking past the three of them on the driveway into the apartment complex. Fifty yards down the road, I glanced over my shoulder to find her glancing over her shoulder. We were glancing at each other. I considered this a good omen. I had sort of met her in the pool that first time by engaging her mother in conversation. Her dad was quiet and watchful but her mom was eager to converse. My poolmate's name was Leslie.

Without getting into too many details, I found myself dating two women, both of whom I really liked. And by utter chance, they each fell into a different one of my arbitrary categories: one, the medical intern; and two, a reading consultant with a master's degree from the University of Buffalo. This was a new dilemma for me. I could analyze it until I was blue in the face but I couldn't decide anything....who was I more attracted to, who was a better match, who was more likely to want a committed long term relationship. At this point, though I hadn't met David Widman yet, I was playing out his constant dilemma...making a decision, because I just couldn't in good conscience date both women and in my heart I knew that if I continued to do that, I would lose both of them.

So, I was driving myself crazy, hanging around my apartment very unhappy and I decided to go with the doctor. I walked over to Leslie's apartment to tell her what I had decided and she was a little upset but how well did we know each other, so she couldn't have been that grief-stricken. I went home and agonized that I had made the wrong choice. So, two hours later, I went back to Leslie's place and told her I had changed my mind and would she 'go steady' with me and see where it led us. She said yes. By default, my doctor began to understand that things had changed and she was so busy, I don't think she cared. What was the final deciding factor? I felt that I was too immersed in medicine and I needed a partner who would pull me into the real world where I would be exposed to culture, food, other professionals with different ideas; and this was a healthy way to live my life. Leslie would save me from myself, so I could become a version of me that would be more interesting and would be more likely to grow, think, feel and act like a maturing adult.

I married Leslie a little more than a year later. All the requisite items seemed in place for a long and happy marriage. Physical attraction, intellectual attraction, mutual respect, desire to have children, and similar values politically, culturally, socially.

Of course, things don't always follow a perfect path. Overall, we had a good marriage as I think about it, and I think Les would agree with me on that. We lived together not quite two years before we married and we stayed married for 36 years, although the last few were marred by separations and three prolonged attempts at couples' therapy. Our divorce was amicable, and we simply split our estate down the middle. Probably the strongest evidence that we had a good marriage was that we had a good divorce, remaining friends, even with Les re-marrying a few years ago. We have two wonderful sons and they in turn have beautiful families with two children each, blessing us with grandchildren.

So why did we get divorced? I got that question a lot when I was dating after the divorce and before the pandemic shut things down. As usual, when it comes to women and relationships, I must fall back on Natasha and Linda and all the minor relationships before and after. I don't know. I don't know the answer. I find myself tearing up as I write this. The complexities of love, intimacy, vulnerability, sharing and caring on a very deep level escape my capacity as an adult physician to give simple answers that have very profound implications for understanding love. Probably my difficulty with this stems from my family of origin, the absence of a father figure, an aloof mother, a younger brother who was too distant age wise to be a best friend as much as I love him. But blaming this trope from psychotherapy seems inadequate and unfair to me and to our marriage. From my vantage point, we hurt each other badly, nasty attachment wounds, that I don't think ever healed even though we brushed them off in couples therapy. I think we just stopped loving each other over time even as we still liked each other and when called for, depended on each other.

I think back to that decision so many years ago between the reading specialist and the doctor, and I think I made the right decision even though the marriage ultimately failed. What I failed to do consistently was adhere to my progressive Cornell self and remember that once Les and I were going to be a married couple, I didn't engage her in conversations and make decisions that were important for us to make together: should I take the fellowship at Yale which meant she would be moving as well; when should the wedding take place; how would we handle parenting once Les started out on a second career; should we try and have another child and many other more commonplace issues that we just allowed to slide away. Or I allowed to slide away. And especially those quiet conversations that are so difficult to begin, like the meaning of love, its definition, were we okay, how could we deepen our feelings for each other and enter a new level. These were the questions that I didn't know to ask and the conversations I was afraid to have with Natasha and

Linda but now I was committed by marriage and that should have made them easier. But they weren't.

I also concluded that I was a failed feminist even though I tried. I tried hard.

This book is a memoir or maybe a hemi- autobiography of sorts. Or perhaps it sits in the goldilocks zone between the two. I have tried to include recurring themes in it that are not about me, per se.

Most people my age can still remember most of the lyrics of the Youngblood's classic which ends with this verse:

'If you hear the song I'm singing

You will understand (listen!)

You hold the key to love and fear

500

All in your trembling hand

Just one key unlocks them both

It's there at your command

Come on people now

Smile on your brother

Everybody get together

Try to love one another

Right now.

If only it was that easy.

For example, the key that Oslerian methodology brings to creating the joy of medical practice has been lost in today's world. Maybe it has been misplaced. I wonder if maintaining the joy of practicing medicine in an Oslerian way remains compatible with how I wanted to grow in my personal life.

Then there is maturity. Early on, I used the Google definition: thought, feelings and behavior characteristic of an adult. I hope that when I finish this project and someone reads it and learns about me at college, then med school, then training and more training, then marriage, parenting, divorce, dating, illness and the unknown, you will have a sense of how I, me, personally matured over time. I have been challenged by a friend to define maturity for myself now. There is no answer because the maturity of a human being is always changing. It is a dynamic and amorphous quality that depends on experience, knowledge, environment, and future.

I'm going to spend some time on my own professional life but will say now that I accomplished all that I had hoped to when I left for Ithaca shortly after Labor Day, 1967.

Chapter 21

The Neurology Story

You will remember that at CUMC we had internship advisers and I thought mine was a Dr. Johnson. Not sure of the name, but positive that he was a professor of Infectious Diseases. As we went through the process of applying, he told me I would need several letters of recommendation in addition to the transcripts, evaluations and various documents from my student days. He told me I should ask Dr.

Fred Plum for a letter, as well as several others, and he would write one as well.

Fred Plum MD was the Chairman of Neurology at New York Hospital. He was a brilliant clinician, a brilliant researcher, a brilliant author, and, well, he was very impressive. But, he was also a reminder to those who observed him, that all humans are fallible and we all have our own small and large quirks.

Dr. Plum's quirk as a professor was precision mated to rigidity. I spent a month on the Neurology service at New York Hospital. The team included the Chief Resident in neurology, a senior medical resident, junior medical resident, intern and several medical students. Yes, there I was at the bottom of the pecking order, again. Dr. Plum made rounds with this team on Thursday mornings at 10 am sharp. To make a point of this, let me share that we gathered in the hall outside the nursing station at 5 minutes before ten, forming two lines on either side of the hall and looking sharp. As the second hand of the wall clock hit 12:00, meaning 10 am on the dot had arrived, Dr. Plum would round the corner at the far end of the hall, a black doctor's bag under his arm, and head toward us. He was about 6 foot tall, ruddy in complexion and his facial features were fixed in a sober stare. There was no chit-chat. He walked right up to the Chief Resident and always said the same thing: 'First case.'

We would all go to the bedside, Plum on one side of the patient and the Chief Res on the other side. The Chief Res would present the patient in sparse terms. Dr. Plum would honor the patient with a brief hello and possibly a hand pat and examine the patient using the neurologist's implements which he took from his black bag: reflex hammer, safety pin, tuning fork, ophthalmoscope. All this was predictable and the same, week after

506

week. Then Fred would say goodbye and we would move out into the hall. Everyone's heart rate increased as the Reptilian brain did its thing. Except Fred's.

Dr. Plum had a traditional way of teaching. He would start with the Chief Resident and begin to question him or her about history, neurologic findings on exam, and so on, each question being slightly more nuanced and with a greater degree of difficulty until the Chief just didn't know the answer. Then Fred would move to the senior resident and repeat the sequence but with different questions. He would work his way down to the medical students, but only question one of us. And you know, he never asked me any questions which made me happy but somehow sad, too, because I never had the chance to go head-to-head with Fred Plum. My guess was that I intimidated him. Not really. That was my only contact with him. This was the faculty member I was to ask for a very important letter of recommendation.

Now, Dr. Plum had a reputation of always agreeing to write a letter for the CUMC student's application to an internship program. But he never promised to be supportive in the letter and there were all kinds of lore at Cornell about how he would trash some student in his letter, ruining their chances of getting into the program they wanted. As an observer of Dr. Plum, honesty and integrity were chief concerns for him. I am sure he was true to those values.

It was with some trepidation that I appeared fifteen minutes early for my meeting with FP to ask for a letter of recommendation. The meeting was scheduled for 4 pm. I was still waiting in his outer office at 4:20 when a buzzer went off on his secretary's desk and she indicated that I could go in.

The office itself was poorly lit with built in bookshelves on all four walls totally packed with books and bound journals. Fred was sitting at a desk that reminded me of the pictures I had seen of the President's Resolute Desk in the Oval Office. There was a powerful banker's lamp providing light for the desk and I could see that he was signing a pile of letters. The entire office was done up in dark woods, like mahogany, that further emphasized the gloom outside of the shining beacon of the banker's lamp. I stood at attention on the other side of his desk while he signed one letter after another. I stood that way for ten more minutes without being acknowledged. Then he paused, sat up straight, looked at me and said, 'Newman.'

I guessed this was my chance to ask him for help and I attempted to radiate confidence and awe at the same time. It wasn't easy. I have no idea what I said to him and, honestly, I don't think it mattered. You just did not schmooze Fred Plum.

Surprisingly, still staring me down, he went on a riff about how medicine was a demanding mistress and I should never forget that there would be other mistresses who would be demanding of my attention, like a wife, children, relatives, friends and the community at large. And I needed to find a middle ground to attend to all these mistresses for the rest of my life. With that, he went back to signing his letters. After a moment, I turned on my heel and left his office, not really knowing what to think. Later, Dr. Johnson told me Dr. Plum had written me a smashing, great letter of recommendation.

Fortunately for all of us at CUMC, we had two Chairmen of Neurology. The other one was Neurology Chairman at Memorial Sloan Kettering Hospital for Cancer. His name was Jerome Posner MD. Together, these two men had written one of the most important monographs (slim volume focused on a single topic) in the history of neurology literature. I still have a signed copy of this book. It was referred to as Stupor and Coma, prompting many jokes about the authors. The correct name of the textbook was The Diagnosis and Treatment of Stupor and Coma; and it was the definitive text on diminished levels of consciousness.

Let me tell you about Jerry Posner. I spent one month of my 3 months of internal medicine at Memorial Sloan Kettering. Just about every patient in the hospital was admitted very ill with some direct consequence or complication of cancer. I was a sub-intern and I was on call. I had established a routine of making rounds with a cart and drawing blood cultures and blood counts on every patient on my unit between midnight and one am, since everyone spiked a fever during that hour. After that, I would visit with a few patients who had the need to chat, couldn't sleep or just wanted another human being to visit them. There were, of course, excellent nurses, including my old girlfriend from Archbald with the famous pothole. She had gotten married in the interim. Anyway, at about 3 am, I would sit down to finish writing notes and orders and thinking about my patients and what else I could do for them.

I felt a shadow fall over the chart I was looking at and a hand placed carefully on my shoulder. Looking up, I found Dr. Posner who asked me.....asked me!.....if I minded if he sat down to discuss the case I was studying. At 3 am. You bet, Dr. Posner, sir. Sit right down. Let's talk. And we spent an hour and a half discussing the case I was reviewing and other cases on the floor as well. I learned more neurology in that ninety minutes than I learned in four years at CUMC. He was enjoying himself in the middle of the night. And I felt that I had found a friend, a colleague, another Oslerian physician.

There couldn't have been two doctors more dissimilar in style and manner than Plum and Posner. But these two men were friends and colleagues. Jerry Posner was the only doc that I ever saw call Fred Plum out in front of the entire department when he was wrong, and Dr. Plum felt he was never wrong. It was at a weekly neuro conference which was totally separate from the rounds I described. Everyone was seated in a large lecture room which had the typical 'Indiana Jones' slope from back to front. Fred had just finished explaining to the department why such and such patient had to have a glioma (one type of malignant brain tumor) of the so and so gyrus of the temporal lobe in the space behind the pituitary isthmus which was a bridge that connected this gland to the reptilian brain. Please excuse me, but I just made the anatomy up out of whole cloth. Even today, I have no idea whether such a location exists in the brain. In making his astounding diagnosis, Fred had quoted three journal articles, journals that I didn't even know existed, one of which was written in Swedish. At that point, Jerry Posner stood up and raised his hand at the same time....raised his hand!

'Fred, aren't you forgetting....'

And Jerry went on to quote an American journal written in English that had been available for nine months which totally shot down Fred's analysis and supported what turned out to be the correct diagnosis. Plum was okay with that. It had come from Posner.

Plum and Posner. Fred Plum, the pompous, rigid, brilliant academic scholar and clinician who delighted in embarrassing young aspiring doctors, some of whom could have been excellent neurologists save for their experience with Fred. And Jerry Posner, the kind, warm, brilliant scholar and clinician who delighted in encountering a young medical student in the middle of the night and talking patient diagnosis and care with him for almost two hours, leaving him uplifted by the encounter and wondering whether neurology wasn't such a bad field after all.

This chapter is devoted to both these men, both of whom had a strong impact on my life even if nobody could see it. I learned a lot about becoming a doctor and what that meant and especially what that meant for me. I was thinking and feeling more deeply about my profession. My idea of Oslerian medicine was shaping itself into a bedrock philosophy from which I would not stray far.

Chapter 22

Errata

"I got life, mother

I got laughs, sister

I got freedom, brother

I got good times, man

I got crazy ways, daughter

I got million-dollar charm, cousin

I got headaches and toothaches

And bad times too

Like you"....I Got Life from Act One, The Broadway Musical Hair circa late 1960's

I'd like to draw you in to this chapter by telling you a personal story that I would often include when talking to large nursing groups, often at awards celebrations of one type or another. This is when I was Chief Medical Officer at Christiana Care, the large healthcare system in Delaware, and would be asked to speak at these gatherings. Nurses loved to give each other recognition and I don't blame them since so few doctors do.

This story starts on my last night on call at HUP when I was an intern. The hospital operator pages me (no cell phones) and tells me my mother is on the line, should she connect us. Of course. I should mention that my mother rarely called me and never when I was on duty.

Her mother, my grandmother and the only grandparent I ever knew, was very sick in the ICU at a hospital in Scranton and could I come. Of course. I knew my Nana was 86, diminutive and obese with aortic stenosis and congestive heart failure and had been slowly going downhill. She and I were very close, and I loved her dearly.

I arranged for one of the other interns on call that night to cover my service since I had a family emergency. No problem. I jumped in the Datsun 240Z and put it through its paces going up a

519

vacant Northeast extension of the PA turnpike. I arrived in the ICU just as the nursing staff were giving report to the next shift.

You must picture what I looked like. I was dressed in scrubs and had a short white coat on. My scrubs were streaked with every manner of bodily fluid. All kinds of stuff were hanging out of every pocket that I had including things like partially eaten Tastycake Krimpets. My hair and body were limp from sweat and fatigue.

Nobody there had ever seen me before, ever. And they immediately all stood up as one. I thought they were going to gang tackle me and have me arrested. But no, this was how nurses responded to doctors walking onto a unit during Osler's day. Scranton hospital medicine had apparently not entered the twentieth century yet. My astonishment and concern vanished. Then I noticed something else. They were all wearing nursing caps. With nursing pins. Wow. I had heard about these things but had never actually seen them. I was now in the grits of nursing. I introduced myself and asked where I might find my grandmother. They told me. If I had been an axe murderer bent on putting geriatric patients out of misery, access to my Nana couldn't have been easier. What a crazy thought. I was just too tired.

I walked into the ICU Bay and saw my mother in a chair on the far side of my grandmother's bed. Above her head I saw a monitor with a continuous heart rhythm read-out. I sat by Nana's side and took her right hand in mine, leaned over her face, kissed her cheek and whispered in her ear, 'Nana, it's Jim, I'm here.' She squeezed my hand.

And she flat-lined. I think she was waiting for me to get there. It was an incredible experience. I walk in, take her hand, kiss her cheek, tell her I'm with her, she squeezes my hand and dies. I look at my mother and say to her, 'she's gone.' It must have sounded very strange and my fatigued brain seemed to echo the phrase.

Over the years I have had several patients, and more than a few nurses tell me similar stories. But when I think about that and how much I loved her, I have no words. It's like, whoa.....did she pass something to me that I didn't understand or was she simply saying I love you, goodbye. Wow.

Now on new topics, shit happens.

And it happens a lot to doctors and their patients, particularly in hospitals. And most especially in teaching hospitals. So presented here as carefully as I can are some instances of shit happening much like Osler himself might have recounted after a night getting pie-eyed in London's East End.

When we were JARs there was an intern named Bill Groh. Dr. Groh. There is a question as to whether Groh started life in dental school, but now he was definitely a HUP medicine intern and admitting at the VAH-spa. One night, one of my closest friends in the inner core, Tim Crowley, chief instigator, spots Groh walking down the hall with a set of pliers. Crowley asks him what's with the pliers and Groh said that he had admitted a patient to the ICU with unstable angina but the guy was also complaining bitterly of a toothache. Groh does an oral inspection and finds a dental abscess in tooth #22 (right lower molar). So, he breaks into the maintenance shop, takes the pliers and pulls the patient's abscessed tooth. The patient's toothache and chest pain immediately both resolve and Groh discharges him out of the hospital at midnight. Bill Groh would have done well in an HMO setting.

Most people are aware that one of the dangers of being an alcoholic was developing repeated bouts of hepatitis or inflammation of the liver. Eventually this could lead to cirrhosis of the liver which is a scarring process and liver failure as the result. Really any substance that inflames the liver repeatedly or continually can cause this: viruses, toxins, drugs. When the liver becomes cirrhotic, it doesn't function well.

The liver is a marvelous organ. Some people worship it and call it the seat of the soul. We call those people gastroenterologists.

This reminds me of a patient who was admitted to the VAH repeatedly with mental status changes. His liver was so far gone from booze that all he had to do was walk by a McDonald's kitchen vent and the smell from the kitchen would knock him out. Another admission for cirrhosis with obtundation due to protein exposure. We got why this patient couldn't understand the need to stick to an impossibly strict diet but his mother would ask us every single time he was brought in...'he just can't shake this thing.' No, dear, he can't quite shake it off.

I mentioned that we shared clinical responsibilities at the VAH-spa with the Medical College of Pennsylvania or MCP. But they always seemed to have more admissions than the HUP service. I already mentioned the social security alterations but there was another way one of our class tried to unbalance the number of admissions to the two different services. If a patient was brought in unconscious, which happened a lot, an un-named

JAR from our group would put a few drops of a dilating agent into one of the eyes of the patient, giving the impression of what we call a 'blown pupil' indicating some catastrophic event in the brain. HUP had no neurology service at the VAH, so acute neurologic problems always went to MCP neuro. Osler might have laughed if he was drunk enough but Fred Plum would not be happy. Disclaimer needed: Osler was not a drinker except when he was spending time in Canada, or Boston, but I have made him a party guy in this chapter because it seemed to fit. Wouldn't you like to head out into the London night for a rare bit of chicanery with Sir William Osler. I sure would.

Long after I had left my HUP residency and was solidly and stolidly in private practice, I got a call from the Chairman of Medicine for the HUP service at the VAH-spa. What was his name? This is one of the reasons it can be a challenge writing a memoir when you are 74. Of course, there isn't much to write about if you are 34. I had a long and odd relationship with this doctor from the West Philadelphia VAH. The best way to describe him is that he was the walking embodiment of a nerd. If you close your eyes and imagine your version of what a nerd looked like that was him. But he was smart and pleasant and, in no way, narcissistic. He would take morning report at the VAH when we were JARS on service there and did a decent job. But he had a way of irritating everyone in my class of residents and we weren't shy about radiating our feelings. He was a kidney specialist and his research somehow connected to frogs and toads, so he thought decorating his personal conference and office rooms with plush or plastic versions of frogs and toads was a super-neat idea. We thought that the idea coming from a 58-year-old Professor of Medicine was nerdy. This one day, the discussion at morning report regarding a patient who was presented became somewhat heated and our Chairman suddenly looked at us and asked why we were giving him such a hard time. This shocked all of us and most of us were at a loss for words. But not me. (Just remembered his first name....Irwin. Yes! Neocortex intact.)

I looked directly at Irwin and said, 'the reason we are giving you a hard time is that we don't like you.' There was no audible gasp or laughter or anything. Just silence. You could say that my filters had failed me. I thought that the situation had come to one of those occasional critical points that required an unusual injection of 'The Truth.'

Then, after a dramatic pause, I continued. 'Irwin, I can only speak for myself, but my guess is that none of us don't enjoy not liking you. We want to like you. We want to be your friend and colleague. But you are going to have to pay more attention to how you relate to your house staff, and we will have to pay more attention to how we relate to you. A good start would be to put away most of these fake frogs and toads. You can leave one or two on your desk that are your favorites, but it's hard to take you seriously when you've got 30 or 40 of these things collecting dust.'

Suddenly, everybody was talking at once, and Irwin Singer MD (now I have his last name as. well) was right in the middle of the conversation and enjoying it

immensely. From that point forward, Professor Singer became part of the team. He was happier, we were happier, our mutual relationship was more productive.

And just to prove we really meant it, morning report ended that day when a gentleman waiting outside for a meeting with Irwin to begin, suffered a cardiac arrest and we all went out and resuscitated him successfully and got him comfortable in the ICU which was across the hall from Irwin's office.

I bet you feel like you are part of our team now, as well.

But I got distracted from telling you why Irwin Singer called me at home one-night years later when I was in private practice. Apparently, the VAH-spa was being sued by the relative of someone who had died on the neurology service around the time I was a resident at HUP. The patient was being cared for by the MCP neuro service as I have previously mentioned but for some reason the HUP internal medicine service was rounding on the patient as well because of a multitude of complications. The MCP neurology resident had basically never seen the patient who was in the hospital for months. Once the lawsuit was filed, this MCP doctor had pulled the medical record and written short notes in between the HUP resident notes. That is, he made up stuff and briefly noted them long after the patient had succumbed to his illnesses. This fails the doctor ethics test. During the prolonged admission, my name was in the chart two or three times when I had gone to see the patient, probably because I was on call and a nurse had requested my presence to restart an IV or whatever. Irwin was emmeshed in this lawsuit and wanted me to review the medical record so I could provide him with some insight about the case.

My response was carefully couched in deeply thought feelings and personal accountabilities. 'Irwin, uh, no. I don't have time to do that. Nor do I have a responsibility to do that. Sorry, can't help you.'

I was the seventh resident he had called without any satisfaction. And because of our little therapy session at morning report way back when, he knew this wasn't personal. It was simply, The Truth.

Moving on, there was a singularly weird move by one of my closest friends with a patient who was brought to the HUP RW unconscious and with many of the outward signs of being homeless, addicted, jaundiced, toothless and food deprived. And, without having had a shower for several days; or weeks. One of my buddies working the RW that night knew that Dr. Groh, of dental fame, was admitting. He took an indelible ink marker and wrote in capital letters, GROH, across this patient's forehead, just in case anyone became confused as to who was going to take care of the patient. The nurses were extremely unhappy with this behavior and even as confused as I can be, I thought we had gotten past this level of immaturity. My JAR friend accepted the nurses' admonishments, but he never apologized for what he felt was an honest mistake in protocol.

Speaking of this particular JAR, there is an interesting story involving me that I would like to share.

During that year, the Philadelphia General Hospital (PGH) closed its doors for good and that was on the same day I took over JAR responsibility in the HUP MICU. Remember that the two interns worked 8 am one day to about noon the next day admitting all patients, while I, with my outstanding sub-intern, who's name I believe was Kate and who was at the top of her class, spent the month with me admitting patients from 1 pm until the next morning at 8 am. Her rotation with me that month reflected the trust our Program Director, Larry Beck MD, placed in my intensive care skills. Very little, apparently. He wanted to make sure I had a sidekick who knew what she was doing so she could keep me and our patients out of trouble.

Well, the combination of the PGH being shuttered and my occasional bad luck combined to create the largest influx of patients into the HUP MICU that they had ever seen. A medical service at HUP on a nursing unit with two interns and a JAR might admit 4 or 5 patients during a day and night on call to a medical floor and never more. The MICU would admit a bit less but with a higher grade of problems. There were 11 beds or what we call MICU Bays at HUP during my time there. Not very many.

Every morning JARS would meet with Dr. Relman to present the patients admitted the previous 24 hours at a fun conference called Morning Report. The presentations were brief and this lasted a bit more than an hour. It was fairly early in the day, so everybody was energetic. And I must add that Bud Relman was a serious guy, obviously, but he did have a sense of humor. Which I will get to in a minute.

After my first night on call in the HUP MICU and no longer having the protective barrier of the PGH next door, my sub-intern and I admitted 18 patients. You might ask, if the ICU only had 11 beds, how could you admit 18 patients. And these were new patients so when they were admitted, those 11 beds were already taken. Now that's 29 patients who required ICU care. So, I sat alone for 15 minutes and tried to remember all the engineering stuff that I had learned from my classmates during that two semester organic chemistry course that I ace'd because none of those engineering students wanted to be there and they spent some of their time boring me with their engineering know-how. Then I gathered up my sub-intern Kate and the head nurse and ran through a list of ideas: of the patients in a bed currently, who could be discharged to a floor bed using fairly loose criteria and get adequate nursing care. Four, sounds good, move them. Giddy-up, rawhide. Eighteen admissions minus 4 discharges equals 14. Now we had 14 to admit to a non-existent bed, most of whom were still in the RW. That prompted a call to my medical JAR in the RW. Send the sickest four up in twenty minutes and see if any of the others can be held overnight in the RW or admitted to a floor unit bed with some adaptations. That yielded three more patients kept in the RW overnight. Good. Move 'em, move'em, rawho.

Now my valuable time was interrupted by a committee of admitting interns and a few residents who were complaining that their evening was being interrupted by my ICU management. Oh really? I huddled with the nurses in the ICU. Could we get gurneys and line them up end to end in the MICU against the wall opposite the bays? Yes, we could do that. Maybe not safe, but we could do it. And could we have patients on those gurneys hooked up to IV poles and heart monitors. Theoretically. Good. Let's do it and see how it works.

We needed to place 11 patients. By doubling the capacity of the MICU with the gurneys we had places for everybody. Another huddle with nursing. Could they upstaff the MICU out of nowhere because all these new patients were going to need orders from me and my sub-intern Kate. Always liked that name.

If I hadn't said it earlier, nurses are a doctor's best friend; and a patient's special best friend. Yep, we'll pull nurses from floors to cover all these patients. Then I took Kate (I hope that is her name) to the on-call room to calm her down and get her to buy into the plan, my plan, which I hadn't thought of just yet. This is what I told her:

'Kate, we are in an emergency situation, so we are going to forget everything you learned in medical school to this point, and we are only going to pay attention to each patient's immediate needs. No need to take an exhaustive history and physical, write a beautiful admission note and a full set of orders. It doesn't matter if they aren't seen by a social worker tomorrow. We want to know why they were admitted, which we can find by glancing at the RW record, what meds they take, what med allergies they might have, and what their chief complaint is. Then we assess: fluid and electrolyte needs, IV's, blood products, medication orders, cardiovascular stability and acute abdominal situations. Finally fever and infection. Don't worry about diet, nutrition, multivitamins. If you have a question, interrupt me and I will answer you succinctly. If you have an idea, tell me quickly. Write orders and move on. You start at that end, and I will start at this end and we will move toward each other. I need to know right away about hypotension, rhythm disturbances, acute MI's,

538

hypertensive crises and potential surgical intervention. And Kate, if we can move any of these patients to a surgical service, let me know and I will make it happen.

We got through the night. Nobody died. I walked into Morning Report, sat next to Bud Relman at the conference table and laid out 18 index cards with our admissions from the past 24 hours as if I was playing solitaire. And that is how the month went, although we got much better at the engineering part and had only occasional patients that had to be treated in the hallway.

But there is another connected story that is worth telling and it has to do with an ambulatory clinic that served as a pressure release valve for the RW. It was staffed by a single JAR and no nurse as I remember. When patients came into our RW, they got a quick once over by a triage nurse and if they appeared to have a minor problem (urinary tract infections, gonorrhea, sinus infections) they were sent to the ambulatory clinic to be seen and treated by the JAR that day. Well on the day I am thinking about the JAR was my friend Tim Crowley. And he delivered care efficiently and expertly until he got to one specific patient. This was a fiftyish Black man with no medical history who was standing in the checkout line at a local ACME supermarket where he was purchasing his lunch. While waiting to pay, he developed some chest pain which was hard to describe, which he had never had before, and which resolved in less than five minutes. That was the whole story. Crowley wanted him admitted to the MICU as a patient with unstable coronary disease. He called me and while I gave Tim a hard time for appearance's sake, I accepted the patient. This is during our PGH crisis month in the MICU, so giving up a bed for a soft admission was a tough call. But I had enormous faith in Tim's judgement, or in this case, hunch. The patient went to one of my interns

540

who went ballistic on me. How could I let Tim Crowley admit this nothing of an admission and take one of our precious beds. My intern had a point. But I wasn't going to back down now. I had faith in Tim and I was supporting the admit. 'Listen,' I said, 'put him to bed, rule out a heart attack (MI), keep him comfortable and we will discharge him tomorrow from the ICU.'

Of course, this patient was on a monitor so we had continuous readings of his heart rhythm and his heart rhythm was a perfect normal sinus rhythm until 3:12 am when he went directly from normal sinus into ventricular fibrillation (a heart non-rhythm which rapidly deteriorated to death) from which my interns successfully resuscitated him and put him on a drug to prevent it from happening again. If he had been sent home, he would have died in his sleep from a lethal arrhythmia that nobody would have known about.

The next morning, I got to Morning Report early with an extended printed rhythm strip on this patient and starting at the door, taped it eye high around the room until I was behind Relman's seat where I stopped because it showed the sudden transition from a normal rhythm to V fib and the code blue and I tore off the strip where he resumed with his normal rhythm. Tim was there requesting all the accolades for his 'gut' instinct that something really bad was wrong with this guy and as a result we saved his life. The man was thoroughly worked up including a heart catheterization and he had diffuse severe coronary disease not amenable to surgery other than a heart transplant which he did not get. He was treated as best we could with anti-arrhythmic medications and discharged and I never found out what happened to him. Probably nothing good.

The reason I like to tell this story is that it is an example of heuristic reasoning. Tim could not really tell you why he insisted the patient be admitted. There was something that tugged at his intuition and prior experience that pushed him to insist. Nobody agreed with his decision, even me, but I was willing to buy into Tim's gut unexplained feeling. There is no research, no published guidelines, no computer derived meta-analyses, no carefully thought out algorithms that would have admitted that patient. But decision making in medicine is still partially an art and sometimes it is not a bad idea to go with your gut. Osler would agree, I'm sure.

Morning report could be very funny. There was a case admitted with Superior Vena Cava syndrome, an unusual problem in which the main vein returning blood to the heart after nourishing the body with oxygen would clot off, usually due to a tumor in the chest. Relman asked our group what the most common cause of this rare problem was when he was an intern. The JAR sitting next to me, Arnie Cohen, immediately responded, 'arrow wounds.'

I started this chapter with a personal story and I am going to end it with a personal story, although not one as mystical and wonderful as the first.

My mother lived to be 93. She lived alone in the home my parents built before my father died along with Pepper who my mother never wanted but stayed with her until 1978, 19 years. She never got another dog or cat. She worked into her seventies and traveled with group tours, usually accompanied by one woman friend or another. My brother who lived in Toronto for most of his career, would drive to Scranton to visit her and around holidays would bring her to Wilmington. I rarely went to Scranton. I talked to her once a week and if there were any family issues to discuss and she would call if anything upset her. Fortunately, she had a close circle of friends, which I find to be much more common in women than men as we age. I respected her and loved her but we weren't close. She was always aloof and never changed and I was, well, me.

Sometime around 1990, my brother Stephen brought her to visit Wilmington, perhaps for Thanksgiving. As was Steve's custom, he would stay for a few days in Scranton to visit with friends from high school who never left and take care of various issues that he kept active in the States. And he would check on mom's life as she was showing her age and many of her friends had passed. On this visit, he found that she hadn't paid any bills for months, let her car insurance lapse and had an unusually empty refrigerator and pantry which was not like her, particularly when Steve was going to be home. He was concerned but I wasn't surprised. I had a growing sense over the prior year or two that she was hiding her dementia but now it was threatening her safety and others as well. We tried to talk her out of driving to no avail although she promised to stay close to home and only take routes that were very familiar to her. That didn't satisfy me and I called her internist who I liked and felt looked after her well. He laughed me off and said he wouldn't do anything about restricting her driving license, even talk with her about it. Now that I'm 73 and often feel older, I understand why taking away someone's driving is really pushing them toward infinity.

I began to have conversations with Stephen about assisted living possibilities. As a caseworker for the State of Pennsylvania, my mother was very familiar with assisted living and nursing homes, and while she generally rejected the idea for herself, she was willing to tell us which assisted living facility she would prefer, just not yet. Meanwhile, I took over the job of paying her bills. Over the next six months, her dementia became progressively obvious and problematic. Sometimes, I thought the only phone number she remembered was my cell phone number. She would call me ten or twelve times every day, repeating the same conversation and this was when I was in private practice and actively seeing patients. Balancing my concern about mom and the pull of my practice and family was wearing on me and migraines that I had suffered through all my life were becoming much more frequent, prolonged and severe.

My conversations with Steve increased steadily about what to do. I was in favor of forcing the issue, he was reluctant. And neither of us singularly or together could have a rationale conversation with her about it. Even though we were discussing an assisted living environment that we had toured and was perfect, and that she had originally picked out as her preferred choice, now the possibility of leaving her home made her strike out in anger and I was the major villain in our family drama. Finally, I had it. I called Steve and told him I was arranging to move Mom to her preferred assisted living complex on a specific date in June. We would meet at home in Scranton the day before. I would drug her if necessary to calm her enough so she would accompany us. And here is what happened:

Steve and I met at our growing up home for a visit. We immediately got into a discussion with our mother about assisted living which she reacted to very angrily, though not violently. Then we decided to go out for Chinese food which was a favorite of mom's. We had a very nice, very calm dinner, went home and immediately started fighting again. It was remarkable.

When she went to bed, I gave her a small dose of lorazepam which is a benzodiazepine anti-anxiety medication which I felt would help her sleep. It did. The next morning, she awoke and got up to use the bathroom and immediately tripped and fell striking her head. Great. I may have contributed to the death of my own mother, the single parent who had made sure that I had a good start in the world. This certainly gnawed at my self perception as an Oslerian physician. What did the Hippocratic Oath say, 'primum non nocere...above all, do no harm.'

We took her to the hospital where she saw an emergency room doctor and had a CT scan of her head. Everything was okay and the same as the last time she came into the hospital ED for much the same reason. No change in the CT scan which showed multiple small strokes which likely occurred because she was non-compliant with her blood pressure medication and was a likely reason for her progressive dementia. So, I didn't kill my mother, but she was still quite calm and even sleepy. Steve and I carried her to the car and took her to the assisted living place and moved her into her apartment. By now, she was back to normal, the lorazepam had worn off, and we went down for lunch. Maybe it was working a bit even at that point because we had a very civil lunch.

Steve and I had planned to give her car as a thank you gift to a handyman named Joe who would check on mom periodically and fix anything that needed attention. We did that. Steve headed back to Toronto and I went back up to visit mom and see how she was doing.

The answer was quite well. She was enjoying her new surroundings, eating well and introducing me to her new friends. Her small apartment was cozy and already looked like her. During lunch she asked me how long she had been living there. I looked directly at her, without any hesitation, said, 'six months.' She looked back at me and said, 'I thought it was about that long.'

A little later she asked me where her car was and I told her that months ago she had given it to her handyman as a thank you gift. And she said, 'yes, that's right.'

My mother lived for two years in assisted living and both Stephen and I would visit her periodically. Her phone calls dropped back to once a week, usually originated by me. She looked healthier than I had seen her in a year or two. But her dementia was worsening and she started to fall. Her assisted living complex did not have the option of moving her to a nursing home environment or dementia unit, so we decided to bring her to Wilmington where I had her admitted to the Kutz Home, a Jewish nursing home with an Alzheimer's wing. That is where she spent the last year of her life. I tried to stop and visit three times a week for a half hour and was pretty good about keeping it up but she had no idea that I was there. She didn't recognize me or say my name. Or anybody's name. She was virtually mute, her brain withered and her body an empty shell. I brought my dog to visit but no luck with that either. Leslie would stop occasionally and my boys. No response. Once, one time only during that entire year, when I was talking to her with the hope of getting some response she called me Jerry, her brother and her best friend. It is the only thing that I hold onto now that she has been gone a long time.

I think I have been unfair to my mother in some ways. What I took as her being aloof was partly stubbornness. She was stubborn to the end. Leslie and I were on vacation in the Outer Banks off North Carolina and on our last day, I got a call from the Kutz Home. They felt my mom was infected. She was running a slight fever and her urine looked dirty. Should they take her to the ED or have a doctor see her? Mom had been in hospice care for five months and that's who I told them to call. The Hospice nurse. No one else. And we would be there the next day, which we were. It was apparent to me that my mother was likely septic from the urinary tract infection which meant that the bacteria was seeding her bloodstream, and this would likely end her life. Two weeks later she was still alive but barely. Her sepsis progressed at a snail's pace even without any treatment at all including fluids and nutrients. I was there every day. The last five or six days she had a barely detectable blood pressure, a heart rate around 30 and deep sighing respirations about once a minute. While sitting there, you would say, this is it, when she would take another breath. She fought death to the very last second. But maybe to spite me, she died peacefully twenty minutes after I left her side that day. May her memory be a blessing......

Chapter 23

Private Practice

"Nobody Knows You When You're Down and Out"....Derek and the Dominos...from Layla and Other Assorted Love Songs 1970

Three years and eleven months since my first day of practice working for Russ MD PA and I was not an equal partner as per our agreement. I was still being paid a salary no longer commensurate with my accounts receivables, which were neck and neck with Russ's and, of course, I had no authority. The practice was clearly Russell's.

I decided it was time to re-consider my relationship with Russ and what I was doing in this practice. Russ was decidedly no mentor. I wouldn't consider him a friend, either. He was a competent clinical rheumatologist, but not a rock star. His reputation in the community was purely based on being the first one to practice rheumatology in Wilmington. I felt okay with him covering my patients, but our relationship was not fun...and I wanted a partner who was fun, plus smart, plus interesting, plus communicative, plus fair. Russ was none of these things in large measure.

In considering these factors, I felt badly because Russ had baggage. He had dealt with family illness. But more recently, he had dealt with the strangest lawsuit I had ever heard of, let alone seen. And even though it was another rheumatologist in town suing Russ for what amounted to restraint of trade, no other prominent and wise physicians in the community could do anything to reach a compromise or settle the dispute which was doing nothing to help the cause of medicine in Delaware.

There are too many bizarre elements to this legal jeopardy for me to re-litigate from my memory all the peculiarities involved. So, I will just say this civil lawsuit came to a trial, featured my old friend Vince Poppitti as the judge, involved famous and well-heeled attorneys on both sides, lasted six weeks, made the first page of the Wilmington News-Journal for four weeks, involved roughly 25 complaints of conniving by Russ to prevent the plaintiff rheumatologist from building his practice, and the jury found for Russ in all but one minor accusation which didn't merit any award. There were twelve co-conspirators of which I was one but none of us were named in the lawsuit. Somehow, I felt dirty being named a co-conspirator. Thank God I wasn't a defendant. Particularly since I hardly understood what was going on that resulted in this craziness.

Defeated, but unbowed, the other guy went back to California from where he came. This debacle was what Russ was recovering from as I pondered our future relationship.

When doctors start a private practice, they tap all resources to take a stab at what practice income they would be content and what their practice expenses are likely to be so they can gauge their personal income. You would think this is easy but it's not. Since I was pretty sure that I was going to be plenty busy, and I wanted to make a middle-class income but had no allusions that I would get wealthy as a rheumatologist in solo practice, if I could get over my guilt deserting Russ, I thought we would be fine...we being my family.

As an aside, there are actuarial tables that list the salaries of rheumatologists and all other specialties of physicians, but these reflect employed physicians and not entrepreneurial private practice docs. Who employs physicians and gives them a salary?

Hospitals, insurance companies, HMO's, corporations and in exotic locales, like California, very large multi-specialty physician groups. More recently, venture capitalists.

In May, 1984, Russ came to me with a new proposal. I wouldn't be an equal partner but rather a 49% partner. And he would be a 51% partner. To me, that meant that every practice decision in dispute would be made by Russ: salary, bonus, benefits, hiring, firing, everything. Plus, Russ wanted me to pay him an amount in cash equal to my current accounts receivable in order to become a 49% partner. This is after he had made a good deal of money from my efforts over the previous 4 years. Alright, so we can add hard-nosed businessman to the list under Russ.

I told him this was new and I would have to think about it. And I had a little think about it. And I discussed it with Leslie. Now I have suggested that I knew what I was getting into becoming a rheumatologist regarding income and I was good with that. I would not have the disposable income like a cardiologist or orthopedic surgeon. Leslie and I were both good with that.

Now I thought about Russ' personal life which included a big house in a ritzy gated neighborhood equipped with its own swimming pool and a tennis court and a new Jaguar sedan in the garage. Russ's math and my math were not the same math even considering that I was lousy at math. Maybe he or his wife had family money, but I didn't think so.

There comes a point where what you want to happen and what happens take divergent paths. My romance with Natasha would be a cogent example. This was one of those times. I told Russ I was leaving. He was on his own, but I hoped we could be good colleagues, continue to cover each other, and work collaboratively as much as possible. I think he was shocked. The only thing he asked me was whether the lawsuit had been the reason. This was a fair question. It wasn't and I told him so in no uncertain terms. And that was totally true. My reasoning was more damning than the lawsuit. At least in my mind.

In the end, one thousand patients signed a release for their charts to be sent to my new office which was pretty much all my patients that I continued to care for over the previous 4 years. Not a bad way to start again. I give Russ a lot of credit here because he didn't complain but rather facilitated the transfer of records and maintained a somewhat cordial attitude toward me. I was asked by some of his physician friends whether the lawsuit had poisoned the well for our practice to which I simply answered no and that was accepted. Everyone wanted the infamous lawsuit to be forgotten. Almost immediately, my schedule book was full and I was off and running, Osler at my side. The more Osler seemed to haunt me, the more he reminded me of that microbiology professor at CUMC who kept me company over coffee before fading into the crowd of students and staff. Funny, I never saw that prof again.

Every doctor has a different style in the office. This was mine. My patients, for the most part, had arthritic problems and often had emotional and psychological issues to accompany them. Rather than have my nurse take them to an exam room, check vital signs, have them change into a gown and wait for me sitting on a table, I would go into the waiting room with the chart of the next patient saying hello to people as I entered and watch my next patient transfer to standing and walk towards me. I would shake their hand and often put a reassuring hand on their shoulder. Then we would walk back to the exam room together, with me reading their body language. By the time we were in the exam room, I already knew a lot about the day's visit. I didn't ask them to put on a gown unless it became appropriate. I would check vitals and sit in a chair opposite them and ask an open-ended question, my eyes on theirs. 'What brings you in today?' 'Are those knees slowing you down?' 'Is your energy level improving?' These questions allowed the patient to set the agenda for describing the chief complaint.

I always thought that an office visit had three components: 1. What the patient needed to tell me; 2. What I needed to know, like medications and med side effects; and 3. General schmoozing about the grandkids, the job, the family, the local sports teams. These elements re-established the doctor-patient relationship and got the critical information on the table, with me recording in a kind of shorthand.

Then the patient would transfer to the exam table, and I would go through a total joint exam and check anything else that needed checking. 'You have a new cough, let me listen to your chest.....under your t-shirt.

The visit would end with any change in the patients' meds, exercises or diagnostic tests that needed to be done and any questions the patients had.

As you are reading this, you might be saying to yourself, that is an awful lot of stuff to cover in the course of a fifteen minute visit. And it is. But as a physician who knows their patient and is focused during the visit, and has developed a level of trust with the patient, it can be done easily. It can also be easy to fall behind, and I hated doing that. My patients had busy lives and part of my job was to keep them busy so I didn't want to waste their time. Plus, I liked having twenty minutes to catch my breath and have lunch.

Sometimes, a fifteen-minute visit was insufficient. A death in the family. A child arrested for drugs. A planned surgical procedure. There were some tricks that could be applied to catch up, like taking the history while doing the physical. Or skipping lunch.

The most difficult patient to fit into the schedule was the new patient. An unknown. These patients fell into several different categories, and discovering which category would help me decide how the rest of my day would go. I was a committed Oslerian, so I would take a complete history from the patient during their first visit. This paid various dividends. It helped establish a relationship of trust with the patient which would save time later and in subsequent visits. It provided valuable clues as to the emotional state of the patient and other problems that could have a bearing on diagnosis and treatment.

I have noticed that over time the complete history has been relegated to filling out a checklist in the waiting room or sometimes at home before leaving for the doctor's visit. And I have noticed that the complete history has been reduced to the history restricted to the organ system which falls under the subspecialist's purview, like a gynecologist or gastroenterologist. And I have noticed that the vital signs are taken by a nurse technician or assistant, and not an RN, who also reviews the current meds and makes changes in the electronic chart to update the med list which now means entering changes into a computer that anybody in the entire community of practitioners has access to when you are in their care for an emergency, for example. Inputting the wrong meds could prove costly because in an emergency, the computer becomes truth. And I have noticed that the entire history of the presenting complaint is often taken by a nurse via zoom or over the phone prior to the doctor's visit. If this doesn't sound familiar to you, it will. This is all in the name of progress.

Excuse my skepticism, but it is all in the name of time and money. Doctors are paid for documentation, diagnosis, and treatment. The evolution I describe reduces the time the patient spends with the doctor. The doctor can see more patients and bill for more patient visits and maybe even for a higher level of service with all that documentation going on by the patient, the office staff, the nurse technician and the RN.

Reading this may make you angry at the money-grubbing doctor. It shouldn't. Both you and the doctor are victims in this social evolution of medicine. Often, the physician is on salary and is being managed by executives of corporations that are demanding greater and greater productivity from the doctor. He may not want to practice medicine this way, but he may have no choice. And the scariest thing of all is that the doctors' bosses may be corporations that have no mention of healthcare in their mission statements, or worse, may be venture capital groups.

So, what is lost in all this. I have already described it. The joy of practicing medicine is lost. The wonder of developing a trusting relationship with another human being in which the physician can use their knowledge, skills, and experience to diagnose, cure and heal the patient. I was determined to structure my own practice so that I did not lose that joy. And I was mostly successful.

When you practice like I did sometimes you are rewarded in strange ways.

I treated a patient who had moved from Pakistan with her husband, and she had mild rheumatoid arthritis. Since she spoke no English, we had to work out a simple regimen that would control her disease and would be safe for her and we could communicate about with some success. She had family back home and would go to visit them every few years for six months at a time. This one time she returned and made an appointment to see me and I found things to be under control. She thanked me and started to leave, but just as she opened the door to exit the exam room, she stopped, turned and asked if she could talk to me. Sure. What she wanted to show me was an inflammatory breast cancer which had eroded through the skin under her left breast. I nodded and explained as best I could what this meant for her and then walked her across the hall to a friend who was an excellent breast surgeon collaborating with the Christiana Care Cancer Center. He took over and much to my satisfaction she was cancer free years later. She hadn't shown that to her family doctor who hadn't examined her during their visit earlier in the week and she didn't have an OB-GYN doc. She trusted me enough to bring what she knew must be a problem to me.

I encouraged colleagues to send their difficult patients to me; difficult because the diagnosis was uncertain and difficult and because the patient was, well, difficult. As a result, my practice was full of patients with auto-immune diseases, rare multi-system diseases and, as a balance, routine degenerative arthritis, bursitis and problems like carpal tunnel syndrome. While it lengthened my days and nights, I cherished the hospital consultations for these were sick patients and often the diagnosis proved elusive, and the treatment had been purely empiric (eg. antibiotics for a fever without a clear infectious process.) For those situations, I could go into full Alan Myers mode.

Perhaps several examples are in order. When I saw a hospitalized consultation, I changed my routine slightly. First, I would review the hospital chart including the nursing notes, vital signs charting, physician notes and diagnostic studies. Then I would go into the patient's room, introduce myself, sit down

571

and go through the entire history again in pure Oslerian fashion. The history will give you the diagnosis 90% of the time and a thorough examination will increase that to 95%.

This patient was a 22 year old woman who had been healthy all her life until she developed high fevers ever day around dinner time, peaking at 104 degrees. With the fever she had severe headaches, sensitivity to light and sound and a very stiff neck. She was admitted with suspected meningitis and while her spinal tap did show some changes of meningitis, no organisms could be found in the microbiology lab. She was seen by excellent specialists, particularly in infectious diseases and neurology. By the time I was consulted she had 3 or 4 spinal taps and the results were always the same and blood tests were uniformly normal except for some indication of inflammation in her system.

I found her lying in bed, the room darkened and a cold compress on her forehead. Her exam was normal. I asked her if we could perform a simple experiment and she agreed. I took the blunt end of my pen and printed my first name on her abdomen. The impression made by the pen rapidly faded. Then I covered her belly with her hospital gown and told her I would be back in 5-10 minutes and she shouldn't look at my 'experiment'. I knew that her doctors had asked me to see her because they wanted to start her on a corticosteroid medicine, prednisone, but she didn't want to take it. I went back into her room, and we uncovered her abdomen. There was my name, Jim, in red letters surrounded by a pale border. I told her that this was called a Koebner phenomenon and was typical of a form of Juvenile Rheumatoid Arthritis called Still's Disease. Despite occurring mostly in children around six years of age, it also occurred in young adults her age and older adults in their fifties, and nobody knew why. She would recover but I thought I could resolve her meningitis and fever with a form of aspirin that wouldn't upset her stomach and she wouldn't have to take prednisone. I prescribed a non-acetylated salicylate in high dose and the next day she felt great. No fever. No headache. She went home. I followed her up in the office and tapered her off the salicylate and she had no recurrence.

Not every hospital consult was this easy, but it proves the point that you could apply the finest health care to a problem, still not have an answer, but traditional internal medicine applied by the right specialist could yield the desired result with nothing more than a bic pen as the diagnostic instrument of choice.

One more hospital consult, because they are so much fun. A young man in his thirties was transferred from the hospital in Dover, DE to Christiana Care for progressive kidney failure. He had an odd history in that he was admitted in Dover with fever and enlarged lymph nodes in his mediastinum (the space between the lungs and under the sternum near where the heart sits.) The doctors in Dover biopsied the enlarged lymph nodes and the pathology report was consistent with sarcoidosis, a benign disease which is fairly common and which didn't explain why his kidneys were not working well. They started him on prednisone in high doses empirically. Empirically sometimes translates into 'just because,' in this case just because prednisone is used for some cases of sarcoidosis. Because of his kidney issues he was transferred to Wilmington to our flagship hospital where he was seen by a gaggle of the best specialists we had, all of them close colleagues and friends of mine. They couldn't figure out what was going on. Someone suggested that they ask me to see the patient. Couldn't hurt. Why not. I reviewed the medical record and walked into his room where I found a 'good old boy and Dallas Cowboy fan'. I hate the Cowboys, being an Eagles fan. We bonded immediately. We sat and talked about his work, his family, his history, how he felt, what the likelihood of the Cowboys going to the Super Bowl again might be. By the time we finished talking I knew what was wrong with him and why my mates didn't get the diagnosis. I thought in this case it was only a rheumatologist who would get things right. He had subtle but definitive skin changes of progressive systemic sclerosis or, by its shortened name, scleroderma. Nobody had asked him if he had Raynaud's phenomenon which these patients always have....a problem where the fingers and sometimes the toes, ears and nose blanch white with cold exposure. But what was really confusing to my colleagues was that his kidneys were getting worse by the day. Scleroderma kidney disease is very real and often progressive just like his was. But these cases were always associated with severe high blood pressure and an unusual anemia called microangiopathic hemolytic anemia which could be diagnosed by reviewing a smear of the patient's

576

blood...but he didn't have high blood pressure and he didn't have an anemia. What was going on, my friends wanted to know. I told them that he had been on prednisone and for reasons that are unclear, patients with scleroderma treated with prednisone did not develop the hypertension and anemia that accompanies scleroderma kidney disease. I also told them that we should move him to the ICU and start him on an anti-hypertensive that blocks an important enzyme for the kidney called angiotensin and this would likely reverse his kidney failure.

They didn't believe me. I couldn't blame them. They were good. Really good. What I was telling them didn't make a lot of sense plus their experience with this was roughly zero or maybe less. They had the courage of their convictions and, like me, they felt they had taken an Oslerian approach to this patient's illness. Except they hadn't cured him. So, we reached a compromise. We moved him to the ICU and started him on an angiotensin inhibitor.

577

The nephrologist did a kidney biopsy which I felt was unnecessary and the infectious disease doctor ordered very specialized antibody tests specific for scleroderma. I told him that only 35% of patients with scleroderma would demonstrate these autoantibodies but when they were positive, it was almost diagnostic of scleroderma. However, a negative test told us nothing but doing it was harmless compared with the renal biopsy which was fraught with peril. This reveals one of my biases. As an Oslerian, I intensely disliked making a diagnosis based on only laboratory findings. They added less than 5% to the diagnosis.

In the end, the scleroderma antibody test was positive, the renal biopsy, showed classic changes of scleroderma in the kidney, the kidney function returned to normal, the prednisone was discontinued, the patient was discharged with follow up in my office, and everybody was happy except for me.

I didn't understand why he had sarcoidosis on the biopsy of his mediastinal lymph nodes. I called my friend Sergio Jimenez MD at Jefferson Medical College who had once been HUP faculty with Alan Myers and asked him whether he knew of a relationship between scleroderma and sarcoidosis. Sergio told me that it had never before been reported in the medical journals or textbooks, but that he had collected five patients that had both diseases presenting at the same time and could I send him the slides and the medical records. Sure. Months later he called me and told me that he was publishing his six patients with sarcoidosis and scleroderma and my name would be on the paper as a principal author. Now I was happy as well. I was always committed to a tiny bit of research, wasn't I? Of course, now we knew that both diseases sometimes occurred together but not why that should be.

Sometimes I admitted patients to the hospital. I just told you about two consultations in the hospital where I looked like a hero, but I didn't feel like a hero. These were sick patients who I was diagnosing, curing and healing. Just doing my job. This next story makes me look at best unlucky and at worst, just plain dumb.

One day in the office, I got a call from the Emergency Room at Christiana Hospital, our flagship hospital between Wilmington and Newark where the University of Delaware campus sits. A nurse there told me that they had a patient lying on the floor of the waiting room acting out and insisting they make an appointment for her to see me in order that I treat her rheumatoid arthritis. Not every patient in Delaware is this odd. It seems she was a patient of a rheumatologist in Newark that was in my coverage group and who I was fond of, named Chris. I called him and asked for the story. He said that she was very difficult and they had frequent falling outs and I would be doing him a favor to take her on as a patient. This is not what you want to hear about a referral from a reasonable colleague. But I knew I was stuck and called the ER back and said, 'send her up'. She was not as difficult as advertised. In fact, she was peculiar personality wise but in a funny kind of way and the two of us hit it off. And she did have very bad rheumatoid arthritis which Chris was managing quite well. I made some slight changes to her meds and started to follow her. At some point she began to complain of lower back pain. Rheumatoid arthritis does not cause lower back pain. This patient was in her sixties, obese, physically inactive. Every human in her situation would have lower back pain at one time or another; it is the most common reason for a person to visit their family doctor in the US. And there was nothing unusual about her lower back pain. Now I see this patient in the office once a month to monitor her medication and RA and every visit she would mention that her lower back pain was no better. After about 3 months of listening to her complaint of lower back pain, I told her that since it wasn't getting better, I thought we should x-ray her pelvis and lower back. She agreed. Normally this patient would want me to treat first and work it up later, but this time she decided to be compliant with my plan.

The pelvis x-ray is done to view the hips, the sacroiliac joints and the symphysis pubis as well as the bone of the pelvis where cancer metastases go to sleep quite often. She had the x-rays done at the hospital, so I stopped by to look at them while I was there to make rounds on a few patients. Except it wasn't there.

It wasn't that the x-ray wasn't there. The pelvis wasn't there. It was just gone. Like she had been born without a pelvis or hips or sacroiliac joints or a symphysis pubis, which was obviously not possible. I found a radiologist and looked at the film with him.

He made some salient points adding up to the conclusion that she appeared to have a soft tissue mass which had resorbed the entire pelvis and she needed an MRI to further define the features of the anatomy. He suspected that this would prove to be a sarcoma which is a terrible diagnosis, in a terrible location. No, he had never seen a case of a missing pelvis. He laughed and went out to grab some coffee.

I was at a loss. I had ignored this patient's complaint of lower back pain for months while something was eating her pelvis and that something wasn't going to be friendly. I called her and arranged for her to be admitted. After the workup, which included a biopsy of the soft tissue mass, she was diagnosed with a rhabdomyosarcoma of the pelvis arising from who knows what tissue and eroding through the entire pelvic structure. By the time the cancer docs took a look, they said there was nothing to do except for pain control. Of course, her pain was getting worse now that she knew she had cancer, but truthfully the tumor was also getting bigger and eating into even more structures. A case like this at Memorial Sloan Kettering would be considered for pelvic exenteration, a radical approach in which the lower half of the body would be amputated in an attempt to extend life. Christiana Care didn't do pelvic exenterations, nor would I have permitted it.

Then the worst happened. Her tumor eroded through the skin of her buttocks and she had an open ulceration that the nurses had to attend to on a regular basis every day. And this just got bigger. We got all the help that was available from the surgical wound specialists, the physiatrists, anybody that could give us some advice. This gigantic wound smelled really bad and this resulted in two additional sad problems. We had to isolate the room from the rest of the floor by reversing air flow so the other patients could breathe. And the nurses on the unit hated me for months. I was the only doc involved in her case that was willing to go into her room to visit. Of course, she did not have a living will and wanted as much done as possible to keep her alive short of intubation and code calling. She survived like that for four months before she died of sepsis. This was a tribute of sorts to her nurses and a black mark across my name. Had I x-rayed her sooner would the outcome be different? I strongly think not but it's always better to stay ahead of a problem than lead from behind. I never forgot her, even after the nurses forgave me for admitting her.

When I started my own practice, I had no doubt that I would be busy. There was no strong competition and the other rheumatologists in Delaware were fine, but they took the attitude that they weren't interested in assuming care for sick patients. Their practices were full of osteoarthritis and shoulder bursitis and fibromyalgia. They hated going into the hospital. And they hated covering my patients because it was well accepted that I was happy to take care of systemic lupus erythematosus, scleroderma, polymyositis, dermatomyositis, Sjogren's syndrome and undifferentiated connective tissue diseases. And I was fine seeing all manner of vasculitis and undiagnosed multi-system diseases. My best consults came from the ICU. I was the Alan Myers of Delaware and my mantra and core values came from Sir William Osler: diagnose, cure, heal through exhaustive history and examination and follow-up.

What I didn't expect was that I would become too busy, beyond my own physical capacity to react when called upon. And it didn't take that long. When I started, I settled on office hours every day from 9am to noon, then 1pm to 4:30 except Thursday when I would start at noon and finish at 5. There were two conferences per week that I wanted to attend and sometimes give: medical grand rounds Thursday at 8am and a community lecture at the Delaware Medical Society on Tuesdays at 7:30am. These created blocks of time before and after office hours to see my patients who were in the hospital, hospital consultations and time after office hours to return phone calls, mostly to patients but also referring doctors who wanted to discuss our mutual cases.

Into this tight schedule, I had family responsibilities. I had a deal with Leslie that while the kids were growing and at home, I would be there for dinner every night at 6 pm and when necessary, I would go back after washing the dishes, which relaxed me. I kept to that promise. I had two sons almost 4 years apart in age, both of whom were very active: little league, soccer, basketball, tennis, band. I tried to attend everything and since I loved baseball so much, I coached little league for both boys over an 8 year period. That was a hoot getting from the office to the field. I also loved to swim and taught both of them to feel comfortable in the pool. During high school, I was at every football game for the band and every band competition on Saturday nights, not to mention symphony band, jazz band and assorted other concerts.

From my point of view, with no father around when I was growing up, I was doing a pretty good job of being a father to my sons. Leslie didn't agree. I was not doing good enough and she felt comfortable pointing out to me when I was failing my fatherhood responsibilities.

There were two patients who were very problematic because of the seriousness of their illnesses and both patients pushed me to the edge of my principles. Maybe that's incorrect. A more correct statement is that I was unhappy with the winding down of their care leaving me feeling empty and confused.

The first patient I will call Tammy. That, of course, was not her real name. I met Tammy in her early twenties when she developed arthritis and pleurisy which is a sharp chest pain with inspiration due to inflammation of the membrane covering the lung. After my evaluation, it was clear that she had lupus....systemic lupus erythematosus but her case on initial diagnosis did not appear to be severe. She responded to treatment and felt well. Eventually, she married and not long thereafter, became pregnant. I had discussed the relationship between pregnancy and lupus with Tammy and her husband, so they knew she would need to be monitored carefully during and after the pregnancy and I recommended she be followed by a high risk obstetrician as well. Lupus can have an unpredictable effect on pregnancy and vice-versa. She did well, however, and gave birth to a healthy baby boy without any indication that her lupus was more active. Everything was going well.

Two years later, I received an unexpected phone call from Tammy. She was in the Dover, DE hospital emergency room with a rash on her legs. I asked her if she felt well enough to come up to the Christiana Care ED and she said her husband could drive her. I met her there.

The rash was what we call petechial, tiny red dots, which usually mean a problem with platelets, one of the circulating elements of the blood which helps small cuts and tears of skin and connective tissue close and heal. A normal platelet count would usually be greater than 150,000. Tammy's platelet count was 7500. My initial thought was that she was having a flare-up of her lupus and had developed antibodies to platelets driving the numbers way down. However, there were no other symptoms or findings that her lupus was more active. Could she be pregnant? She didn't think so and she wasn't.

She had to be admitted because her platelets were low enough that she could bleed and potentially this could be life threatening. I admitted her to my service and started her on high doses of intravenous corticosteroids which was the initial treatment for this complication of lupus.

It was at this exact moment that I allowed my own arrogance or narcissism or stupidity or empathy or some combination of all these factors sway my decision about something that I would later regret all the way to my soul. The day this happened was the Friday of the beginning of the Memorial Day weekend holiday. I was on call for my coverage group and I was unusually busy, but it did mean that I would be in and out of the Christiana Hospital every day through Monday so I knew I would be seeing Tammy regularly. Across the physicians' area I saw a close friend and colleague of mine who was a hematologist and a specialist in platelets. He was talking to a cluster of residents vying for his attention and looked very overwhelmed. I started to write an order to consult him to see Tammy that night, assuming he was on call for the weekend like I was, but then thought better of it. I thought to myself that if I tucked Tammy in and started what I felt comfortable was a good treatment and saw her early the next morning, if I had a concern, I could consult him then and I would be sparing him another patient to see that evening without any harm being done to my patient.

Everything was going well the next morning except Tammy's platelet count was no higher on the steroids she had received overnight, which surprised me. Was something else going on? There was nothing in her history, exam or labs that suggested an alternative explanation. But now I thought I should send a request for a consultation to Phil, my friend. Except I had been wrong. Phil was not on call for the weekend. In his place was a pediatric hematologist who I liked personally but had much less faith in her experience with adults who had lupus. Her opinion was to continue   steroids, it was too soon to judge a response. She said the same thing on Sunday and Monday. I was back in my office early Tuesday morning when I got a call from Tammy's nurse. She was having seizures; her blood pressure was spiking and her kidney function was falling. I didn't take the time to say goodbye and hang up the phone. I was on my way to the hospital. On my way, my cell went off. It was Phil. He told me his group had discussed Tammy early that morning and they felt she had TTP: thrombotic, thrombocytopenic purpura. This is a very rare and often fatal condition that was only connected to lupus by a few anecdotal case reports. It had no universally successful treatment, but some patients seemed to respond to a procedure called plasma exchange. Tammy was on her way to the MRI machine. I asked him if he could arrange for the plasma exchange to be done in the ICU where a bed was waiting and I would meet her in MRI Imaging. I personally brought her up to the ICU and she was attached to the machine which was sort of like a dialysis machine and started plasma exchange. It was in vain. After twenty minutes, she coded and died.

I met with her husband and parents and explained everything that happened and what we now thought was the problem. Could we do an autopsy? I thought it was critical to understand what had killed their daughter and wife and the mother of her child. They agreed. Every organ in her body had classic histopathologic findings of TTP. Including her brain. I still have the slides.

Periodically I ask myself was I negligent in this case. I failed to diagnose her correctly, I failed to cure her and I had no chance to heal her, although I did have the chance to heal her husband and family and I did my best. It is too painful for me to think I was negligent since I felt I had a working diagnosis which fit the patient and I treated it correctly. I was wrong, because I had no experience with an alternative diagnosis which presented atypically. But you see, had I not been empathetic to my friend Phil and prevailed on him to see Tammy Friday night, and had he considered the diagnosis of TTP and we had started plasma exchange sooner, maybe the outcome would have been different. I didn't feel guilty, but somehow, despairingly, I did feel guilty. I also felt overwhelmingly sad. My patient had bad luck twice and I had not seen what was happening. When I finished talking with Tammy's family after her death, her husband asked me what I had learned. I told him that I had learned never to make assumptions no matter how clearcut the situation seemed and I thought to myself that TTP and it's very loose possible connection to lupus was now firmly cemented in my neocortex and would be part of my intuition and heuristic analysis in difficult cases with similar findings.

There was another intervening factor that weekend. I was incredibly busy, not just at Christiana Hospital but at all five of the hospitals in Wilmington. Even worse, one of the patients I admitted was a good friend who had developed an atypical pneumonia which proved to be due to a tumor obstructing his lower airway. He was cured of both the pneumonia and the tumor which was a low grade malignancy. So I was stressed and pre-occupied by too many patients.

There were many lessons from that weekend. Everything that happens is a teaching opportunity.

There was a second young woman who became my patient and she also had systemic lupus erythematosus. Sylvie was in her early thirties when I first met her and she had already been diagnosed with lupus. I put her through the process which you are by now thoroughly familiar and there was no reason to suspect anything but highly expressed lupus and she had the lab results to convince the most doubting skeptic. She had lupus in capital letters with the findings brought in and dropped at my nurse's feet by a gigantic grey wolf with eyes that glowed a feral yellow and enormous canines from which fell large drops of foamy saliva which stained the blue and white lab sheets the wolf carried in its jaws. The wolf's coat was smooth and a reddish brown. This was systemic lupus erythematosus, the red wolf that devours, named for the red rash that inflames the cheeks and face of its victims sparing the fold between the nose and the cheek. Fully expressed and powerful, it was terrible to behold.

But this wolf was biding its time inside Sylvie, teasing us with abnormal lab tests and mild symptoms and the incredible strength of the woman it had chosen to inhabit. With time it would make its presence felt for many of us, least among us, Sylvie herself.

Sylvie had three characteristics that make her memorable to those who knew her. She had the worst disease process I have ever seen. She was the most irrepressible human being I ever knew. And she never failed to wear something purple every day of her young life. For the period I was her principal physician, she was a graduate student at the University of Delaware although I can't remember her field of study even though she worked on her graduate thesis for all the years that I cared for her. She lived with a young man who must have been her lover because I don't think they ever married. Her favorite mode of transportation was her bicycle and, on occasion, a skateboard although by necessity she had to drive to her appointments with me. She had no children or pets. She loved pizza. And she was always happy regardless of what was happening around her or to her. She was fearless.

I remember the last chapter in her young life like it was yesterday. She came in with her partner convinced that there was something wrong with her heart or lungs because she had become very short of breath over the previous ten days. I thought I knew better, because what I noticed was the extraordinary pallor of her skin. I examined her, of course, before saying, 'I am going to put my bet on anemia.'

I was right. In private practice I was occasionally wrong but too often right. Her hemoglobin was 3.0. It was hard to believe she was walking around. Against her objections, I admitted her and this time I had my friend Phil see her straight off, for I had only on rare occasion ever seen a standing human being with a degree of anemia that severe.

Together, Phil and I discovered a treasure trove of lupus induced hematologic misery. She had anti-red blood cell antibodies blowing up her red blood cells; anti-platelet antibodies feeding her platelets to other suddenly famished blood cells; and a dangerous low level of neutrophils, the white blood cells that fight off infection. Initially, Phil posited that she had developed leukemia that was shutting down her bone marrow but this wasn't the case. Her loss of bone marrow derived blood cells was totally due to auto-antibodies attacking the stem cells from which the red cells, white cells and platelets were derived. We proved it in our laboratory and had it confirmed at a university research lab. I had never heard of this happening let alone saw it in a lupus patient.

We treated her with powerful drugs to turn off her immune response including prednisone and Cytoxan, which at best tuned down the problem. As if in anger, the red wolf created another challenge.

Sylvie came to me complaining of visual problems, small holes in her vision. I had her seen by an ophthalmologist immediately who took photographs for my chart of tiny infarcts in the retinas of both her eyes. She seemed to be going blind in small bite sized attacks. We discovered that she had a new enemy antibody, with the unlikely name of the lupus anticoagulant (now referred to as anti-phospholipid antibody and anti-cardiolipin antibody). While the lupus anticoagulant made it sound like it caused undue bleeding, it actually caused undue clotting. Originally the name was derived from the antibody's tendency to prolong those tests used to assess pharmaceutical anticoagulants like heparin which 'thinned the blood.' Her retinal infarcts were due to this class of pro-clotting auto-antibody.

I huddled with Phil. She was at risk for clotting anywhere. I told him that I was going to treat her with an anticoagulant in broad use in those days called coumadin in combination with baby aspirin. He reminded me that her platelet count was running about 10,000 and aspirin would poison platelets so she could bleed from that. I couldn't think of any other options: low dose aspirin and tight control of coumadin anti-coagulation. I explained the risks to Sylvie. She said, 'go ahead.'

It worked. The retinal infarcts stopped as judged by her visual dropouts and serial photographs of her retinas. She didn't bleed anywhere. But we weren't making any progress on her cytopenias, meaning her anemia and low white cell counts as we continually adjusted her steroids and Cytoxan and considered other cytotoxic and cytostatic therapies consulting with colleagues at the NIH and investigators in our fields around the country.

My nurse and I arranged for Sylvie to be granted her PhD slightly early since she was really finished with all but the defense of her thesis. She received it in a hospital bed when she was admitted with fever which turned out to be a false alarm. Despite having a full bore immune response run amuk, high dose immune-modulatory therapy, anti-coagulants in the face of severe thrombocytopenia, profound anemia; Sylvie continue to ride her bicycle and skateboard around the UD campus wearing her purple blouse or jacket or jeans or scarf.

Then the week before Thanksgiving, she spiked a fever and I admitted her. She had a cavitary pneumonia meaning an infiltrate on her chest imaging in the right upper lung field that was destroying lung tissue. Infectious disease consultation and radiology felt this was likely a fungal pneumonia, most likely invasive aspergillus fumigatus. This was going to be a terminal admission. I was slated to go to New York for Thanksgiving with my family and I had instructions from Leslie that I had better own up to my promise. But I was torn. Sylvie and I had been through a lot and I truly respected everything about this brave woman . But I didn't love her. I loved my family. I said goodbye to her on Thanksgiving morning and left for New York with my wife. Sylvie died that afternoon. Her family asked that I eulogize her at the funeral the following Sunday. I did.

Sylvie, may your memory be a blessing.......

This was the nexus point of adulthood for me: balancing the family demands while my sons were still at home and my practice demands for my patients. Both were growing at unreasonable rates and colliding at every opportunity. I already had high blood pressure but that was controlled with medications. Now I was beginning to note more frequent migraine headaches which went untreated simply because there was no good treatment. When I was working, I employed a trick to deal with them involving the mind castle in my brain, borrowed from Sherlock Holmes, whose creator was himself a physician, Sir Arthur Conan Doyle. I simply would sit alone for five minutes and place the headache and all that went with it into an empty room in my mind castle and lock the door on it, sequestering it away from my focus with the patients I still needed to see. You may think this sounds crazy, but it worked. At least for a while.

Now I found that the list of patients was growing longer and more acute. The wait for a new patient appointment to see me in the office was four months. I was getting daily calls from referring doctors about a patient they were sure had active lupus, a wife that insisted she would only see me asap, a nurse in the ED that had a painful swollen knee, a judge on Chancery Court with crippling arthritis who could no longer travel to Baltimore for his care. So, my carefully planned office hours were being hi-jacked by the demand. I found myself starting office hours at 7am and occasionally 6am, which was hours way before my staff got there and finishing up after 7pm but only after the boys were off to college. Leslie and I were becoming accidentally estranged by the hunger of my practice for my availability.

This was unhealthy. This was especially unhealthy for me.

What to do? After another call interrupting our dinner from a very good neurologist asking me if I could see his mother-in-law for atypical shoulder pain that wouldn't go away; this week; and it was Thursday night; and I agreed, I knew I had to make some changes. I washed the dinner dishes and retreated to my study. Leslie was already on the phone talking to her friend Leslie.

I turned off the overhead light and turned on the banker's light that only illuminated my blotter. I was surrounded by books that I loved to read, books and journals I referred to, the various flotsam and jetsam of my life: a baseball glove, several MLB baseballs, an old worn ball signed by Mickey Mantle, two bats, a hockey stick for a right wing, a bucket of pucks, an antique but broken coffee grinder bequeathed to me by a patient who liked to poke around yard sales. I focused on the banker's light and let my mind empty of the day's events. There is always a solution for every problem. I stared at the light. I flinched as a memory of Fred Plum whizzed through my brain. Then Jerry Posner replaced it. As brilliant as they were, both men offered no solace for they each had a lifestyle that fit their own philosophies and suited them, but neither worked for me.

607

Then a new picture came into focus of a younger version of me sitting alone in the MICU on-call room thinking how are we going to deal with this mess and stay true to my mantra, my values with a bit of flexibility built in. Then, in this mind picture, I found Kate and pulled her into the room, saying, 'listen, Kate, this is an emergency situation and I have an idea.'

There is always a solution. I reached for a blank legal pad that littered my desk and put it in the middle of the blotter grabbing a pen at the same time. And this is what I wrote:

Find a psychotherapist and start therapy.

Hire another rheumatologist.

Make new rules and stick with them that ease your schedule.

Eat lunch every day.

No coffee after 4 pm.

Buy Leslie flowers twice a month.

Discuss your headaches with your internist.

Feeling much better and more in control, I went to watch the third period of a hockey game. The Rangers won on a breakaway with less than a second on the clock as the puck crossed the goal line.

I found a therapist on the Main Line in Philly, a Penn PhD whose philosophy therapy-wise was eclectic. Her office was in an old home where she had an office on the first floor across the street from a parking garage. I ended up seeing her weekly for twelve years and that commitment of time and treasure was worth every penny. I learned a shitload about myself and my world and developed a huge toolbox to deal with problems. I wasn't the best patient she ever had. I never would consent to yoga classes or meditation. I think we worked well together, nonetheless. Her name must remain anonymous.

I got in touch with a physician who I liked very much when he was an internal medicine resident at Christiana Care. I knew he was doing a rheumatology fellowship and he was married to one of his co-residents and she was from Wilmington, so there was a good chance they would be coming back to practice. I asked him if he would want to work with me. He said yes. His name was Peter.

I held an office meeting and discussed phasing in some new scheduling tactics. The start time would be rigid at 8 am. The finish time would be rigid at 4 pm. No patients scheduled before 8 or after 3:45. No more than 3 new patients per day no matter how long the waiting list became. Hospital consultations would be seen within 24 hours but no guarantees for same day. I would take 30 minutes for lunch and the staff would not let me drink coffee after 4. Nan, my RN, would work with me to handle messages through the day rather than a whole pile of them at the end of hours. Any emergency visits to the office would be pre-screened by Nan.

I visited a flower shop that Leslie favored and arranged for her to get an arrangement twice a month. But I didn't go to my doctor about the headaches. I had had them all my life. It wasn't a tumor! What could they do.

The neurologist's mother-in-law turned out to have a pancreatic cancer that was invading her diaphragm over her liver (remember the diaphragm is that big muscle that does most of the work of breathing). A peculiarity of anatomy is that sometimes pain is referred to a spot where you don't expect it to be. Irritation of this muscle over the dome of the liver causes pain referred to the shoulder. No wonder it was confusing. She was my last Saturday office patient.

Things changed slowly as I knew they would but they did change. My office hours became more manageable, I was less irritable and less hungry, and I slept better at night. Even though it was more difficult to get an appointment to see me, especially as a new patient, nobody got angry and stopped referring patients or stopped coming to see me. They understood and they were good with it. And I was able to stay true to Osler: diagnose, cure and heal.

When Peter was to start, I sat him down and told him what I would like to do. He could agree or, if he didn't like it, he could start on his own and we could still be friends and work closely together. I told him in confidence about my conversation with myself regarding my failed relationship with Russ. I told

Peter that we would share my office with his name on the door, he would have his own private consultation room like I did, and we would direct as many new patients referred to me as possible to see him instead, plus, if I had 'stick-in' appointments, we would put them in his schedule. Those new patient appointments would become his patients. He would join the call group for nights and weekends with the other rheumatologists in town. We would practice as though we were partners.

But we wouldn't be partners. He would have his own practice legally which he could set up any way he saw fit. The two of us would make all practice decisions together from the start. I explained that at the beginning he would have almost no accounts receivables and he would have no salary. I would carry the practice costs all by myself so he wouldn't have any practice expenses. I expected but couldn't accurately predict how many months it would take for him to have accounts receivables and payments that would allow him to share the overhead. At that point, we would sit down and mutually decide what constituted joint overhead expenses that sounded fair to both of us and we could revisit this as needed. By the end of the first year I expected him to be pulling in enough cash to cover half of our mutual expenses and take a salary for himself. I gave all this to him at no cost. An opportunity to establish himself by working with me and showing his value to the community. I thought the first year might be tough for him but if he could tough it out, it would be worth it. And what did I get? Eventually lower overhead, less demand on my time, collegiality, fun, joy. He agreed it was a good plan. There was no other physician in Wilmington, DE that would give him a deal like that. Their attorneys and accountants were too greedy.

I told him one other thing. I owned the condominium which was our office. That meant that he would be paying me half of my mortgage since he was responsible for half the overhead, but he wouldn't be gaining any equity in the condo. So, if we were working well together after a year, I would sell him half of the condo at the going rate, and we would be equal partners in our office space. I didn't want there to be any reason that Peter would resent me for taking advantage of him financially. This arrangement worked for a dozen years, then he left.

Chapter 24

Marriage and Medical Practice

"I got something to say that might 'cause you pain

If I catch you talking to that boy again

I'm gonna let you down

And leave you flat

Because I told you before

Oh, you can't do that"....You Can't Do That...The Beatles, Hard Day's Night

They say that medical practice is like a marriage, and I suppose it's tempting to draw parallels. Both require compatibility, compromise, collaboration but only marriage encourages consensual sex. To me, it seems foolish to make a comparison because marriage is born in a spiritual chamber of family, religion, friends and the prospect of children. Medical practices that join two doctors are born from need as I have described in my case, but also can be born in the cauldron of profit.

While I have gone on quite a bit about my life, my search for the meaning of love, my understanding of human growth and potential, maturity and my profession, I have veered away from love. Except, perhaps, to mention that I remained confused and in

618

doubt about love between a man and a woman. And this despite having found a life partner that in full bloom I both loved and was in love with by the end of my SAR year.

Leslie seemed the perfect partner for me. I found her beautiful and sexy, intelligent and articulate, cultured and sophisticated. She looked smashing in a simple black dress. The dress seemed to survive our entire 36 years of marriage and never looked worn and never failed to fit and accentuate her figure. And she never failed to tell me that she got it on sale at a dry goods store for forty dollars. So, thrifty as well.

She was an exceptional cook. A chef, really. Just as I found doing the dishes a relaxing chore, Leslie would decide to make a modified new recipe mid-week to chill out. Drinking a glass of white wine with an ice cube in it, she came up with the most delicious dinner. Occasionally she would play a trick on me. One time she served unusually large, tender, stuffed lamb chops and when I asked why the lamb chops were so big and tasty, she told me without a hint of irony, 'that's because they are stuffed pork chops.' Aside from moo shu pork at a Chinese restaurant, I had never eaten pork before, and certainly not growing up in a Kosher home. I asked for them again, frequently.

That first year, when we were dating, and after I moved in with her and sublet my apartment to Smilin' Art, everything that I suspected regarding her sociability, her keen interest in art, movies, theatre, and cooking were confirmed. She had a natural affinity for people and made friends easily. I loved all that about her. We were both liberal politically and shared similar personal values. And we both wanted children. While our first pregnancy miscarried early, I remember the feelings I had when she called me to say she was pregnant again, the warmth that spread through me. We were living in Connecticut then but the baby, Michael, was to be born soon after our settling in our home in Wilmington. I was starting work and fatherhood at the same time and as confident as I can sound in this memoir, doubts pestered me as to whether I could succeed in my new world of private practice. Would I be able to support our family, send my kids to college and more if they wanted. I asked myself the uniquely American question, could I provide my children with more experiences and more opportunities than I had growing up.

Leslie settled into motherhood and typically for her found a small circle of new mothers which she adopted as friends. I could tell she was already looking outward to see how she could participate in the larger community.

We had a very warm house to live in which we bought from the original owners who were getting too old to manage a house. And we made it warmer by our presence and the birth of Michael. It lacked two things that summer. Air conditioning. And furniture. We did have a bed, kitchen table and chairs and, of course, Michael's room was fitted out. The air conditioning was a problem so one of the first things we did was to install central air conditioning. Wilmington enjoys hot, humid summers not dissimilar to DC. We took our time with furniture. In fact, consistent with our taste and principles, the first investment we made for our new home was artwork. Not a lot but a few things to put up on the otherwise bare living room walls. Eventually, over several years, things fell into place and our house was clearly our home.

Leslie and I were together for 38 years if you include our two years together before we got married. When I sit back in my chair and think about those years, they seem to naturally divide into thirds.

The first third, everything was new and exciting. We were meeting new people, my practice was growing, our house was becoming our home. We loved each other. I loved Leslie despite not really knowing what that meant exactly. I think she loved me. And we were, at times, in love with each other again just like in the Blythewood Pool. But life intrudes into a successful partnership creating turbulence. Our marriage was no different as I remember it.

The first tragic event in our lives was Leslie's next pregnancy. Michael was two years old. The pregnancy proceeded normally until, if memory serves me, about 35 weeks. Then the baby was becoming small for dates on ultrasound. 'No need for alarm,' said Les' obstetrician. But things got worse. Les had an amniocentesis and I hand carried the precious fluid to SmithKline labs in King of Prussia, PA to evaluate for signs that the baby's lungs were maturing normally. The results were equivocal.

When the baby was delivered by Caesarean Section, it was immediately obvious that the small boy had a serious genetic anomaly, trisomy 18, and incompatible with life according to our pediatrician, Howard Borin MD who Leslie and I considered to be next to God. The next day, I was holding my newborn son when he took his last breath and died in my arms. I went to tell Leslie, who was recovering from the C-section in a hospital bed. I was distraught. But Les chided me that I had no right to be so upset. After all, she reminded me, that she had carried the child for nine months and had nothing to show for it but a scar. She seemed angry with me, but I quickly decided that she was correct as usual. I was forgetting myself. My role here was that of the physician: diagnose, cure and heal. I had to be available to heal

624

my family. Leslie, of course, but I had faith in her strength, and there was Michael and how this change in our family course would affect him. And there were the grandmothers who needed my empathy. And our friends who would reach out and my family needed to be shielded if their concern became too intrusive. I loved her for her wisdom and her strength and quickly forgot my personal loss.

Even those you love can make mistakes. And because you love them, you always forgive them first and put aside any other reactions. This event went deep into my subconscious where I denied its existence for years. It only emerged during our first round of couples therapy late in the second third of our marriage, actually awakening me from sleep. I had buried it so deep that when I awakened having relived the scene in my dream, I wondered if it had really happened. By the next day, I was convinced it had. That awakening was the first time I recalled the events of my second son dying. I shared it at our next session and Leslie recalled the incident just as I remembered it. I forgave her, of course, but she never apologized. I'm not sure she needed to apologize. I can't begin to imagine the emotions that had to be pinging around her brain at that time. But as insignificant as I make that event sound now, it denied me the opportunity to mourn the loss of my son; and more importantly, it denied Leslie and I the opportunity to mourn the loss together. And it re-enforced in me the defense mechanism that had been so useful ever since my father died, burying raw emotions so deep that they cannot be felt, examined, mourned and placed in closure. That is the kind of thing twelve years of psychotherapy can unlock.

Michael was disappointed, Leslie recovered from her surgery, I went to work, and life went on, but something had changed for me and for Leslie. I know that I didn't realize it at the time, but I think the loss of that child was the beginning of a wall that was being built between the two of us. Very slowly.

Les will have to write her own memoir to learn what she feels about it. We went on and got pregnant again and that pregnancy gave us the joy of Craig, a totally unique and brilliant son in the best and truest sense of the word brilliant to complement Michael. I was at peace with our family. Leslie was not.

Emotionally, I came to suspect that Leslie didn't appreciate me as a life partner as much as I appreciated her. I was committed to our marriage and to our family so I found that possibility both sad and frightening. Worse, I would awaken wondering if Les could ever appreciate her husband. That thought went right back into my subconscious. If Les reads this memoir, I wonder what she would think of these thoughts.

Leslie had been educated as a reading consultant with a Masters degree from SUNY Buffalo. And her jobs had been in her field. After

627

Craig was born, she increased volunteering, mostly in the Jewish community agencies which she had begun after Michael was born. She gained experience with strategic planning and that led to a part-time job opportunity with a non-profit agency called The Children's Bureau, to do strategic planning. Part of her work led to a merger between her agency and a much larger agency called Children and Families First. Leslie's part-time job became full time and she spread her wings over the city of Wilmington and the State of Delaware. Eventually, she became the CEO of Children and Families First. I was very proud of her work and her accomplishments outside of our home while still being chief parent and homemaker. I have said elsewhere in this memoir that I had no role model for the job of husband and father, but I was determined to create one for my sons as best as I could. I thought I did well. I never felt that Leslie agreed. And with this issue, like so many others, we never had the difficult conversations that would have drawn us closer and helped to dismantle that wall, growing ever higher and wider. Even with the aid of three rounds of couple's therapy.

It's tempting to speak for Leslie about one issue or another but it's not fair. She really does have to write her own book. And I will tell you it will be a great read. But I will share something which was very painful for her, and which was my doing and likely put the final cap on the wall. Leslie always wanted a big family. Six children. And she desperately wanted a daughter. So far, she had given birth to three sons. She came to me when we were in our mid to late thirties and told me she wanted to try again to get pregnant and I should think about it. I did. I am not going to go through my think on this because to write about it would be too painful for both of us. In the end, I said no. I don't know if my decision was the best thing for me or the right thing for our family, but I know it was a terrible blow for Leslie. It was what the psychologists call a severe attachment wound.

This decision was the very weak keystone in the last third of our marriage.

We were separated a number of times but dating. Several years earlier we had purchased a small beach cottage in Lewes, DE and we were spending the weekend there. We were invited to dinner at the home of one of Leslie's friends who I didn't really know very well. This woman and her husband had been married for quite a long time, went through a family tragedy, and ended up divorcing. Then they started dating and re-married and seemed quite happy. Later that night, Les and I discussed divorce. Neither of us wanted to divorce, neither of us wanted to stay married, neither of us were sure about whether any love (whatever that turns out to be) remained or even whether that mattered. We decided to divorce. We cried ourselves to sleep and cried over breakfast in the morning. Then I went back to Wilmington and Les stayed in Lewes. We had a simple divorce. One lawyer for both of us. She lives in the beach cottage, and I lived in our warm home until I sold it and moved into an apartment.

Four months before Peter left our practice, he came to me and said he wasn't happy practicing subspecialty rheumatology with me, and he wanted to explore other options. I encouraged him to do just that. I was too young when my father died to have learned much of life's lessons from him, but I do remember him saying that it is a blessing to love what you do to make a living. I loved what I did. Peter should have that chance as well.

The day he came to me and told me he was leaving, he shared that he had looked at working for pharma, for the Veterans Administration, for corporate America, but in the end, he decided that what he wanted was his own practice distinct from mine. And that's what he did. From all descriptions that have come back to me, it was quite different from mine and reflected his own needs and values and style.

Peter told me that day that he could never feel that he had established himself in Wilmington as a unique and valuable physician because he was living in my shadow. He felt the secretarial staff gave new patients appointments to me bowing to the patients' insistence or the insistence of the referring doctor. I didn't believe that was true, but in this case, he had twelve years' experience gathering that opinion and for him it was truth, so for him it didn't matter.

I knew where his office was, but I really didn't know how busy he was or whether he was happier because I never had an opportunity to speak to him again. What I did know in my heart was that Peter would have scoffed at my commitment to Sir William Osler's teachings, my feelings regarding the joy of medical practice, and the sense of victory when diagnosing a complex case and offering a treatment that cured, leading the patient and their family toward healing.

Peter had changed after returning from his fellowship. He was no longer funny. He could become sarcastic and scornful of his fellow physicians. Not me. Not ever. His life choices changed. He divorced his physician wife and left her and 3 children to marry a nurse with whom he was probably more compatible. I wished him all the best, until one decision he made turned me away from Peter and my fellow rheumatologists in Wilmington.

Once again, I found myself sitting at my desk at home staring at the banker's lamp glow and wondering how I was going to deal with my medical practice. I loved the patients, I loved the problems, I loved my staff, and I loved the community that I was serving. But I was going to be dragged down by the business of running a practice as successful as mine. This time there were no solutions written on the yellowing legal pad.

The next day I was making rounds in the Wilmington Hospital which was our City Hospital at the edge of downtown Wilmington. On a whim, I dropped in to see if Bob Laskowski MD was in his office there. Dr. Bob was the new President and CEO of Christiana Care and I had been on the committee of the Board of Directors that had hired him. He was in and had time to chat.

Bob was an internist and geriatrician with an MBA who had been the Chief Medical Officer at Lehigh Valley Health Care before coming to

Wilmington and was one of the new breed of health system executives that were also physicians.

Impulsively, I asked him if he would consider hiring me into a position which would mix administration with practice. I would bring a sizable number of patients with me and spend half my time as a medical director, a job he would need to define, at the city hospital. Christiana Care had just hired a Chief Medical Officer whose office was at the Christiana Hospital, our flagship, down I-95 toward Newark. His name was Keith Doram MD. My position would be an associate CMO for the Wilmington Hospital.

Dr. Laskowski loved the idea and took less than a minute to say yes, absolutely. I guess that necessity is the mother of invention. Certainly, for me. Maybe for Dr. Bob. I hadn't discussed this move with Leslie and needed to do that, but it felt right to me. I had become deeply involved with the politics and relationships between Christiana Care and the private physicians that made up 75% of its medical staff during the period when Peter was working with me. It seemed to me that this was an extension of the direction my career was going.

I walked out of Dr. Bob's office elated. In one fell swoop, I had become employed by a health system that I had adopted from my first week in Delaware, gotten rid of running a business, maintained a patient practice curated by me to include the most interesting and sickest patients, reduced my practice stressors and rekindled my excitement about medicine. Wow.

I met Keith Doram. Great guy, no problems that I could see working with him. I already knew all the doctors and nurses. I decided on office space in the Wilmington Hospital as an adjunct to an internal medicine practice made up of the faculty of the Department of Internal Medicine.

Keith called me and asked if I could come to a meeting of the rheumatology section at the Wilmington Hospital the next afternoon. Russ as the senior rheumatologist had been the head of the section but had become ill and I was asked to take that over and, in turn, I suggested Peter take it on since I was always looking for opportunities to bolster Peter's status in the medical community. Eventually Russ had to retire from practice. Peter was in a great position to spread his wings and, as he would have put it, get out from under my shadow. This is what he did.

The meeting with the rheumatology section was at the request of the private practice rheumatologists (my old on-call coverage group.) These doctors, led by Peter, gathered that afternoon to notify Christiana Care that they were all resigning their privileges at the health system effective immediately. This meant that they would not be available for consultations in the hospitals, they would not be admitting any patients, they would not see their own patients in the event another physician admitted them and wanted a rheumatologist involved, they would not participate in any Christiana Care conferences, teaching rounds or any activities at all. They wanted to go to their office and go home. The patients' needs be damned. Their colleagues' needs be damned. It remains one of the most selfish and immoral acts that I have ever witnessed by a group of physicians. They were leaving the entire city without the benefit of rheumatic disease care for hospitalized patients. With the one exception of me. I would be available for the patients, for their patients, for the medical staff, for the health system, for the resident teaching, for the community.

And to show their egalitarianism, they did the same thing to St. Francis Hospital, the only other hospital in town.

Right, I would be the only available rheumatologist at Christiana Care to see patients. There would be no rheumatologists at the St. Francis Hospital. My elation turned to gloom, and my gloom turned to anger. Not only were they turning their backs on hospitalized patients, but they were also turning their backs on me. This was a classic moment when those years with my therapist came to support me and let me fully embrace my anger. And I needed all those filters to remain somewhat civil and remember 'primum non nocere' so I wouldn't kill Peter. Because he was the ringleader.

After thinking about it, I concluded that it wasn't personal. They were just selfish. They wanted to create a professional life that catered to their needs. Going to the hospital to see patients in need of their expertise wasn't included. Hoo, boy. I wondered what Alan Myers would have thought of this.

Meanwhile, Keith Doram and I got together and began to develop a plan to hire rheumatologists for Christiana Care. And we did, initially six of them. They were quite proficient. I doubt it bothered the community rheumatologists. They were doing their thing, whatever that was.

I came on board CCHS (Christiana Care Health System) during a time of great change in the organization of health care delivery which has not slowed down. Two months in, I was as happy as a pig in shit, when Keith came to me for a private conversation. He was going to be leaving to take a job in northern California for the Adventist Health

System. I was the only person he was sharing this with, not even Bob, until he had worked out all the details. He liked working at CCHS but he and his family were Seventh Day Adventists and there was no community for them in Delaware. Plus, his passion was flying small planes, and I knew he owned one. The job in California involved being a regional Chief Medical Officer covering more than one hospital or health system in more than one city, giving him a reason to fly from town to town for meetings and appearances. I wasn't happy, since I enjoyed and respected Keith. But this was Keith's decision, and I would sit back and watch it play out.

What happened was that Keith remained at CCHS for a little more than a year, then moved his family to northern California and I became the Chief Medical Officer of Christiana Care. This was exciting but it was also a sad time because I had to give up direct patient care. I transferred my patients to the new rheumatology group of Christiana Care so I could begin the full-time job of a CMO.

Let me give you an idea of what that job entailed. The easiest overview of my new job would be to imagine that I continued to have a practice as an employee of the hospital system. Except I didn't have patients with rheumatic disease problems. My patients represented a carefully culled group: doctors, nurses, executives, senior managers, Board members and those individuals that randomly interacted with Christiana Care. In a way, I continued to diagnose problems and I used the same Oslerian methods I had used in medical practice: careful history taking, examining the physical attributes of the complaint, collecting data and always reaching inside for heuristic intuition. Then I would suggest a treatment in the hope that it would cure the problem, finally getting everyone used to whatever changes they needed to endure so that they would heal from the upheaval in their professional routines. Yes, that is what I did. The big change for me was that non-compliance was the rule and not the exception for my 'patients'.

This is where I needed to develop my own personal skills, some of which were nascent and needed to be developed, like compromise, negotiation, conflict resolution, patience and leadership. I had to learn to broaden and sharpen my filters to be used appropriately. And at the right time, I had to use such unfamiliar techniques as anger, shaming, and foolishness. I found that I was quite good at public speaking and very articulate when supporting a point of view without ever resorting to the 'Harvard method.' You remember, talking about something else about which you were very familiar in order to bore your audience to death to the point where they forgot what point you wanted to make, and they would agree with you just to get you to shut up.

And I found that I had an important tool in my toolbox. I had been in the community long enough, in private practice long enough, engaged with all sides of any argument long enough, and working inside Christiana Care long enough that I could draw from my extensive understanding of our history in Delaware as a medical community to make important points and get things done.

So, what did Dr. Bob think my job description was?

You need to have an idea of the scope of Christiana Care Health System. There were two acute care hospitals, which I have described as the city location and the flagship location where most of the high-end tech stuff was located. CCHS had the potential of opening 1200 acute care beds at the two hospitals for an emergency, like Covid. Since opening a bed meant staffing a bed, this was an expensive proposition and the job of the Chief Operating Officer and Chief Nursing Officer.

In addition, on the campus of the Christiana Hospital, there was a free-standing Cancer Center (my small contribution to the site since a previous CEO, also a doctor, asked me to chair the project,) outpatient surgery-center, medical offices, outpatient imaging practice, and a wellness walking trail around and through the whole place. Finally, like Penn and many others, CCHS had metastatic practices throughout Delaware and extending into Pennsylvania, New Jersey and Maryland.

Many people reported to me in my role as CMO. These were my direct reports. I was not their 'Visit'. I was their friend. Most of the time. I reported to Dr. Bob and considered myself the number two or number three executive on the 'org chart' depending on the issue. If it was an issue that touched patients, I was number two. If it was an issue that touched the operations and physical plant including staffing, number two was the Chief Operating Officer whose name was Gary Ferguson, who was great at his job and I valued him as a friend and advisor.

I tried to meet with my direct reports once a month. Some of these folks were a bit needy and wanted to meet twice a month and I would try to accommodate them. Others would notify me of a problem that couldn't wait, and they would sneak in an extra meeting. On average, it was monthly.

I was responsible for their budgets, employed physicians, strategic planning, research, education and relationships with other departments. Most of these direct reports were physicians who chaired their departments or had equal power positions in the clinical structure of the healthcare system:

Chairman of Internal Medicine

Chairman of Surgery

Chairman of OB-GYN

Chairman of Family Medicine

Chairman of Pediatrics

Director of the Center for Heart and Vascular Health

Director of the Cancer Center

Chairman of Emergency Medicine

Chairman of Radiology

Chairman of Anesthesiology

Director of Medical Informatics (Dual reporting to me and Chief Information Officer)

Chairman of Maxillo-Facial Surgery

Director of Trauma Medicine

Chief Academic Officer

Chairman of Orthopedic Surgery

Chairman of Podiatry

Director of Credentialling and Medical Staff Relations

Collaborative relationship with Nurse Chief of Quality Assurance

And I continued a role that I started when I was first employed as Patient Safety Officer.

Then there were the trailers. These were sometimes unexpected problems that came to my attention because I was a trusted source of influence. Some examples of this included our Diabetes program and who would be calling the shots; the pros and cons of joining the Christiana Care Medical Group which I was

not directly involved in but again, community physicians would use me as a trusted source if they wanted to come in from out of the cold. This came to involve neurology, cardiology, maternal-fetal medicine, neonatology and a number of others.

As CMO, I had to sign off on all contractual relationships that were connected to grants, research and educational projects. I was totally dependent on the Chief Academic Officer for this, since I had no experience with this sort of thing. This was a mistake that I made and a good example of being hoisted on your own petard by the Chief Academic Officer. For years the Chief Academic Officer, whose name was Brian, wanted me to advocate for the hiring of a vice-president who could organize and review all our relationships with other institutions with whom we shared grant and research and educational funds. This was a tough one to get past the CFO (Chief

Financial Officer). But with persistence, Brian finally got what he wanted. Six months later, this very bright woman who had spent most of her career doing just what I hired her to do at CCHS while at MD Anderson Cancer Center in Houston, came and asked to speak to me in private. Of course. She came to my office requesting some time to discuss all the ways CCHS was in jeopardy because of poor documentation and failure to follow proper protocols when it came to grants, research and education and at the same time, putting our partners in those areas at risk. I shared all this information with Dr. Bob who was displeased. Eventually Brian decided to leave, and Bob asked me to fill the gap, at least temporarily. This was a bad idea, and we are getting to the end of this part of the story.

I could write two hundred pages about all the problems and funny and not so funny things that happened during my tenure as Chief Medical Officer which lasted a bit over eight years. But I am not going to do that.

I have avoided going into detail regarding my hiring by Bob Laskowski, first as Medical Director and Associate Chief Medical Officer for the Wilmington Hospital, then Chief Medical Officer for Christiana Care, and finally as Senior VP and Director of The Value Institute and Chief Academic Officer, a project I started but hardly lasted in for more than 5 months. I was a long way from sophomore year at Cornell University turning my back on Comparative Anatomy of Vertebrates. I was a long way from Year 2 and 3 at CUMC where I tried and failed to find and understand love. I was even some distance from Osler when I read his journals in the small museum at the PGH as an intern at HUP. But I was exactly where I wanted to be when it came to the joy of medicine, what I thought we were losing, and what I wanted to ensure we wouldn't.

651

I haven't mentioned it but during the years Peter and I worked together, I was given the opportunity to become involved in multiple discussions and attempts to re-organize care delivery in northern Delaware by organizing physicians into large groups that would partner with CCHS. Those attempts failed largely because of persistent suspicions by private practice docs that the health system would not look out for their interests. My own attempts to resolve conflicts were only partially successful. But my involvement got me a seat on the Board of Directors at CCHS which, I believe, partly led to Dr. Bob's enthusiasm about hiring me.

I had spent 25 years in private practice after landing in Wilmington, DE, and, while at times it was exhausting, it was always rewarding, and it was almost always fun. There was a lot of joy. I spent another nine years as an executive in a major health system in

Delaware and found that rewarding as well. I feel good about the job I did and the contributions I made before I was employed when I was a private medical staff rheumatologist and when I was CMO.

Circumstances led to my retiring early and these circumstances were not fun. There was no joy. And they have just added to my despair over the loss of passion, value and joy in today's world for physicians.

Peter died unexpectedly as a young man several months ago. May his memory be a blessing....

Now what were those circumstances? Read on....

Chapter 25

Migraines

"My friends tell me, that I've been such a fool

I stood by and took

 it, babe, all for lovin' you

Drown myself in sorrow, as I look at what you've
done

But nothin' seems to change

The bad times stay the same

Oh, I can't run

Sometimes I feel, sometimes I feel,

Like I've been tied to the whippin' post

Tied to the whippin' post,

Tied to the whippin' post,

Good Lord I feel like I'm dyin'."

.....The Allman Brothers Band from The Allman Brothers Band 1969

I sat on the stage of Summer Jam in 1973 and listened to these boys rock this iconic song of theirs and the words and the guitars still ring in my head. Unfortunately, the band's founding member Duane Allman had died in 1971 from a tragic motorcycle accident but the band continued emphasizing live performances over studio albums. Gregg Allman died of cancer in 2017. At the time of his death at age 24, Duane Allman was named the second greatest rock guitarist of their top 100 by Rolling Stone, just behind Jimi Hendrix.

Ever since I was a small child, I can remember headaches. They occurred infrequently through childhood and adolescence, perhaps four times a year, but they were nasty and would put me down for a whole day. By description, those early headaches were no different from the headaches I began to get more frequently as an adult. They always began around my right eye and were throbbing. There was no aura that you read about. Over several hours they came to involve my cheek, right side of my nose, forehead and eventually my entire head, neck and upper shoulder blades. I would become nauseated but did not vomit. Light and sound were bothersome and at times I had to lay down. With time I began to identify triggers that could prompt the headache. The biggest trigger was weather change, then came alcohol of any type, then stress, chocolate and a range of foods. When I finally asked a neurologist about the headaches at CUMC, he told me, 'son, you have common migraines and nothing can prevent them or help them. Take a couple of Bufferin or Tylenol every four hours; or both together to see if it helps.' It didn't.

Common migraines. Not special migraines, not jack rabbit migraines, not flaming migraines, and not super deluxe migraines. Just common migraines. Live with it. I later learned that at the time migraines were a family of vascular type headaches that were given names depending on their pattern and mine were 'common.'

I stopped drinking any type of alcohol. Eliminated chocolate, cured meats, herring and anything else that seemed to be a trigger. I couldn't do anything about the weather and stress. Fortunately, at that time in my life the headaches were still relatively infrequent, occurring maybe three times a month. That would change.

In my mid-thirties, having survived the loss of my second child, Russ's lawsuit, surgery for a recurring collapsed lung and the start-up of my solo practice, I found that I now had hypertension, moderately severe. I was fortunate because this was at the cusp of new families of anti-hypertensive drugs that were easy to take and did a great job controlling my blood pressure. Just a few years earlier, the only drugs available for high blood pressure were reserpine, aldomet and hydralazine all of which were impossible to take regularly. I didn't notice any correlation between BP control and migraines. Too bad.

When I was practicing medicine, one time I got a migraine so severe that it wouldn't go away for three days. Status migrainous, it's called. I dropped in on my neighborhood neurologist who sent me for a CT scan. Totally normal. He prescribed a drug called fioricet with which I was unfamiliar and I don't think is available anymore. It was a combination of acetaminophen, caffeine and butalbital, which is a weak derivative of phenobarbital. That got rid of this static migraine but couldn't be taken on a regular basis. But I could take it on an intermittent basis and I was getting these headaches three times a month, so some good news.

The good news didn't last. My migraines began to occur more frequently, became more intense and lasted longer, up to 24 hours. Weather changes would predictably trigger a migraine especially if there was barometric pressure change. As I got older, my stressors at work and at home started getting worse and my headaches became more frequent. I was getting headaches up to fifteen times a month by my mid-forties. I couldn't rely on fioricet because I would be taking it too often and likely getting rebound headaches as a result. But I discovered a mind trick that did help me deal with the headaches. Like Sherlock Holmes, I relaxed in a dark room and went into my mind castle and locked the headache in a closet. It was still there, but by compartmentalizing it in my brain, I was able to focus and analyze better and continue to keep up my bruising schedule in the office. Over time, I did find there was a cost. Keeping the migraine in the closet seemed to drain my energy reserves and I would become exhausted at day's end. Overall, though, I was doing better.

In my fifties, I had acquired a new internist named Vickie who was smart and empathetic, and I went to see her for the headaches. She researched the entire subject. There was a relatively new migraine medication available, a family of medicines called triptans. While they were promising, they were contra-indicated in patients with high blood pressure or with a family history of coronary disease. Too bad. We then went on a journey trying every crazy drug on the market without side effects that anecdotally helped one person or another with migraines. No luck. I even tried acupuncture which I had seen work for post-operative pain and behavioral conditioning...also a bust. Finally, she told me that Jefferson Medical College in Center City, Philadelphia had opened a headache clinic and they were beginning to start selected patients on botulinum toxin injections for migraine with some good results.

Did you ever reach way back in the pantry looking for a can of tomato sauce that you remember you might have bought five years earlier, found it, but it was bulging at the top, bottom and sides, so you threw it out before it exploded. Good idea. It was contaminated with a bacteria that produced one of the deadliest toxins for humans on the planet. Today, we use tiny pharmaceutical doses to temporarily smooth out crow's feet and forehead wrinkles. But these Jefferson guys were giving people 25 shots into their face, scalp and neck to prevent migraines. I told her it was a bit early in our experience with botulinum toxin for me to go to Jeff for treatment.

In 2009, I was well into my tenure as CMO at CCHS and the constant pressure was getting to me. Too many problems were ending up on my lap.

Migraines were frequent and were aggravated by a car accident I had back in 2003 which screwed up my lower neck. My mind palace trick wasn't working anymore. I saw Vickie again to see if anything new had come to her attention. She suggested a radical idea: opiates on a regular basis.

Opiates are a family of naturally occurring and synthetic drugs which had been around for a long time. Morphine, codeine, hydrocodone, oxycodone, heroin, methadone, and several others, currently culminating in fentanyl.

Opiates were almost perfect drugs as defined by having a single pharmacologic function, which was predictable, dependable and caused no untoward side effects. The single pharmacologic function of opiates was pain control.

But I said almost. Most opiates caused minor and predictable side effects like constipation, nausea, sedation which in the settings in which they were used for brief periods were not a problem: trauma, surgery.

By 2009, several forces were in play that were suggesting that opiates could be used on a regular basis in chronically painful conditions, migraine being one of them. Doctors and nurses and hospitals had been under the gun for a while at that point by no less an authority than the Joint Commission on Accreditation of Health Care Facilities for inadequately assessing, documenting and treating pain. It was partially true. For those of us in the profession of medicine, there had always been discomfort with the patient complaining of a subjective experience like pain even when they had some reason to have it and treating them with an opiate.

Why?

Because of the one huge side effect of all opiates, enhanced tachyphylaxis. Most medical students are aware that some drugs lose efficacy over time and there needs to be a dose adjustment usually to a higher dose. This has a fancy name and is called tachyphylaxis.

We think opiates block pain by inducing specific receptors on specific brain cells in the Reptilian brain thought to be a pleasure center. The oldest part of the brain, you may recall. With more receptors on the surface of these cells you need more drug to interact with these receptors to get the cell to do its thing. Control pain. Induce pleasure. And not only do opiates   induce a pleasurable response orchestrated by its target cells in the Reptilian brain but these cells communicate with newer parts of the

666

brain to effect behavior directed at maintaining this pleasurable response and dull the painful sensations.

But here's the thing, when you take the opiate away and there is nothing to interact with all those receptors which have multiplied by taking the opiate on a regular basis, these cells communicate with the newer parts of the brain to effect behavior aimed at getting more of the opiate. If the patient can get more opiate, the cell produces even more receptors, and as a result now needs even more opiate. Behavioral changes occur directed at obtaining more opiate. This is a neurophysiologic response that Dr. Lenneberg would understand even though it has nothing to do with language development. The old brain teaches the new brain that it must find sources of opiate. The patient becomes drug seeking. Fascinating, a cellular response deep in the ancient brain trains the complex new brain to develop ways of obtaining a drug. This is called addiction.

By the way, this addiction thing can occur with a wide range of pleasurable neurophysiology experiences like sex, gambling, horse racing, caffeine, Tylenol, amphetamines, barbiturates, benzodiazepines, cocaine, shopping ...just about anything that induces these receptors in the Reptilian brain. Now, most addiction specialists think that once this receptor induction response is established, it is permanent, particularly for powerful inducers of these receptors, like opiates. Therefore, once addicted, it is a lifetime chronic illness.

If only society regarded addiction as an illness instead of judgmentally regarding it as a crime or character flaw or sociopathic disorder, maybe we would be making greater progress in controlling it.

Now I am sure it is more complicated than what I described above but I am a rheumatologist and not a neurophysiologist like Dr. Eric Lenneberg, my unfortunate first Major advisor at Cornell as an undergraduate.

So, if opiates perfectly reduce the experience of pain, but the patient becomes addicted to them, what's the harm in just taking them permanently as overseen by a physician. This question was being asked by pain specialists in the early 2000's and some of these specialists usually drawn from the ranks of physiatrists, anesthesiologists and psychiatrists with a few neurosurgeons thrown in, were actually treating patients with ever increasing doses of opiates, even more than one opiate at the same time. I saw patients in my practice who were being treated this way by other physicians. Thankfully, not many. It was this trend line in the practice of medicine that pushed my internist, Vickie, to suggest a trial of regular opiate use to prevent and/or mitigate my migraines.

So here is the harm. Eventually, once you are in this cycle of addiction to a drug, you begin to get sick from the untoward effects of the drug. Take the example of the moderate opiate, hydrocodone, often used short term for trauma like a fractured ankle. If you continue to take hydrocodone on a regular basis, and then try stopping you feel anxious, agitated, achey, paranoid. You lose weight because you aren't hungry. Your behavior changes and you can't do your job, so you get canned. Socially, your friends start staying away. You run out of money, so you start robbing people. You get arrested and go to jail. There is no easy way to get hydrocodone in the slammer so you become some chronic lifer's bitch. You get HIV, then AIDS, then you die miserable and alone looking for one last hit and your family has disowned you so there is nobody around to mourn your loss and nobody around to bury you. This is, of course, worst case scenario......Boot Hill.

Alternatively, you realize you are addicted to the opiate and you seek help. You go to a residential rehab center for a month, or 3 months or 6 months. You are carefully detoxed from the drug or drugs so you don't suffer some of those nasty withdrawal symptoms. The food is good and plentiful so you start gaining weight and you are encouraged to use the gym and work with the trainer. The staff and your fellow addicts are a support structure for you. And before you leave, you create a plan to ensure you don't relapse.   Recidivism is always a risk for an addict. Why? According to addiction specialists, because your brain has been changed permanently you will be pulled back into addiction given the right circumstances.

Now I am sitting in Vickie's office, and I am discussing starting on an opiate for my migraines, having exhausted all other avenues except botulinum toxin which I am not ready to try. I am very reluctant. The only opiate I have ever taken was one Percocet of undetermined strength after anesthesia wore off from a hernia repair and that Percocet made me so nauseated that I swore I would never take another one. The memory of almost throwing up after a hernia repair because I took one Percocet tablet is still strong in my memory banks 30 years later. You don't want to throw up after a hernia repair, especially one done the old-fashioned way, without that mesh.

Vickie is encouraging me to give it a try. I don't have to take Percocet (which is oxycodone and Tylenol). How about Lortab (hydrocodone and Tylenol)? Okay, but just the lowest dose, 2.5 mg taken four times a day. She wants me to take it every day on a regular schedule. I sign a pain contract which is routine and somehow reassuring. But 2.5 mg of Lortab does nothing.

It is a pediatric dose. She increases the dose to 5 mg with some relief and no sedation or side effects that I or anybody else notices. Over the next 18 months, the dose is increased to 15mg four times a day and for 18 months I have had pretty good relief of headache pain and think I am functioning better: less stressed, eating more, exercising, handling problems like I did the night that they shuttered PGH and the HUP MICU went crazy.

Then things went south. I started to note that I would be agitated at times. I would get anxious easily. My weight was dropping again. While I didn't crave the medication, I made sure that I had it on hand. My dealer: Vickie, her office staff, the CCHS pharmacy, all treated me like everything was normal. But I was not normal, and I honestly didn't know why. I discussed all this with an honest broker, my psychotherapist. She suggested a psychiatry consult and referred me to a psychiatrist in Bala Cynwyd, a suburb of Philadelphia. I immediately disliked him, but he did listen to my story and at the end he looked at me and said with an Oslerian glint in his eye, 'you've told me the diagnosis by reviewing your history; you're an addict.'

I paid him $225 in cash and walked into the parking lot, when what he said hit me squarely between the eyes. Yes, I was addicted to hydrocodone and I needed to deal with it promptly and totally.

I went home and told Leslie what I had learned. She was shocked and upset and angry all at the same time. The next day I told Michael and Craig who were upset but needed to process what this meant in the context of their own experience.

They were not drug users, not counting alcohol, but they had known plenty of kids who were addicts.

Meanwhile, my therapist found a rehab center fairly close to home that had good reviews. I signed up with plans to stay a month, get detoxed, and begin a program to prevent relapse. The only thing left to do was to inform Dr. Bob that I would be out of commission for 6-12 weeks taking FMLA. I seem to remember that all this came together with amazing speed. The only fly in the ointment was Leslie who wanted me to go to the Betty Ford Center in Los Angeles for six months. She must have been really angry.

The night before I was to go to the rehab center, I considered my situation and kicked myself for making such a bad choice when Vickie had presented opiates as a plausible treatment for migraines. Should have gone for the Botox. The next morning at 8, I had a presentation to make to the Quality Assurance Committee of the Board of Directors. At that time, I was the Director of the new Value Institute which Bob had asked me to create and had given me ten million dollars to create it with. The idea was to study ways that ever improving health care could be delivered by ever decreasing cost. Value equals quality divided by cost. Sounds impossible when you think about it, but I believed there was so much waste in the system that it could be done and CCHS could be a leader.

The presentation went very well. I was pleased. Next, I had a meeting with Dr. Bob during which I told him I needed some time off and was taking FMLA but I planned to be back, hopefully in six weeks. He asked me if I was abusing drugs.

I have thought about that question a lot since then. The question was both illegal, breaking two federal statutes, one of which was HIPAA, and none of his business. I should have told him that and walked out. At the very least, I should have said that the only drugs I was taking were prescribed by my internist who was an employee of the Christiana Care Medical Group. But I wasn't prepared for the abruptness of his question, so I said, yes. In my mind, it wasn't even true since 'abusing' really wasn't the correct description. I was prescribed opiates for a chronically painful condition on an ongoing basis which was consistent with the then current practice of internal medicine at that time and for which nothing else had proved effective or tolerated.

Still, I left CCHS confident that I would return ready to start again and be welcomed back by an organization whose values included treating patients as you would want to be treated if you are a CCHS employee who becomes ill. In my mind, I was ill with an illness called addiction. Now that it had been diagnosed, I was seeking as close a cure as I could find and heal from the trauma it had caused. In essence, I wanted to be treated by my caregivers the way I treated my patients. Not asking too much, was it? I would add that the second line of the Hippocratic Oath states that you will be 'loyal to the Profession of Medicine and just and generous to its members.' During my thirty years in Delaware I had dedicated myself to the growth and excellence of Christiana Care in collaboration with my colleagues and we had largely succeeded.

That's not the way it went down. I did my part. CCHS was not true to their own values. Without firing me directly, they did everything they could to separate me from the organization and destroy my ability to practice medicine. As I think about it now, it still angers me. Bob Laskowski and the Executives in the C-suite should have welcomed me back, nurtured me to good health and function and eased me into whatever responsibilities I could handle and helped me make sure that there was no relapse of my addiction. I was aware of an amazingly similar case at

Dartmouth where that was exactly what happened. If I was CEO, that is what I would have done if the shoe was on the other foot.

But bias and judgmentalism is a tough problem for addicts. I'm not going to make excuses for Dr. Bob. I suppose he wanted to protect the health care system and he thought this was the safest and best way to do it. Everything I had done for the Medical Center of Delaware which became Christiana Care Health System from the day I started in 1980 until the day I left for rehab in December 2010, counted for nothing to these former colleagues of mine. Nor were those proud values printed in all our literature. They made me report myself to the State of Delaware as an impaired physician and I signed a contract with the state Attorney General's office that made me swear I would agree to the actions listed in the contract on pain of forfeiture of my license to practice medicine, the language of which made me feel like a criminal. During those days and for a long time afterward, I felt like if given the opportunity, I would gladly have kneecapped Dr. Bob, but the truth is, I'm not that kind of man and I'm not that kind of physician.

Primum non nocere. You know, above all do no harm. I couldn't avoid it. It was the Prime Directive for us physicians like on Star Trek.

There are two chapters left in this memoir. My story finds me divorced, retired, no longer a practicing doctor or an executive at a rising health care system. My accomplishments and legacy have been expunged from the history of Christiana Care. Doctors whose careers I advanced and programs I supported and residents and students I taught who I thought were my friends won't return my calls or emails. No matter. What's done is done and I have made my peace with it. And what I accomplished matters more to me than anybody remembering that

I did it. I did eventually start Botox injections and found they worked quite well at controlling migraine headaches although I have no idea why they should. Must have something to do with cell receptors. When the weather changes and a front comes through, my doctor, no longer Vickie, prescribes low doses of oxycodone for a few days if I get a bad headache. This works fine and I don't find myself craving opiates, thank goodness. If my brain has changed into that of an addict, it didn't stop me from writing this book. There are certainly other things in my life that could have slowed this project but didn't. Now please excuse me for a while so I can shower and scrub off the memories of Dr. Bob. See you for the   last   chapters.

Chapter 26

MORTALITY

"I'm learning to fly,

But I don't have wings,

Coming down,

Is the hardest thing."

Tom Petty

"Yes, I'm free,

Free-fallin'

Yes, I'm free,

Free-falling, yeah."

Tom Petty

Tom Petty died last year. For those who loved his music and his poetry, it was a great loss. That includes me. But I can still listen to his music. And I do all the time.

I have been aware of death as part of life and inevitable since early in my high school years. At my father's funeral, I remember my mother taking us through his viewing where we stopped for a bit and contemplated his unmoving, lifeless body. I can't remember my thoughts or feelings at that moment, only that I knew he wouldn't be there anymore, and the rest of my life awaited me. There would be many reminders over the next year that my dad had died, but whatever I felt was buried deep in my subconscious. Many years later, my psychotherapist would tell me that I had a very strong defense mechanism for dealing with hard realities and what she called attachment wounds. It was the ability to bury these hard realities deep within my brain where I didn't have to work through them, understand their significance, grieve if necessary and find closure.

With therapy and on my own I have come to understand that this defense mechanism was very protective of me for so many things that I faced throughout my life, but it came at a cost. The cost was energy, psychic energy that was needed to keep my attachment wounds bottled up deep inside. To release that energy, to make it available to me going forward, I had to learn to reach the place where I had caged so much of life's sadness and allow those things to be released and come up through my physical body and my invisible thoughts so that I could consider and understand their significance, feel their weight and force and help shape my adult self. If I was successful, I would find myself as a mature adult.

I see the same things happening with my friends and contemporaries as we reach our seventies. We are all striving to finally become adults.

To be mature always across the spectrum of human endeavor. I have doubts that very few of us ever reach that level of maturity. When we look at politicians, celebrities, sports heroes, and others in the public space, there seems to be only a few who we can use as examples. A few. Not many. A shame.

Why is this happening to me now? Why am I writing this memoir? I think that it is because I am feeling death creeping up behind me. And one day, soon, hopefully not too soon, it will be my lifeless body in the viewing....and everything that is part of my life now will be absent from who I was.

That I know of, I escaped dying three times up to this point. When I was 35, my left lung collapsed spontaneously and eventually I required surgery to keep it expanded and working normally. But the real danger occurred because it was not appreciated that I had a mild variant of hemophilia and I almost bled to death after the surgery was finished.

At age 50 or thereabouts, I was involved in a head-on motor vehicle crash and sustained a fracture of my lower neck that would have either killed a person outright or left them paralyzed from the neck down for their remaining life. The diagnosis was delayed for three weeks. I was left with a sore neck on occasion and no other symptoms.

And about ten years ago, early one winter morning, while walking my dog, I slipped on black ice and came down on the back of my head hitting frozen macadam on my driveway. Woozy, I found my scalp was bleeding heavily and after tending to my dog Gabriel, I found my way to the emergency room where a non-depressed skull fracture was diagnosed, the laceration was sutured, I was given directions to rest and sent home. With no one around on that cold morning, had the fracture been depressed into my brain and with my bleeding tendency, I easily could have laid there unconscious, dying in front of a helpless Gabriel. But I didn't. Had a bad concussion, though, which took a while to subside.

Now I face a different challenge. In the summer of 2019, before Covid became a pandemic, I started to have bouts of intense fatigue in the afternoon forcing me to lie down and sleep for an hour. I called these 'fugue' states and they were totally different from an older man's afternoon nap. Soon the fugue states were accompanied by mild infectious illnesses. Head colds, sinus infections, diarrhea, bronchitis. This was very unusual for me. I was proud of my robust immune system which seemed to keep me healthy during bouts of community epidemics.

I was a patient in the Penn system at this point and I went to their patient portal and pulled up my labs. A quick survey confirmed that I had a disturbing trend in my complete blood counts over several years. I had become modestly anemic but more worrisome was the absolute number of white blood cells called neutrophils which are the first cells that fight infection. A healthy adult will have greater than 1900 neutrophils in their blood count. I had 600, a reduction that could put me at risk for life threatening infections if it got much lower. I shared all this with a friend of 50 years, Dr. David Henry, who was a phenomenal hematologist-oncologist at Penn ever since the two of us finished our residency together. We had been in the same class and David went on to become Chief Resident in Internal Medicine.

Dr. Henry re-assured me that I had myelodysplastic syndrome, a slowly evolving malignancy of the bone marrow which he would still be treating twenty years in the future. He could give me some treatment that would fix my low neutrophil count, get rid of the infections and improve my anemia as well. But I knew David very well and I detected some wary unease below his calm demeanor. That night I did what every HUP resident would do, re-acquaint myself with myelodysplastic syndrome which I hadn't encountered since my residency. David had given me good information, but he had left out one part. MDS did evolve slowly but it tended to cause some chromosomal breaks and changes within the early cell forms which normally would mature into normal blood cells. This could be a harbinger of a second hematologic malignancy. Acute Myelogenous Leukemia. My familiarity with AML, with one exception, was totally restricted to our residency when it was considered the most horrible admission an intern could get. Why? Back in the late 1970's, patients with new onset AML were incredibly sick: no bone marrow function, terrible infections, sometimes severe bone pain, and the treatments back then made patients feel sicker than their illness. AML was one tough disease. Survival, at best, was 3-6 months with patients dying from both the treatment and the leukemia; nasty stuff.

The next day, I called David and asked for a bone marrow biopsy. And in his usual mild-mannered and understated way, he said, 'that's sounds reasonable.'

Over the next 5 months I had four bone marrow exams and by the last one, I had definitive findings of AML. I needed treatment. Now the decision was a choice: stem cell transplantation vs chemotherapy, which had improved greatly from the therapy I remembered. Dr. Henry helped a great deal in making the decision, which was chemotherapy. It was the right decision, because three years later I am in a sustained remission and writing this memoir. I am not totally healthy, however. There are several chronic problems that I am left with as consequences of leukemia and its treatment. But these problems are manageable. I am also left with the very real possibility that the leukemia will relapse. We can cross that bridge when we come to it.

So how do I feel about mortality, particularly my own mortality. Viewing my father's body in its coffin made little impression on me at age 15. I found ways to mourn the loss in my life and find closure that I am comfortable with today. My middle son, born with a fatal chromosomal trisomy, died in my arms on the second day of his life. At the time, I resorted to my defense mechanisms and buried my thoughts and feelings deep in my subconscious mind because I felt that I needed to shroud myself with the role of the clinician and the healer in order to care for my wife and my young son at home. That wasn't a healthy thing to do but I felt I had no choice and so I accepted the role. With time, I believe I have mourned that loss and successfully dealt with the attachment wound.

Now I face the greatest loss of all. My existence. My sentience. My future. All that will stop forever. I don't know if there is anything remaining after death to experience. I can accept that. When I first got sick with AML, I felt I was ready to die. Now I know that the disease and the treatment messes with your brain, so I doubt I was in my right mind to explore the meaning of dying. I am in a better place for that now. I am not afraid of death or dying. One meaning of its inevitability is the end of suffering and not just physical pain but mental anguish, psychosocial questioning, individual growth, further maturation. That is what I think. Google says that maturity encompasses the thoughts, feelings and behavior of an adult. Death is the end of adulthood, the end of maturation.

James   Newman   MD

Postscript

"Build it, and he will come."

Soon after I brought Peter in as my partner in practice, I took the longest vacation I had ever had. Three and one-half weeks. Leslie and I took Michael and Craig, who were around 8 and 11, with us on a two thousand mile driving trip visiting the Western National Parks. At least many of them. It was one of my favorite vacations. I remember Michael had a birthday while we were on the trip and we had a birthday dinner for him somewhere outside Bryce Canyon in a small town. There were many high points and a few low points, but the point of this postscript is unrelated to the trip. I remember that somewhere along our trail we went to a movie which had been out for a while and I had really wanted to see: 'Field of Dreams' with Kevin Costner. I am a huge baseball fan and baseball was one of the few things that I had very powerful memories of sharing with my dad, also a huge fan. Before I was born, Scranton had a minor league club and some of the players made it to the majors. I couldn't have been more than 5 or 6 when my dad gave me a baseball with Jimmy Piersall's autograph. Piersall played four years in the minors and 17 years in the majors for five teams, although I believe the Scranton minor league team was a White Sox property and he never played for the White Sox. His most prominent years were with the Boston Red Sox and he was elected into the Red Sox Hall of Fame.

My dad told me that he was the dentist for a number of players for the Scranton franchise and he believed Piersall was special. He was a center fielder, won two gold gloves and was elected to the AL All-Star team twice. Throughout his long career he was considered one of the best defensive centerfielders in the majors.

But what made him special was that he got to the majors with undiagnosed bipolar disorder which became increasingly worse. During his rookie season with the Red Sox, bizarre behavior on the field and in the clubhouse which began in a game against the Yankees when he engaged in a fistfight with the Yankee second baseman in the middle of an inning, a second baseman named Billy Martin, who was loosely wired himself. This led to a psychiatric hospitalization where he received electroshock treatments which did not work and an experimental drug called lithium which vastly improved his rapidly cycling mood swings. Settling down, he became one of the most effective position players in the game with a lifetime .292 batting average and just over 100 home runs. But he still had his moments. He celebrated his 100th homer by running the bases in the correct order but ran them backwards.

Piersall's life has been well documented by a non-fiction book about his struggles with serious mental illness, an autobiography, a major motion picture starring Anthony Perkins and Karl Malden and a made for TV movie as well. He was one of the first celebrities to attempt to normalize society's thinking about mental illness. My dad continued a written correspondence with Piersall until my father's death.

On our trip out west, I finally got to see Field of Dreams which I have now watched about twenty times. If you don't know the story line,

Kevin Costner and his wife and two small children are trying to keep the family farm in Iowa going despite some difficult years financially. One late afternoon, Costner is standing out in his cornfield when he hears a voice coming from nowhere, "Build it and he will come." Build what? Who will come?

Throughout the movie, Costner gets several more mysterious messages via this 'voicemail' which, at first, he thinks he hallucinated but is quickly pulled into the quest, eventually recruiting a reclusive author played by James Earl Jones, who he drags to Fenway Park to watch a ball game where the scoreboard flashes a message, "Go the distance," which only Costner and Jones can see.

It all comes down to Costner building a ballfield in the middle of his cornfield while his brother-in-law, a banker, is trying to convince him to sign over the farm to the bank and Jones, who hasn't written anything in decades but had written a famous novel in his youth is sitting there disconsolately. Suddenly ball players in old, old uniforms, but appearing youthful, start walking out of the corn rows and taking positions on the field and warming up, led by 'Shoeless' Joe Jackson. Jackson was indicted with seven of his teammates for conspiring to 'throw' the 1919 World Series, the infamous Back Sox Scandal that rocked baseball. The players, members of the Chicago White Sox, went to trial and were acquitted but the Commissioner of major league baseball banned them for life from the game anyway and as a result, Jackson, a fabulous player in the prime of his career, never reached Cooperstown. The movie 'Field of Dreams' is in part a redemption for players whose careers were cut short for various reasons.

As the players are throwing around baseballs on Costner's field in the corn, James Earl Jones gives one of the most memorable speeches of sports feature films:

"Ray, people will come, Ray. They'll come to Iowa for reasons they can't even fathom. They'll turn up your driveway, not knowing for sure why they're doing it. They'll arrive at your door as innocent as children, longing for the past.

"Of course, we won't mind if you look around," you'll say. "It's only twenty dollars per person." They'll pass over the money without even thinking about it. For it is money they have and peace they lack.

And they'll walk out to the bleachers, and sit in shirt-sleeves on a perfect afternoon. They'll find they have reserved seats somewhere along one of the baselines, where they sat when they were children and cheered their heroes. And they'll watch the game, and it'll be as if they'd dipped themselves in magic waters. The memories will be so thick, they'll have to brush them away from their faces.

People will come, Ray.

The one constant through all the years, Ray, has been baseball.

America has rolled by like an army of steam rollers. It's been erased like a blackboard, rebuilt, and erased again. But baseball has marked the time. This field, this game – it's a part of our past, Ray. It reminds us of all that once was good, and it could be again.

Ohhhhhh, people will come, Ray. People will most definitely come."

Now it's dusk of the same day, the players have gone back into the rows of corn with James Earl Jones but Shoeless Joe tells Kevin Costner that he can't follow into, the wherever in the corn. Costner returns to home plate watching the setting sun when a young ball player in uniform emerges from the corn. As he slowly walks towards the infield, Costner realizes that it is his father as a young man, a father that he was estranged from as a young teenager. They greet and shake hands and his father asks him if he wants to have a catch. They start to throw the ball back and forth as the credits roll.

Having a catch with my dad was one of the few things that burns in my memory of him. Physically, it was about all he could do given his unstable heart disease. But I cling to the memory even today.

And I wonder sometimes if Sir William Osler is out there in the corn trying to teach Shoeless Joe Jackson how to play cricket.